CATEGORIES OF MEDIEVAL CULTURE

CATEGORIES OF MEDIEVAL CULTURE

A. J. GUREVICH

Translated from the Russian
by G. L. Campbell

ROUTLEDGE & KEGAN PAUL
London, Boston, Melbourne and Henley

First *published as* Kategorii srednevekovoi kultury, *Moscow,*
1972

This edition first published in 1985
by Routledge & Kegan Paul plc

14 Leicester Square, London WC2H 7PH, England,

9 Park Street, Boston, Mass. 02108, USA,

464 St Kilda Road, Melbourne,
Victoria 3004, Australia, and

Broadway House, Newtown Road,
Henley-on-Thames, Oxon RG9 1EN, England

Set in Linotron Garamond
by Input Typesetting Ltd, London SW19 8DR
and printed in Great Britain
by Billing & Sons Ltd, Worcester

Library of Congress Cataloging in Publication Data

Gurevich, Aron IAkovlevich.

Categories of Medieval culture.
Translation of: Kategorii srednevekovoĭ kul'tury.
Includes bibliographical references and index.
1. Civilization, Medieval. I. Title.
CB351.G8713 1985   909'.07   84–9906

British Library CIP data available

ISBN 0–7100–9578–3

CONTENTS

[v]

ILLUSTRATIONS

ACKNOWLEDGMENTS

Extracts from *Egil's Saga*, translated by Gwyn Jones (The American-Scandinavian Foundation, New York, and Twayne Publishers, Boston: 1970) (© 1960 by The American-Scandinavian Foundation), are reprinted by permission of The American-Scandinavian Foundation.

Excerpts from *The Elder Edda*, translated by Paul B. Taylor and W. H. Auden (© Paul B. Taylor and W. H. Auden 1969), are reprinted by permission of Faber & Faber and Random House, Inc.

Excerpts from *The Prose Edda of Snorri Sturluson*, translated by J. I. Young, are reprinted by permission of the University of California Press.

The illustrations are used by courtesy of the British Museum.

CHAPTER I

Introduction: the 'world picture' of medieval man

The Middle Ages – the very words bring a succession of familiar images flooding into the mind: feudal castles and Gothic cathedrals, crusades and baronial wars, the glitter of the tournament and the flames of inquisitorial fires. But these are all external trappings, a sort of ornamental screen behind which real people lived and worked. What sort of people were they? How did they see the world they lived in, and what guided them in their actions? The moment we try to reconstruct the mental world of medieval man, to analyse the spiritual and cultural resources by which he lived, we find that his world is almost completely swallowed up in the dark shadow cast upon it by classical antiquity on the one hand and by the Renaissance on the other. It is hardly possible to see this period with an unprejudiced eye. The concept of the 'Middle Ages' (*medium aevum*) which came into use a few centuries ago as a handy label for the period dividing Graeco-Roman antiquity from modern times, carried with it from the outset a pejorative sense suggestive of a downfall, a lacuna in the cultural history of Europe, which it has retained to this day. Seeking an adjective to describe backwardness, lack of culture, lawlessness, we say 'medieval'; the word is virtually synonymous with whatever is dark and reactionary. Properly, it is the earlier period of the Middle Ages that is usually called the 'Dark Ages', but the Oxford English Dictionary goes further and extends the term to the whole of the Middle Ages.

Such a view of the Middle Ages was no doubt understandable in the seventeenth and eighteenth centuries when the ascendant bourgeoisie had every reason to hasten the overthrow of feudalism by helping to discredit the ages when the church and the nobility had ruled supreme. But it has long ceased to be justified. It should never be forgotten that it was precisely in the Middle Ages that the modern European nations were born and the present-day European states began to take shape; it was then that the languages we speak emerged, and it is from the Middle Ages that many of the cultural values underlying our own civilisation are derived. The contrasts are obvious; but the connecting links and their continuity are beyond doubt.

We should be taking a very one-sided view, however, if we saw in the Middle Ages no more than the 'childhood' of the European nations: a sort of preparatory step to modern history. The Middle Ages have their own independent historical value. The German historian Leopold von Ranke used to say: 'Every historical epoch has its own immediate relationship with God' – an idealist way of putting a profound and undeniable truth: every epoch is interesting and important for its own sake, in and for itself, regardless of its relations with the subsequent course of history. In fact, we do not study the past for teleological reasons only, to discern, that is how the present has arisen from it. Study of different periods of history, including those remote from us, and, perhaps, unconnected in any clear or direct way with our own, enables us to see both the unity and the diversity of mankind. Once our eyes are opened to the recurrent strains in history, when we keep on coming across the same human needs and the same human responses, we gain a deeper understanding of human society and the laws that govern it. Contact with human existence in all its variety in other historical periods, in other civilisations, in other cultural environments, helps us to comprehend our own particular originality, our own place in the historical process. Thus, we have to take account of the individual as well as of the general, of common factors as well as of diversity.

Historical knowledge is always, in one way or another, self-knowledge; studying the history of another epoch, we cannot but compare it with our own. Is this not in the long run the meaning of cultural history? But, in the process of comparing our own epoch and its civilisation with other epochs and other civilisations, do we not run the risk of applying our own standards to them? To some extent, this is unavoidable. But let us be clear in our own minds about the pitfalls. What we regard today as basic values for our lives may not have seemed so to people belonging to other periods of history and to other cultures; and, conversely, what seems to us false or trivial may have been true and vitally significant for those belonging to another culture.

When Laplace was explaining the movements of the heavenly bodies to Napoleon, the latter is said to have asked him what role in all this he allotted to the Creator: to which Laplace answered: 'I had no need of such a hypothesis.' And, in fact, modern science manages very well without a Prime Mover, Supreme Reason, God, Creator – or whatever else this supernatural power might be called. But we shall understand very little of medieval culture if we limit ourselves at the outset by assuming that all was ignorance and obscurantism in the Middle Ages because everyone believed in God. For medieval man this was not a 'hypothesis' but a postulate, the very core of his world-view and of his moral awareness, and without it he would have been at a loss how to explain the natural world or orientate himself therein. What is 'erroneous' from our point of view was not erroneous for medieval man; rather, it was the highest truth round which all other concepts and ideas revolved, and with which all medieval cultural and social values were bound up.

If we are to understand the culture of a past historical period we must proceed on rigorously historical lines, applying only such standards as are strictly relevant. There exists no one single standard which is applicable to all civilisations and all epochs, since no man in one civilisation can be an exact replica of his counterpart in another. And yet the conviction that human nature – especially human psychology – remains an invariant throughout the course of history, was still cherished even by the greatest of the eighteenth- and nineteenth-century historians. As the starting-point for his *Weltgeschichtliche Betrachtungen* Burckhardt took man 'as he is, was and ever shall be'. As a result, the contemporary Western European masqueraded as the man of another time and another culture.

Human society is in permanent motion, change and development. At different times and in different cultures men perceive and interpret the world in their own fashion, and in their own fashion they organise their impressions and their knowledge, and construct their own historically conditioned world-view. And if we wish to know the past as it really was ('wie es eigentlich gewesen ist', to quote Ranke once again) we must approach it with adequate criteria, study it from within and try to discover its own internal structure; and we must be constantly on our guard against foisting our own contemporary values and standards on to it.

This general caveat is particularly applicable to any attempt to understand an epoch as distinctive and peculiar as the Middle Ages. The structure and the processes of medieval thought are so alien to us that often they seem hardly accessible to modern ways of thinking. Does this not perhaps go some way towards explaining the prejudices we entertain *vis-à-vis* the Middle Ages? We know a fair amount about the historical events but far less about their inner motivation, about the motives which led people to do certain things, and which gave rise to social and ideological conflict. All social movements are movements of people, of thinking, feeling beings equipped with a particular culture and a particular set of ideas. What people do is motivated by the values and ideals of their time. Without taking into account the value-judgments and the criteria by which people were guided in feudal society, we cannot pretend to understand their conduct. Consequently, we cannot pretend to offer a scientific account of this conduct as part of a historical process.

Nor can we, if we ignore the system of values underlying the *Weltanschauung* of medieval people, pretend to understand their culture. The most widespread and popular kind of literary production in the Middle Ages was hagiography – the Lives of the Saints. The most typical architectural product is the cathedral; in painting the icon predominates, in sculpture the personages of Holy Writ. Medieval master-craftsmen, writers and artists ignored the visible outlines of the earthly world surrounding them and kept their gaze firmly fixed on the world beyond. The result is a highly distinctive way of seeing things. Almost without exception the artists and poets of the Middle Ages ignore the visible facts of nature, they depict no landscapes, they pay no attention to individual peculiarities; they seem to be unaware that at other times in other countries people dressed differently, lived in a different sort of dwelling and carried different arms. People are type-cast rather than individualised. Instead of trying to penetrate into the manifold variety of living phenomena, the artist takes as his starting-point the ineluctable opposition between the sublime and the base, an opposition polarised as absolute good and absolute evil.

The world as thus created by the medieval artist is very much *sui generis* and very strange to the eye of the modern beholder. It is as though the artist is unaware that the world is three-dimensional, that it has depth. In his pictures, volume is replaced by flatness. Was he also unaware of the passage of time? In pictures by medieval masters, it is usual to find consecutive actions depicted simultaneously. Thus we find collocated in one and the same picture John the Baptist standing before Herod, John being beheaded by the executioner, and Herodias bringing Herod the dish bearing the head of John, whose lifeless body lies alongside. Or again, we see a nobleman riding along a path; he rides into a castle, leaps from his horse and enters a room, where he meets the lord of the castle and exchanges with him the kiss of friendship obligatory on such occasions: all of this shown not consecutively in serial fashion but integrated in compositional unity within the framework of one single picture. This way of representing consecutive events, which are dispersed in time, on one artistic plane – so alien to our present-day concept of the picture as representing one temporal event or state and no more – is still found in Renaissance art. For example, in his illustrations to Dante's *Divina Commedia* (dating from as late as the 1490s) Botticelli has tried to show the progress of Dante and Virgil through the circles of hell by placing their figures several times in one and the same picture.

Again, it seems that the medieval artist did not distinguish any too clearly between the earthly world and the supernatural world: both are represented with the same degree of clarity and precision in lively interaction within the confines of one and the same fresco or miniature. This is something very remote from what we call 'realism'. Let us not forget, however, that the word 'realism' is also of medieval provenance – but at that time the only 'realities' were certain categories to which we today would deny reality.

The list of incompatibilities, as they might be called, which arise if we take up our critical stance on modern principles of art and the *Weltanschauung* underlying them, could no doubt be extended. Of course, it is easy to talk of the 'primitiveness' and the 'childish ingenuousness' of medieval artists, of their 'clumsiness'. It is easy to point out that linear perspective in the representation of space had not been discovered, and so on. But all such verdicts do no more than reflect our failure to understand the inner world of the medieval artist or poet, and our proneness to judge the art of other times in the light of contingent criteria totally alien to these times.

But, it may be objected, the language of art is always conventional, and it is not easy to pass from it to an understanding of the social awareness and the *Weltanschauung* of men of other ages. This is certainly true; but it is not in art alone that the 'oddities' of the medieval mind reveal themselves. For example, is it not puzzling, from our point of view, that word and idea in the medieval system of thought possessed the same degree of reality as the material world, as things to which universals correspond? Is it not strange that concrete and abstract were not differentiated, or at least the frontier between them was not clearly drawn? That repetition of the thoughts of ancient authors was laudable, while the expression of novel ideas was frowned upon? That plagiarism was not an offence while originality might well be seen as heresy? That in a society in which the lie was regarded as a cardinal sin, the preparation of false documents in justification of property claims and other privileges could rate as a means of establishing the truth and as an act pleasing to God? That childhood was not regarded as a particular stage of human growth and development and children were treated as undersized adults? That the outcome of a lawsuit depended not upon the accurate presentation and objective assessment of the circumstances, or at least not so much upon this as upon due observance of procedure and recitation of formulae; and that right and wrong in litigation could be established by the application of boiling water or a red-hot iron? That not only a human being could be accused of a crime and brought to trial, but an animal as well or even an inert object? That land measures with the same name could vary quantitatively, that is, were in practice incommensurate? That in the same way, the unit of time – the hour – was of varying duration according to the season of the year? That among the feudal lords wastefulness was prized far more highly than thrift, the favourite virtue of the bourgeoisie? That in this society freedom was not simply the opposite of dependence but could also be combined with it? That poverty was seen as a state more pleasing to God than riches, and that while some strove to enrich themselves, others voluntarily relinquished all they possessed?

Perhaps these examples will suffice. They are the first to come to mind as examples of those sides of medieval life which do not tally with the rationalistic way of thought fashionable today; they have not been specially selected to afford yet further illustration of the well-worn thesis of the 'backwardness' and the 'savagery' of the Middle Ages. They are intended to show that all these medieval 'absurdities' and 'incongruities' stand in need of both explanation and an adequate degree of understanding. We have to discover the inner content, the innermost meaning of this culture, so remote from us not only in time but also by reason of its temperament and structure.

The difficulty in comprehending the spiritual life of the people of the Middle Ages is not simply due to the fact that it contains much that is strange, indeed incomprehensible, to us today. The content of medieval culture is not something that readily lends itself to analytic dismemberment, the tool we are accustomed to use in our study of contemporary culture. In the context of the Middle Ages, it is hardly possible to differentiate clearly between such spheres of intellectual activity as aesthetics, philosophy, history and economics. Or rather, it is possible to differentiate between them to some degree, but the very process is harmful both to our understanding of medieval culture as a whole and of the discipline in question in particular. When medieval thinkers turned their attention to the study of the beautiful, it was inevitable that such study should turn upon comprehension of God – the creator of all visible forms, which do not exist in themselves but only as a means to comprehension of the divine reason. In exactly the same way, history did not present itself to the medieval mind as an independent process, spontaneously generated by its own immanent laws: this stream of events unrolling, developing, in time acquired meaning and significance only in the light of eternity and the fulfilment of God's design. The attitude of medieval scholars to wealth, property, prices, labour and other economic categories was an integral part of their analysis of the ethical categories: what is justice, how should man conduct himself and his affairs (including his economic affairs) in order to ensure that he is not thereby jeopardising the supreme and final aim – the salvation of his soul? Philosophy was 'the handmaiden of theology', and in the eyes of the medieval philosopher the role thus allotted to philosophy was for a long time its sole justification, in that it endowed his arguments with a deeper significance.

Does this mean that all medieval knowledge reduces to theology, and that the aesthetic or philosophical thought of the age of feudalism cannot be isolated for particular study? Not at all. But it does mean that when we select creative art, law, historiography or any other sphere of medieval intellectual activity for analysis, we must not try to isolate this particular sphere from the wider cultural-historical context; for it is only within the framework of this whole which we call medieval culture, that we can rightly understand its individual components. Theology represented the highest generalisation of medieval man's social behaviour; it provided a general semiological system in terms of which the members of feudal society apprehended themselves and saw their world both motivated and explained.

From what we have said it will be clear that what mainly distinguishes the medieval world-view is its integrated structure; it is this that explains the specific non-differentiation, the inseparability of its various spheres. Hence also medieval belief in the unity of the universe. Just as each detail of a Gothic cathedral recapitulates the grand architectonic design of the whole structure, just as in each separate chapter of a theological treatise the constructional principle of the *Summa*

Theologica can be traced, just as an individual event in earthly history exemplifies an event in sacred history (the eternal experienced in the temporal) – so was medieval man aware of himself as the unity of all those elements from which the world was created, and as the final purpose of the universe. In the particle the whole was subsumed; the microcosm was a replica of the macroscosm.

This integrated nature of the medieval world-view, however, in no way guarantees its freedom from contradiction. The contrasts of eternal and temporal, sacred and sinful, soul and body, heavenly and earthly, which lay at the root of this world-view were also deeply imbedded in the social life of the period – in the irreconcilable contrasts of wealth and poverty, dominion and subjugation, freedom and bondage, privilege and deprivation. The Christian world-view of the Middle Ages 'transferred' the real contradictions to the higher plane of the all-embracing transcendental categories. On this plane, the contradictions were to be resolved in the fulfilment of earthly history, as a result of the Atonement, the return of the world, through its development in time, to the eternal. Hence theology gave the medieval community not only the highest generalisation but also its sanction, its justification and sanctification.

Evidently, as applied to the Middle Ages, the very notion of 'culture' has to be construed in a much wider sense than is customary when we speak of the culture of the modern age. Medieval culture does not simply comprise certain aesthetic or philosophical categories, nor is it restricted to literature, art and music. If we are to grasp the determining principles of this culture we must go far beyond the boundaries of these domains; and then we see that in law, in economics, in property relationships, and in much else – at the root of all medieval activity, creative and practical alike – there can be discerned a unity, outside of which none of these separate spheres of activity can be fully understood. They are all tinged with this cultural unity.

No doubt the culture of any epoch can and, indeed, ought to be studied in this broad perspective, as an all-embracing semiological system. In the case of medieval culture, however, it is particularly important to take the whole picture into account. The various spheres of human activity in the Middle Ages do not have 'professional languages', in the sense that we today have a language of politics, of economics, of art, of religion, of philosophy, science and law. Let us take some examples: mathematics was studied in the Middle Ages and consequently there was a language of mathematical symbols. But these mathematical symbols are at one and the same time theological symbols, because mathematics itself was for long a 'sacral arithmetic' used for the symbolic elucidation of divine truths. Consequently, the language of mathematics was not independent; it was, rather, a 'dialect' of the wider language of Christian culture. Number was an essential element of aesthetic thought, a sacral symbol, a divine thought.

Another example: poverty was endemic in the Middle Ages. But poverty was not regarded – or, at least, not until a rather late date – as an independent social and economic problem; rather, it was seen in the light of other problems of more import for the medieval mind. Poverty was interpreted in terms of the corporate and juridical division of society: poor people were accounted as base, devoid of privileges, and therefore no logical incongruity was seen in the opposition 'noble'/'poor' since these concepts were not limited to economics and property. Again, poor people were seen as God's elect; the *pauperes Christi* were those who had spurned earthly goods in order to attain the kingdom of Heaven. That is to say, the language of economics appears in its turn as a sort of 'dialect' of a cultural meta-language, in which the concepts and terminology of economics, theology and law are not sharply partitioned.

Let us take another example: the Provençal troubadour sings of his Beloved, but he does not find, indeed he does not seek, individual, original words to express his feelings or describe her beauty. Without exception, the concepts and the terminology he uses will be those of medieval institutions: 'service', 'donation', 'feudal oath', 'seigneur' and so on – a ready-made lexicon of love upon which he will draw for his amorous lay. The Beloved is dearer to him than anything on earth – dearer, that is to say, than the cities of Andalusia or the Orient, dearer than possession of the Triple Crown or the Holy Roman Empire.

In the course of this book we shall come across many more examples of this sort of thing, but for the moment let us turn to consideration of the densely polysemantic nature of the language of medieval man. All the most important terms in his culture are polysemantic, and only take on a particular sense in a particular context. As a good example of this we may take the 'etymologies' and 'summae' which were so popular in this epoch. The ability to give a multi-tiered interpretation of any text is something the medieval intellectual never lacks. Thus, in order to understand the 'language' of any given area of human activity in feudal society, it is necessary to know the cultural language of which this special 'language', far from being a closed autonomous system, is a dialect. All professional, all guild 'languages', continuously merge into each other, and are 'meaningful' not only within but also beyond the confines of the relevant specialised skill or craft. There is in fact only one language, one all-embracing semiological system, variously and specifically decoded in relation to the various specialised spheres of human activity in which it is employed. The general use of Latin in medieval Europe is perhaps connected with this.

But if medieval culture does possess this very special structure, this close interrelationship of all its component elements, the question arises: how then can we study the Middle Ages *as a whole*? Research should take as its starting point the *specific* character of an object, and bear this constantly in mind. Much has been done to increase our understanding of the characteristic traits and concrete content of the philosophy, the art and the literature of the Middle Ages, of its ethical and aesthetic thought, its education methods, its law, the economic doctrines of the church and many other manifestations of the *Weltanschauung* and the culture of the Middle Ages. As scientific knowledge progresses, it naturally and inevitably brings with it an ever sharper degree of differentiation between the individual aspects studied; and in this process the common ground underlying the manifold aspects of medieval culture is unfortunately not always sufficiently clearly brought out. The forms of medieval cultural life are all functions of the social activity of the people of the period, the product of their way of 'shaping' their world.

Evidently, in order to understand the life, the behaviour and the culture of medieval people, it is important to try to reconstruct their ways of thinking and their system of values. We have to try to discern their 'habits of mind', the ways in which they evaluated the world that surrounded them.

But is it possible to penetrate into the secret thoughts of people removed from us by so many centuries? Are such attempts not the province of the novelist rather than of the scholar? The cultural historian has no right to rely only on his imagination; his intuitions must be underpinned by scientific method, he has to find ways and means of ensuring a relatively objective approach to the available material. In my opinion, it is best to try first of all to identify the basic universal categories of a culture, those without which it cannot exist and by which it is permeated in all its manifestations. These categories are then, at the same time, the defining categories of human consciousness in that culture. By this I mean such concepts and perceptual forms as time, space, change, cause, fate, number, the relationship of the perceptible to the supersensible, the relationship of the part to the whole. This list could be extended, developed and refined. But that is not the point. The point is that in any culture these universal concepts are mutually interrelated to form a 'world model' *sui generis*, a 'network of coordinates' through which the bearers of this culture perceive reality and construct their mental image of the world.

I introduce the term 'world model' with a proviso: the word 'model' is not used in any special cybernetic sense, and in what follows it will be used interchangeably with 'world picture', 'world image', 'world-view'.

By the 'world model' latently accepted in a given society, a member of that society will be guided in all his actions. With the help of the categories that compose it he will receive sensa and impressions from the external world which he will then transmute into the data of his own internal experience. These basic categories precede, as it were, the ideas and the world-view which develop among members of the society or of its particular groups. Hence, however much the ideology and the beliefs of these individuals and groups may differ among themselves, at the root of all of them will be found the universal concepts and representations which are canonical for the society as a whole, and without which no theories, no philosophical, aesthetic, political or religious ideas or systems can be constructed. The concepts I have listed form the basic semantic inventory of the culture. The obligatory nature of these categories upon all members of the society must not, of course, be understood to mean that the society consciously imposes these norms upon its members by requiring them to perceive the world and react to it in this particular way; society is unaware both of the imposition and of the acceptance, the 'absorption', of these categories and images by its members: always bearing in mind that ruling groups or classes may appropriate and take control of certain cultural categories and concepts, thereby preventing their free interpretation and ensuring that those who depart from their own 'orthodox' interpretation are stigmatised as heretics and apostates; as indeed happened under feudalism. These categories are imprinted in language as in other semiological systems (e.g. in art, science and religion), and it is as impossible to think about the world without making use of these categories as it is to think without the category of language.

As I said above, our list of the basic cultural categories is incomplete. Other ways of experiencing the world exist, of greater social import, and are found in any and every society – for example, the individual, society, labour, wealth, property, freedom, law, justice. In contradistinction to the cosmic categories listed above, these might be described as social categories. But the division of the world into the natural cosmos and the social cosmos is always to a greater or less degree conventional; indeed, in many societies it is essentially impossible to make such a division, since the cosmos is anthropomorphic and the world of men is weakly or not at all divided from the world of nature. Hence, the social categories like those here listed are in many civilisations tied up with, intertwined with, the cosmic categories in the closest possible way. Both sets of categories are of equal value in the construction of the world model which is to be valid in any given society.

Each civilisation, each social system, is characterised by its own special way of perceiving the world. When we say that the basic conceptual and perceptional categories are 'universal' we mean that these categories inhere in man at every stage of his development. As regards their content, however, they are not invariable. In different social structures we find utterly dissimilar categories of time or of freedom, we find varying attitudes to labour and varying understandings of law, varying perceptions of space and varying explanations of causality. We may assume that within the framework of a civilisation these categories do not represent a fortuitous selection, but form in aggregate a system in which change of certain forms is bound up with change in others.

The basic concepts and images of a civilisation are formed in the course of practical human activity, on the basis of human experience and traditions inherited from previous ages. To a certain stage in the development of production, in social relationships, and in man's alienation from his natural environment, there correspond associated ways of experiencing the world. In this sense, these ways of experiencing the world reflect social practice. But at the same time these categories determine the behaviour of individuals and of groups. Accordingly, they influence social practice, contributing to the process whereby it is cast in forms reflecting the 'world model' in which these categories are grouped.

All of this underlines the cardinal importance of studying the relevant categories if we are to understand the culture and the social life of historical epochs other than our own. A daunting task! Indeed, we may well ask ourselves whether it is possible at all. For in their actual historical manifestation, the categories we have mentioned inhered in people belonging to a completely different epoch from ours. Comprehensible to these people, they become, when these people no longer exist, hieroglyphs, which posterity has to decipher. Torn from the living tapestry of medieval culture, they come to us in fragmentary form and – the main obstacle – deprived of the significance with which they were invested by medieval people. For us, they can no longer yield up their original meaning. The danger of grafting new and alien meanings on to these categories is real, if not inescapable.

These doubts lead us to confront a more general problem: are we capable of comprehending the past without foisting our own way of looking at things, a way dictated by our own time and place, on to its categories? The answer would seem to be in the negative. In fact, our interest in a bygone age, the criteria we employ in selecting material from the sources, our ways of evaluating this material, the generalisations we make, the conclusions we draw – all these are inevitably conditioned in one way or another by the concepts and the values which inhere in our own society. Yet, none the less, 'history' cannot be a closed book. It is instructive that Spengler, putting forward the thesis of the non-communicability of cultures, which he depicted as closed monads without windows or doors, felt nevertheless obliged to make an exception for the historian (that is to say, for himself) and to allow him the possibility of comprehending the principles informing the inner life of each of these systems. Which was, of course, a *non sequitur* from his own premises, but a very natural one. For the researcher who commits himself totally to the principle that it is difficult or impossible for the representative of one culture to understand another, is doomed to creative paralysis and must remain silent.

The difficulties attending the setting up of a dialogue between ourselves and the people of other ages must not deter us from making the attempt. The success of such an attempt will depend in no small measure on the methods employed by the researcher and on his being aware of the dangers besetting his path. His approach to the historical investigation of another culture must be such that his 'kit defects' – that is to say, his congenital preconceptions and value-judgments – are, if not cut to a minimum, at least taken invariably into account. It is not possible to rid oneself of them altogether; but – an important question – are they merely 'hindrances' to getting to know another culture, or do they not perhaps also act as a stimulus, goading the researcher on?

I believe that the way of studying medieval culture applied

in the present book – by means of the analysis of its various categories and the clarification of their meaning as elements in a unified socio-cultural system – deserves attention. It is a method which, of course, generates its own difficulties.

In the first place, since the categories listed above permeate all aspects of the lives of both individual and society, and can be discerned in language and in all other semiological systems, the only way to throw light on their role in a former culture would be to study all the surviving texts and monuments of that culture, for it is in these texts and monuments that the categories are attested. But such a task is Utopian, and completely exhaustive research must remain an ideal.

In the second place, the 'selection' of categories which go to make up the 'world model' remains unclear. It is reasonable to assume that in some civilisations this model includes, along with the genuinely universal categories, other components specific or peculiar to these civilisations or social systems, and that categories which are of essential significance in some cultures may be rather less important in others.

We have taken only a few of the components of the medieval 'world model': time and space, law, wealth, labour and property. This selection may be questioned as arbitrary. And indeed, what common ground is there between the categories of time and law, or between the categories of labour and space? They belong to different areas of human experience, to disparate planes of man's perception of reality. But perhaps just because of this, some attention to them may be of special interest; we may be able to trace some common factor in these concepts and representations which differ so greatly in many respects – some common factor uniting them in one single world picture. We want to carry out, as it were, random tests in various compartments of the edifice called 'the medieval world' with a view to establishing their common nature and their mutual interrelations. By selecting categories of both cosmic and social order, we are able to approach the manner in which the medieval person perceived the world, from different standpoints, and accordingly describe it more fully. In selecting these categories we have been guided by yet another consideration: we want to show that not only in such concepts as time and space, which are directly related to art, but also in representations of law, property and labour, apparently remote from culture, it is possible and necessary to discern a 'cultural' content, without which their social significance and even their economic value would remain incomprehensible. The question whether our categories are well selected for the analytical purpose in hand may be more expediently answered by a perusal of this book. If it helps to make some features of the medieval world picture emerge more clearly than before, it will not have failed.

In attempting to isolate the various components of the form in which were cast the images and impressions of medieval man, we have to pause and consider by what principles we are to be guided. The 'world model' is a fairly stable figuration, defining human perception and experience of reality over a long period; in the Middle Ages when development and change took place very slowly, incomparably more slowly than in modern times, the general world picture inevitably appeared exceptionally stable, if not static. Evidently we may speak of the 'medieval world picture', having in mind the several centuries during which it dominated human consciousness. But let us look more closely at its sources. Attention is usually focused on the continuity of the late classical and the medieval world pictures, with a special role in the formation of the latter being allotted to Christianity. Far less attention is paid to another component in the medieval world-view – the conceptual system of the age of barbarism. In antiquity, most of the peoples of Europe were barbarians; during the transition to the Middle Ages they came to share in Christianity and in Graeco-Roman culture, but their traditional ways of perceiving the world were not necessarily effaced. Under the cloak of Christian dogma, the old beliefs and notions lived on. Thus it is proper to speak not of one but of two 'world models': the barbarian (in the case of Western Europe, the Germanic) 'world model', and its replacement, the 'world model' which grew up on this basis under the powerful influence of the older and more advanced Mediterranean culture, including Christianity.

Accordingly, in each section of this book we shall discuss

the way in which one category or another was perceived, first in the age of barbarism and then in the Christian Middle Ages. In this second part of his task, the author can fall back on the research carried out by historians, art historians, linguists, and historians of literature, philosophy, and science, who in pursuit of their own interests have excavated a great deal of material laying bare medieval man's ways of perceiving and experiencing the world. But material for the first part of the task – identifying the cultural categories of the age of barbarism – is far less plentiful. The greatest interest here seems to lie in the Scandinavian culture of the early Middle Ages. The Germanic cultural traditions lasted longer in the north of Europe, and are much more plentifully attested in northern texts and other monuments than anywhere else. With all its peculiarities, the Scandinavian culture of this period is an adequate reflection of the most important traits of the barbarian culture of Europe as a whole.

In the search for some of the basic components of the medieval world-view we soon become aware that the picture as we have it needs to be refined and sharpened. In spite of the relatively stable nature of the medieval world-view, it did develop and change – and, accordingly, we must show it in motion, pointing to differences in the treatment of this or that cultural category at different periods of the Middle Ages. But in so far as we are bent on sketching a general cultural 'model' by analysing its separate components in greater detail, we feel justified in more or less ignoring any development which led to the deformation of this 'model'. Where apposite, the factors making for disintegration of the world-view we are studying will be indicated. But it is enough for our purposes if we set out the structural categories which are relevant for us; if the results turn out to be worthy of attention, it may then become desirable to fill them out with more concrete content, and to order them more precisely in chronological sequence. The same applies to differences in the world-views belonging to different people of Western Europe in the Middle Ages; here we cannot even touch upon them.

In the contemporary humanities, the problem of the

synchronic/diachronic relationship looms very large. Historical research is diachronic by definition; it sets out to 'show' history in action, that is, to exhibit change in time. But society is a coherent whole, and therefore has to be considered as a structural unity, which presents the researcher with the problem of synchronic analysis of the system. Combining these two different aspects is fraught with not inconsiderable methodological difficulties. It should be stressed, however, that the synchronic examination of a socio-cultural system does not contradict the historical approach; rather, it complements it. Synchronic analysis does not assume that society is static; it is simply a special descriptive method. As I have already said, each of the categories of medieval culture which we examine is presented in both aspects, synchronic and diachronic: first of all, as an element of the archaic Germanic culture, and then as a component of the culture of feudal society. In this process, the problem of the transition from the earlier state to the subsequent one is, of course, left unresolved.

Then again, the 'world model' of the barbarians and the 'world model' of the feudal Middle Ages are very different from each other. The former took shape in a relatively homogeneous society invested with an as yet uneroded system of tribal norms. Hence, the culture of the barbarian world was also strikingly homogeneous, and its values met with universal acceptance within the framework of the society. This does not mean that culture in the pre-class society was 'simple' or 'primitive' – all it means is that its language was generally significant, representing a semiological system which was interpreted in near-identical fashion by all groups and members of the society.

The 'world picture' of the Middle Ages, on the other hand, appears much more complicated and full of contradictions. The reasons for this are to be sought first and foremost in the social make-up of feudal society, divided as it was into mutually antagonistic classes and orders. 'The thoughts of the ruling class' here became 'the ruling thoughts', but even these ruling ideas and concepts themselves – principally the Christian *Weltanschauung* – fail to oust completely other forms of social consciousness, preserved in the lower social classes. The essential point is that the same concepts and symbols are variously interpreted in and by various social groups.

In fact, the 'world picture' apprehended by representatives of differing social strata and classes of feudal society was not invariant over this wide spectrum. The knight's relationship with reality could hardly tally with that of the burgher; the university professor could hardly see things the same way as the peasant. This consideration must always be borne in mind; and when we come to discuss the experiencing of time in the Middle Ages, we shall try to show how radically attitudes to time were to change in the towns in keeping with the urban rationalisation of life; and our analysis of the problems of labour, property and wealth will take into account the varying reactions of peasants, burghers, courtiers and clergy. Similarly, the question of human personality in feudal society, even in the limited form which our discussion will take, will differ in detail according to the social position' of the individual representatives selected for investigation.

Our attention will focus, however, not on medieval ideology nor on a world picture consciously constructed by men in keeping with their social status, but rather on those representations of the world which were not always clearly realised by medieval people, and therefore did not fully reach the ideological level; when we speak of the 'experiencing' of such categories as time, space, etc., we are positing a relatively immediate relationship to them, a relationship not yet wholly transmitted through a system of social attitudes and class interests. In other words, we shall try to discover those cultural elements which are of interest to us, not so much on the ideological level as on the social-psychological level; on the level not so much of understanding the world as of sensing it, although of course we recognise the extent to which these two spheres are mutually connected by innumerable transitions and modulations. It is, of course, impossible to study social psychology if ideology is ignored, and we shall not attempt to do so. The question is, what should be stressed? On what should research concentrate? In the above list of the categories of the medieval world picture, it is primarily the social-psychological aspect that interests us.

Is such an approach to the history of culture justified? I am convinced that it is not only permissible but inevitable, and experience in the humanities in the last few decades – and especially in the last few years – convinces me of this. The study of a socio-psychologic 'section' of social life is being more and more widely recognised as a task of cardinal importance. It is impossible to limit oneself to an 'objective' or rather 'objectival' method of research into, and description of, society – a method in which society is studied as though it were a physical object, that is, from the outside; in addition, it is necessary to try to penetrate into the depths of human consciousness and human ways of perceiving the world, and clarify their structure and their role in the general historical process. The object of historico-cultural analysis is man – living, thinking and feeling man in society, whose behaviour is determined by society, and who, in his turn, acts upon society and its kinetic patterns. The first, as yet isolated essays in concrete examination of the way in which people thought in the Middle Ages are deeply interesting and show that this approach holds promise for the future. Such works show that there are grounds for speaking of a spiritual orientation which is proper to the Middle Ages: a specific manner of thinking that dominates the epoch from beginning to end.

Since this book sets out to present certain fundamental categories of the medieval world-view and certain peculiarities of medieval culture, our interest centres on its *general* characteristics. The cultural 'model' which I present is an 'ideal type' rather than a painstakingly accurate reproduction of reality. I have selected and tried to interpret those components of the culture which should be subjected to more rigorous examination in the future. My method is to paint a broad picture of the path to be followed, leaving the detail to be filled in more precisely and more meticulously at some future date. We are concerned less with the content of medieval culture than with the categories underlying it as basis. We peruse not the 'text' itself, it might be said, so much as the 'dictionary' which is its key.

It should perhaps be emphasised once more that our concept of 'medieval man' is an abstraction. As we reveal the common ground in the categories which go to make up the Middle Ages, we must always bear in mind that medieval society was a society of lords and peasants, burghers and villagers, clerics and laymen, educated and illiterate, orthodox and heretics. Polarisation of the various groups and classes of medieval society, while not destroying (at least until a later stage) the general 'world picture', rendered it unstable, ambivalent and full of contradictions. The task of revealing these cultural antagonisms must be left to specialist studies.

My book concentrates, then, on the mass phenomena of medieval culture. The views of great medieval thinkers on specific issues in the field are of interest to us mainly in so far as they can be described as 'typical', and generally instructive for the study of feudal society and the system of value-judgments obtaining in it.

Since scientific reconstruction of the medieval 'world-view' is only just getting under way, my interpretation of the results must necessarily be of a provisional character; and the results themselves must be checked by later and more penetrating study. May I claim that this book puts the questions; it does not give all the answers.

CHAPTER II

Ideas of space and time in the Middle Ages

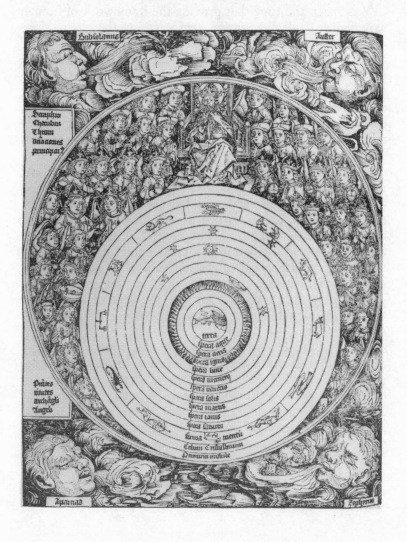

W e apprehend the world in terms of space and time; and it is space and time that provide the framework of human experience. Today, common sense accepts the abstractions of 'time' and 'space' and is guided by them in everyday activity. Space is understood as a three-dimensional, geometrical, evenly extended form which can be divided into commensurate sections. Time is conceived as pure duration, an irreversible succession of events proceeding from the past, through the present towards the future. Time and space are taken as objective, in the sense that their properties are not affected by the matter occupying them.

The complications in our understanding of space and time introduced by the theory of relativity, by particle physics and by the psychology of perception have been largely ignored by most historians, and have had no effect on their traditional attitude to these categories. For the historian, 'space' is the arena of historical geography and cartography, or, at most, something which crops up as an 'ecological factor' in his study of the 'external conditions' of historical development. Time for the historian is essentially the time of synchronic and diachronic tabulation. Neither category gives rise to any special problem.

In fact, the categories of space and time are usually accepted by historians simply as objective 'forms of the existence of matter'. They tend to forget that the 'matter' of history is, to a very high degree, specific, and that the categories of space and time cannot be understood in one and the same sense when they are applied to the natural world on the one hand and to human society on the other. There is often a failure to realise that time and space not only exist objectively but are also subjectively perceived and experienced by people; in different civilisations and societies, at different stages of social development, in different sectors of one and the same society, even by different individuals within the same society, these categories are perceived and applied in varying ways. This has been confirmed by results reached in many sciences – linguistics, ethnology, cultural anthropology, the history of art, the history of literature and psychology, and it is of enormous importance for historiography as well, particularly for cultural history. Both practically and mentally, man is guided by these basic categories of his world picture; and his manner of interpreting them largely shapes his personal behaviour, the behaviour of social groups and the development of whole societies. Study of the perceptual and conceptual cultural inventory should help us to understand its nature and, consequently, to clarify the conditions under which the human personality has been shaped in this or that period.

Where medieval studies are concerned it is especially important to have the problem put in this way. Our present-day attitude to the world differs fundamentally from the way in which medieval people perceived and experienced the world. Many of their ideas are not merely strange to us: they are barely comprehensible. And accordingly, the danger of imputing totally alien motivation to the people of the Middle Ages is a very real one, as is the danger of totally misinterpreting the true causes behind what they did and thought.

Man is not born with 'a sense of time'; his temporal and spatial concepts are invariably conferred upon him by the culture to which he belongs. Industrially developed society is characterised by an intense awareness of time. Modern man handles temporal concepts with great ease: even the most distant past is conceptually available to him without any special difficulty. He can foresee the future, make forward arrangements, and plan the development of the sciences, technology, production and of society itself far into the future. This facility can be explained in terms of the high degree of regularity in the temporal systems we use. Time and space are treated as abstractions which alone enable us to construct our mental picture of a unified and well-ordered universe. For us, these categories have taken on an autonomous character; we can use them freely as tools, without reference to particular events.

Even in antiquity, in the Middle Ages and in the Renaissance there were thinkers who pondered the problem of the irreversibility of swift-flowing time; but it seems true to say that, if we take society as a whole, never before has time been so highly valued as now, and never has it taken up so much of man's attention. Modern man is 'man in a hurry'; his conscious self is shaped by his relationship to time. Time holds man in thrall: his whole life unfolds *sub specie temporis*. A sort of 'cult of time' has been established.[1] Even rivalry between social systems is now understood as a competition in time: who will clock up the fastest development time, for whom is time 'working'? The face of the clock with its relentless second hand could well be the symbol of our civilisation.

In the same way, our understanding of space has altered in modern times: we have discovered that it can be compressed. New methods of communication and of locomotion have enabled us to cover far greater distances per time unit than we could even a few years ago, to say nothing of the more remote past. As a result, the world has become much smaller. People have learned to attach enormous importance to doing things quickly – to speed, a category which unites the concepts of space and time. The whole rhythm of life has been radically changed. We have grown accustomed to this; but nothing like it was ever known before throughout human history.

Our modern categories of space and time have very little in common with the time and space perceived and experienced by people in other historical epochs. In the so-called primitive or mythological consciousness these categories, as pure abstractions, do not exist at all, since archaic ways of thought are mainly concrete, directed to particular and palpable objects. They comprehend the world in its diachronic and synchronic aspects simultaneously; that is, their thinking is 'outside time'. 'We are therefore presented with the paradoxical situation', writes G. J. Whitrow, 'that in his first conscious awareness of time, man instinctively sought to transcend or abolish time.'[2] Are we perhaps justified in saying that the attempt to annul the passage of time by returning to the mythological prototype, to the primordial *illud tempus*, was none other than an attempt to overcome the isolation and the circumscription of individual human existence? Through its myth of the regeneration of time, archaic culture gave man the possibility of overcoming the transitoriness and singularity of his life. By not detaching himself, either in thought or in conduct, from the ancestral social body, man sought to cheat death. In this system of consciousness, past, present and future are arrayed, as it were, on one plane, and in a certain sense they are 'contemporary'. Time has been 'spatialised', it is experienced in the same way as space; the present is not separated off from the main body of time, composed by the past and the future. Ancient man saw past and present stretching round him, in mutual penetration and clarification of each other. An event which took place previously and an event happening now can be perceived by the archaic consciousness as manifestations in one and the same plane, extended in one and the same temporal duration. Time and space as perceived by primitive man may seem unordered to the modern mind. Temporal orientation in the primordial society is extended only to the immediate future, the recent past and current activity, to phenomena in man's immediate surroundings; beyond these limits, events are perceived indistinctly, and loosely coordinated in time. While very well able to orientate himself in space, primitive man was hardly aware of it beyond his practical needs.

It is essential to remember that members of primitive society understood space and time not as a set of neutral coordinates, but rather as mysterious and powerful forces, governing all things – the lives of men, even the lives of the gods. Hence both space and time are axiologically and emotionally charged: time and space can be good or evil, beneficial for certain kinds of activity, dangerous or hostile to others; there is a sacral time, a time to make merry, a time for sacrifice, a time for the re-enactment of the myth connected with the return of 'primordial' time; and in the same way there exists a sacral space, there are sacred places or whole worlds subject to special forces.[3]

Completely clear partitioning between past, present and future becomes possible only when the concept of time as linear and irreversible becomes dominant in social consciousness. This is not to say that distinctions of time are totally lacking in archaic society: after all, his own daily experience enables man to discern sequence in his actions and in natural phenomena. But the chronological sequences in which the everyday life of primitive peoples is organised are separated in their consciousness from the cyclic time of the myth; the forefathers and their living progeny inhabit different temporal dimensions. Festivals and rituals form the ring connecting these two concepts of time, these two levels of perception of reality. Thus, linear time does not predominate in primitive consciousness; it is subordinate to the cyclic perception of vital phenomena, for it is recurrent time that lies at the root of the mythological images forming the world-view of primitive man.

A combination of linear time with cyclic time – with a mytho-poetical 'dream-like compression of time' (Thomas Mann) – can be found in various forms throughout history; the question is, how are these two different ways of perceiving the flow of time correlated? In one way or another, the thinking processes of many of the peoples which produced the great civilisations of antiquity are circular. At the base of the system of values on which the ancient Oriental cultures were built lies the concept of an eternally enduring present, indissolubly bound up with the past. The traditional ancient Chinese conception of time was a cyclical sequence of eras, dynasties, reigns, liturgically ordered and subject to an unchanging rhythm.[4] The expressive symbol of the ancient Indian concept of time was the wheel. The wheel of cosmic order turns eternally; it is the perpetual rotation of birth and death, constantly self-renewing. The Egyptian pyramids serve as majestic monuments to the 'suspended' time of the ancient Near Eastern civilisations. Time continues to flow onwards in everyday life, but this is the time connected with the outward appearance of the visible world; true time is the eternity of the higher reality which is not subject to change. The world, in the eyes of the ancient Egyptians, came ready-made from the hands of the creator; time past and time future subsist in time present.[5]

The attitudes to time characteristic of the civilisations of the ancient East can hardly be reduced to a single formula. In this connection, it is worth bearing in mind J. Needham's warning against making too much of the static element in ancient Chinese culture. Needham refers in particular to the great Chinese historical tradition.[6] In the case of certain other ancient civilisations, on the other hand, it is the total lack of historical texts that is striking. Before we are in a position to make sweeping statements it would seem wiser to study each of the ancient civilisations in more detail. And here we have to remember that the perception of time characteristic of this or that people will be presented in one way in their theories of the natural world and in their historiography, and in quite another way in myths, cults, rituals, which are more immediate expressions of the popular mind.

Antiquity is rightly considered to be the cradle of modern European culture; and in the Middle Ages, and even more so in the Renaissance, the classical heritage had a powerful fertilising effect on European culture. But perhaps nothing reveals more clearly the profound gap between ancient and modern culture than an analysis of their attitudes to time. While vectorial time dominates modern consciousness, it played very little part in that of the Hellenes. For the Greeks, the perception of time remained deeply affected by the mythological interpretation of reality. Time was neither homogeneous nor chronologically sequential; like space, it had not yet become an abstraction.[7] The world was perceived and experienced by the ancient Greeks not in such categories as change and development but as remaining at rest, or as orbiting in a great circle. The events that take place in the world are not unique: the epochs that succeed each other will be repeated, and people formerly existent and events that once took place will recur after the closure of the 'great year' – the Pythagorean era. Man contemplates a perfect harmonic cosmos – 'a plastically fashioned whole, like some large figure or statue or even a most accurately constructed musical instrument giving forth a particular kind of sound'.[8]

A. L. Losev even writes of the 'sculptural style of history'. The cosmos of the ancient Greek was a 'material, sensual and living cosmos, an eternal rotation of matter, now arising from amorphous chaos to generate its harmony, symmetry, rhythmic organisation, its still and noble majesty, now collapsing in ruins, dissipating its structural harmony and

[31]

once again transforming itself into chaos'.[9] The plastic arts of antiquity incorporate this attitude to time with extraordinary and powerful immediacy. The treatment of the body in ancient art bears witness to the fact that in the present moment the ancient artists saw a fullness of being complete in itself and not subject to change; 'was', 'is', and 'will be' are 'aspects of time which imitates eternity and which runs in a circle according to the laws of number' (Plato, *Timaeus*). The Hellenic consciousness is backward-looking; the world is governed by fate, to which not only men but also the gods are subject, and, accordingly, there is no place for historical development. Antiquity is 'astronomic' (Losev) and therefore devoid of history; it is static. 'The Golden Age' as imagined by the ancient Greeks is behind us, in the past, and the world does not proceed by qualitative change. The ancient Greeks seem to be people who 'jib at the future', who move towards it 'with their backs turned to it'.[10] This mytho-poetic and static-cyclic world-view, natural to the Greeks, is transformed in Rome: Roman historians show themselves much more receptive to the concept of linear time, and they no longer see the course of history in mytho-poetic categories, but take their stand on definite moments in actual history (the foundation of Rome, etc.) And yet in spite of the enormous development in philosophic thought, the ancient world did not develop a philosophy of history going beyond the confines of general historical pessimism: the ancients did not apprehend history as a drama – as a field of action in which man's freedom of will could be exercised.[11]

In antiquity, man was not yet able to break out of the sphere of natural existence and stand up for himself against the natural environment. His dependence on the natural environment, and his incapacity to apprehend it as an object upon which he could act from outside, finds its cultural reflection in the idea of the inner analogy between man the 'microcosmos' and world the 'megacosmos' which have the same structure and consist of the same elements; and also in the image of the 'cosmic' human body – incomplete, not clearly differentiated from the surrounding world into which it merges, open to this world and absorbing it into itself. In his fine analysis of this image, which he calls the 'grotesque body', and which plays a leading role in the cultures of antiquity and the Middle Ages, M. M. Bakhtin shows how the image has persisted in the popular mind over a whole series of epochs, right up to the Renaissance which signals a transition to another way of perceiving the world, and to man's new awareness of himself (individualism and the conception of the human body as something 'exclusive', 'alienated' from the world).[12] We may assume that to this particular way of perceiving reality in grotesque images there corresponded a particular relationship with time.

In his work on Polybius and Ssu-ma Ch'ien, N. I. Konrad showed that these two outstanding ancient historians, living in totally different socio-cultural milieux, display an amazing degree of unanimity in their interpretation of history as a process of cyclic return. It is true that they both reach the conclusion that cyclic return does not mean repetition pure and simple, but repetition in which there is, to some degree, a new content. 'Return to something does not necessarily mean repetition of that which was.'[13] Nevertheless, neither the Chinese historian nor the Greek is able to get beyond the confines of the world-view and the perception of time inherent in his epoch and culture; for them and for their compatriots, history was no more than the eternal return in a prescribed order of the same political forms.

Thus, the irreversibility of time which seems to us so natural and self-evident, something without which time would be totally inconceivable, is not seen in this light once we step out of the confines of our own historical conditions and concomitant mental attitudes. Linear time is only one of the possible forms of social time; but it is the one which has ousted all its rivals and is now unquestioningly accepted as the only way of reckoning time in the European cultural milieu. But its victory was the result of a long and complicated process of development.

How did this development take place? How were time and space perceived in the Europe of the Middle Ages? Approaching the study of these basic categories of human consciousness, we find a sort of desert, a 'no-man's-land' between the ancient world and our own. One gets the impression that in the intervening period the human mind remained stuck in a state of primitive crudity. This is the attitude of those authors who aver that human personality was distinguished by its absence in the Middle Ages, and began to find expression only in the Renaissance. As the new personality of Renaissance man emerges, so too do new conceptions of time and space; planted in the centre of his newly discovered world, Renaissance man discovered in his own self a new point of reference. But what can we find out about the structure of human personality in earlier periods of European history? There is no ready answer to this question, though Spengler did his best to find one.[14] Searching for the 'world model' of a given society, which stamps all sides of human activity within that society, we are also searching for a human personality, whose relations with the world and whose self-consciousness are expressed in the shape of that 'world-view', whose categories include those of time and space.

But here again we have to reiterate the conditions and limitations to which we referred above. Is it possible to speak of uniform categories of time and space in relation to the whole of the Middle Ages and to the whole of Europe in that period? Obviously not. Were these categories not differently perceived by different sectors and different classes of society, even within the boundaries of one country at one and the same period? Undeniably they were. But it is permissible to put the question another way: is it possible to discern a common content in these categories, a kind of substratum, from which all subsequent differences, however substantial, have been generated? We take as our starting point the assumption that up to a certain moment and to a certain degree there was such a common substratum in the medieval experiencing of time and space; and that this must be clarified before we proceed to identify the discrepancies.

As the historical watershed marking the point at which the differences in the perception and the understanding of these categories became crucial, I take the late medieval upsurge of the urban class, whose economic practice and whose style and rhythm of life marked them off from the way of life of the rural classes of medieval society. It is in this period that the categories of time and space begin to be transformed, to lose their traditional content. The transition from 'biblical time' to 'time of the merchants' (to use J. Le Goff's expression) begins. But it was a very long-drawn-out and a very slow process, and it was still not completed by the end of the Middle Ages. Consequently, and for the better understanding of this transition period, it is necessary first to be clear in our minds about the 'model' of time and space prevalent in the preceding period of the Middle Ages. New categories of time and space bound up with the activities of the merchants and artisans, and with the onset of scientific investigation, etc., were to remain within the framework of the medieval 'world model' for some considerable time yet, albeit transforming it more and more significantly from within. The upsurge of urban culture does not mean the end or the 'withering away' of the Middle Ages, but it brings in its train a deepening differentiation within the traditional world picture, which previously had been relatively uniform for the whole of society.

I said above that the world picture or some of its individual elements are incorporated in all the semiological systems operating in society. It follows from this that traces of it are best sought in the literary and artistic creations of the age. It seems to me, however, that we must be cautious in our use of this material in a study of spatio-temporal conceptions. This is because the process of perceiving and reproducing the world in terms of art generates its own autonomous categories of space and time, whose conventional character must always be borne in mind. The artistic time and space with which we are confronted in literature and painting, have specific characteristics, arising in the main not directly from the manner of perceiving the world and history particular to the society producing the works of art in question, but from the special ideological and artistic problems facing writers, poets and painters. For example, let us assume that medieval man loved and admired nature (for the moment this is an assumption, the accuracy of which we shall not go into). But the author of a poem or the painter of a picture would not necessarily reflect these sentiments: instead, he would give a totally conventional image of the milieu surrounding his characters, one arising from the needs of the religious-symbolic interpretation of the world. To the medieval mind,

[35]

it was not the world of appearances but the world of the divine essence that was supreme and authentic reality; and hence it was felt that the individual traits of the visible world were unworthy of reproduction, and if they had to be shown at all, it was enough to fall back on a conventional stereotype. In practical life, people could hardly fail to be aware of spatial dimensions, or to see differences in the volume or size of bodies situated near to or far from their eyes, and they must have been aware of proportional differences; but in medieval art the work of art is either monoplanar, or uses the principle of 'inverse perspective'. The artistic representation of the world in the Middle Ages can be explained by reference to definite aesthetic and ideological principles which were obligatory for the artists of the period. Of course, these same general traits can be interpreted as symptoms of a particular relationship to everyday reality, and we have to discover the world-view and the associated mental disposition that could give rise to such an aesthetic. Besides, we can assume that in the Middle Ages artistic time and space did not possess the same degree of autonomy with regard to the social perception of time and space as is the case in modern painting and literature. Have we not grounds for ascribing to medieval man a more integrated awareness of reality? Was the separation between artistic cognition and practical cognition not perhaps less in his case than in ours? Nevertheless, the transition from analysis of the means of poetic and graphic expression used by medieval artists and writers, to consideration of the world-view of the period, is a very complicated one. This does not mean that we can attempt a reconstruction of the medieval world-view without analysing the literary and artistic works of the period: such an analysis is indeed necessary. But we have to bear in mind the general difficulties bound up with the study of artistic creation.

The categories of artistic time and space in the medieval literature of Western Europe have been studied by several specialists, and D. S. Likhachev, who undertook a similar analysis of Old Russian material, is right when he emphasises the specifically 'artistic' treatment of these categories.[15] But the problem of the specific character of cognition in different epochs and in different civilisations is wider than the problem of shift in aesthetic categories, even if this movement is considered in connection with the evolution of socio-political ideas. The study of a culture presupposes an analysis not only of the ideo-conceptual sphere, but also of the socio-psychological networks and of the forms of human behaviour.

Epic and myth must be drawn upon if we are to lay bare the basic categories of the medieval way of thinking. These reflect, however, only a rather deep-seated and archaic layer of the culture. In addition, we have to study the histories, the chronicles, the Lives of the Saints, business documents, letters, tracts and other material, the authors of which did not always – or at least to a lesser degree than the poets and writers – bother about the artistic means of the media and gave more immediate expression to their thoughts. It is in such sources that the epoch is able to 'let the cat out of the bag' and let us observe its specific conceptions of time and space in operation.

Much can certainly be learned about the categories of the medieval world model from a study of the languages, the terminology, and from the oft-recurring set phrases, commonplaces and word combinations. Ritual and procedure played a very large part in the social and cultural life of medieval man. Clearly, it is by a study of the written sources that the historian can most readily recover these patterns. But at the same time we must not forget J Le Goff's pithy saying: 'Feudalism is a world of gestures, not of the written word.'[16] The written record does not give us the whole of medieval man's way of perceiving and representing his world. Much has been irretrievably lost.

Precisely in this connection, analysis of medieval art in this light becomes important. The graphic arts were almost entirely anonymous in the Middle Ages. But even if the artist was known, it is still true that he saw as his main task the reproduction of the traditional and unchanging modes, and the expression of commonplace notions and ideas. His individuality showed itself, if at all, in the inventiveness with which he handled these inherited skills in the rendering of his set theme and images. This applies both to the age of barbarism and, in no small measure, to the art of the Middle Ages

[37]

proper. The well-known authority on the religious art of the Middle Ages (and art in the Middle Ages was predominantly religious, serving the needs of the liturgy) Emile Mâle writes that in this epoch countless generations of men speak through the mouth of the artist; and that although his individuality was not disclaimed, he had to submit to the requirements of the 'sacred mathematics'. The key elements in the work of art, in artistic creation of any kind, are construed as religious hieroglyphs; the artist is not at liberty to give full rein to his imagination, for he is first and foremost in the service of the 'theology of art'.[17] The reasons for this lie not only in the dependence of the artist upon theology, a dependence fostered by the church, which kept a tight grip on art; art spoke to medieval man in the language he knew and understood. Hence, decipherment of the categories lying at the root of this language of medieval art can (even with the provisos set out above) go a long way towards helping us to understand medieval man's ways of perceiving his world: particularly medieval understanding of space and time.

When studying the products of medieval culture, we must not forget that for a long time there was no clear differentiation between the real and the imaginary. What the writers and poets of the Middle Ages recounted was very largely taken by themselves and by their listeners and readers as true accounts of fact. Categories such as 'true' and 'false' are not strictly applicable to the epic; but even in historical writing there was a strong dash of the fairytale and the legend. 'Poetry' and 'truth' (in the sense of 'what actually happened') were not yet sharply distinguished; just as there was no clear division between sacred and profane literature. Neither by function nor by style can works setting out to give an account of events happening in real historical time be distinguished from works in which subjective, artistic time provides the setting. Therefore, the works of medieval historians are no less significant for our understanding of the medieval perception of time than the epic, the lyric poetry or the courtly romance. The essential point is that in all literary (in the wide sense) and artistic production the category of time, like certain other components of the 'world model', was employed in a spontaneous and unaffected manner.

[38]

Ideas of space and time in the Middle Ages

Let us turn now to a more detailed consideration of the problem of spatio-temporal representation in the Western Europe of the Middle Ages.

CHAPTER III

Macrocosm and microcosm

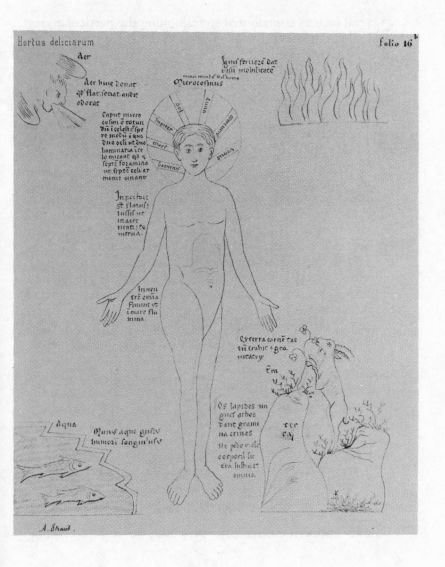

Several factors contributed to fashioning the particular way in which medieval people perceived the space surrounding them. There was first of all their relationship with nature, including the use they made of it, i.e. their production patterns; and then there was the dispersal factor, the distance from one settlement to another, providing a mental and physical horizon which in turn depended on the state of communication between centres of population, and on the religious and ideological postulates governing the community.

The landscape of Western and Central Europe in the early Middle Ages was very different from what it is today. A large part of the land was covered by forests, which did not disappear till very much later, as a result of population expansion and the exploitation of natural resources. Much of the non-woodland area was marshland and swamp. A long time was to pass before the forest yielded to the plough and the swamp became pasture. Points of human habitation were usually scattered here and there in the forests – lonely oases, remote from one another. Small hamlets with a limited number of farmsteads, or isolated farms, predominated. Larger settlements were rarely met with, and then only in specially favoured localities – in river valleys, on the coast or in the fertile regions of Southern Europe. As a rule, the settlement was surrounded by deep forest, which was both attractive because of its resources, such as fuel, game and fruits, and terrifying because of the dangers hidden in it – wild animals, robbers and other miscreants, ghostly beings and werewolves, with which human fantasy liked to populate the mysterious world surrounding the settlement. The forest landscape still persists in popular imagination, in folklore and in the poetic fancy.

Links between settlements were very limited, consisting

mainly of irregular and superficial contacts. A natural husbandry is characterised by the effort to make do for oneself in all basic requirements. In any case, there were practically no roads to speak of, while such rude paths as existed were often impassable. The old Roman highways, in those regions where they existed, fell more and more into disrepair; new routes were rarely cleared and thereafter very difficult to maintain. Such attention as was paid to means of communication by the state authorities did not go beyond their own immediate and very limited needs. Yet, even to satisfy these minimal needs was not easy. While granting immunity to the ecclesiastical institutions and to the thanes and giving them wide powers over the peasants, the Anglo-Saxon kings retained for themselves the right to require the people to take part in the construction of forts and the repair of roads. The building of roads and bridges was accounted work pleasing to God. Swedish runic inscriptions on stone make special mention of bridge-building as a signal service; it was usually carried out as a memorial to a dead relative. The legendary Swedish king Onundr earned himself the nickname 'Road-builder' because of his services in founding new settlements and connecting them by roads.

Travel in the early Middle Ages was a dangerous and protracted business. Dangerous because robbers were virtually a fixture on the roads; protracted because the means of transport were in no better shape than the roads themselves. The most one could expect to do on horseback in twenty-four hours was a few dozen kilometres, while pedestrians moved even more slowly on the wretched roads. The journey from Bologna to Avignon took up to two weeks, from Nîmes to the Champagne trade-fairs took twenty-four days, and even to get from Florence to Naples took eleven or twelve days. A letter from Pope Gregory VII written in Rome on 8 December 1075 reached Goslar in the Harz on 1 January 1076. Two examples will give some idea of the speed with which news of important events was transmitted: news of the death of Frederick Barbarossa in Asia Minor reached Germany four months later, and it took four weeks for the English to learn that their king Richard the Lion-heart had been taken prisoner in Austria. Special couriers were used to carry tidings such as these. The courier run from Rome to Canterbury normally took up to seven weeks, but specially urgent news could be delivered in four weeks.[1]

It was quicker by sea than by land; but here the traveller was threatened by even more fearful dangers than his counterpart on land: storms and other natural hazards, and pirates. Boat-building was in a rudimentary state in early medieval Europe, the boats were ill suited to conditions in the open sea and accordingly preferred to hug the coasts. The exception to this was provided by the Vikings, the fearless mariners whose ships ploughed all the seas of Europe – from the Black Sea and the Mediterranean to the North Sea and the White Sea; they even crossed the North Atlantic. But we do not know how many of their fast ships perished in storms or what price the Vikings paid for their voyages to the White Sea and to the coasts of Greenland and North America. Even the Normans tried not to stray too far from coasts or islands; for navigational aids on the open sea were extremely primitive.

The absolute predominance of the rural population in the Europe of the early Middle Ages was bound to tell on the relationship of the people – of whatever social class – with the surrounding world: the peasant farmer's way of seeing the world and reacting to it was typical of the rest of society in general. Bound to the soil by his work, absorbed in the tasks of rural husbandry, man perceived nature as an integral part of himself instead of treating it as an object pure and simple to be manipulated, utilised or disposed of. Nevertheless, the bond between the peasant and the soil does not mean that he was indissolubly attached to his allotment. Historians have more than once emphasised the very high degree of population mobility in medieval Europe, even in the period following the end of the great *Völkerwanderung* and the definitive occupation of Europe by the barbarians. People were always on the lookout for good sites for settlement and easy ground to till. The process of internal colonisation involved a large number of peasants. The attachment of the peasant to the earth was not lessened by this movement, however, for what impelled the migrants was precisely the desire to acquire their own strip of land and cultivate it.

Clearing new arable land, burning scrub and rooting out tree stumps – these were the crucial factors in the establishment of a medieval rural community: before the internal colonisation process got under way, such a community was of much looser construction since the peasants lived on their farmsteads or in small settlements, separated from other populated areas by very considerable distances.

Culture is, as it were, a 'second nature' created by men in the process of their social practice. In the Middle Ages the creation of this second nature was (as it had been in antiquity) profoundly influenced by man's relationship with nature. Man's links with his natural surroundings were particularly strong in the age of barbarism. The dependence of the barbarian tribes on nature was still so deep-seated that their world-view had many features clearly indicative of their inability to make any sharp distinction between themselves and their natural environment. In Old Scandinavian poetry, parts of the human body are often compared to natural phenomena; and, vice versa, components of the organic or inorganic world are designated as parts of the human body. The head is the 'sky', the fingers are 'branches', water is 'earth's blood', rocks and streams are its 'bones', grass and trees 'earth's hair'. These were to become conventional metaphors, but at this stage they reflect a world-view which makes no clear distinction between the human body and the world it inhabits; and transition from one to the other was across frontiers which were fluid and indefinite.

This link between man and nature was the key determinant in his consciousness. Man's properties as an individual and as a member of a group (family, clan, community), on the one hand, and the properties of the earth he tilled within the confines of that group, on the other, were not sharply delineated, but remained intertwined in the social mind. In Scandinavia, a free man was called an *óðalmaðr*: i.e. the possessor of an *óðal* – the hereditary landed property of the family. But the word *óðal* referred not only to land but also to the totality of rights that went with that land to its possessor. *Óðal* presupposed the right to hereditary and indissoluble possession of land, a right which could not be vitiated as a whole even by alienation of a parcel of the property. Even in the case of transference to third parties, this ultimate right was retained by the odalmen, the holders of the *óðal*, who could have the alienated portion returned to them on payment of a redemption fee, even if the portion in question had been alienated several generations earlier. The point is that the right of *óðal* was a function not of the portion of land but of its owners, from time immemorial, 'from the time of the kurgans' associated with that land. The odalman was a free-born man, and the word *óðal* is etymologically related to the word *ethel* (*edel*), designating the noble birth, the noble provenance of a man, his belonging to a free kin. The qualities of the owners were transferred to the land, which was also regarded as 'free', 'noble'. The term *allod*, used by the Franks and other Germanic tribes on the European continent to designate free ownership of land, seems to be related to the term *óðal*, with which it shared the meaning we have indicated.[2]

In these terms, then, we see a close conjunction in as yet unimpaired unity of two sets of concepts – those concerning hereditary characteristics of the person, his origins and his membership of a clan or kin, and those concerning landed property and its relationships.

Things in general could incorporate the qualities of their owners; this applied not only to land but to swords, horses, ships and jewellery. It was, however, the relationship with the earth which united in a particularly organic fashion the individual, the group to which he belonged and nature. Only as a member of a group – family or clan – could he appropriate a plot of earth and its fruits and benefit from certain well-defined privileges. It is significant that the word *eigen* originally meant not possession of objects, but a man's belonging to a community, and it was only later that the term was extended to material possession. Even at a later period, property, ownership of land remained the personal characteristics of the owners.[3]

So it is risky to construe man's relationship to the earth in the early Middle Ages as one of private property, presupposing a subject–object relationship involving the right of free disposal of the latter. In contradistinction to movable property, the earth could not be the object of unrestrained alienation or of any sort of property deal. Between man, or rather the human group, and landed property there existed a much closer bond, one which was in essence indissoluble.

This special relationship within the land owned by the family also determined its central role in the structure of the early medieval cosmos. The farmstead of the landowner served as a model of the universe. This is well illustrated in Scandinavian mythology, which retained many traits of the beliefs and notions once common to all the Germanic tribes. The world of people was Miðgarðr (Midgard), literally 'middle steading', the cultivated, tilled part of world-space. Miðgarðr is surrounded by the world of monsters and giants which are hostile to men – Útgarðr, which means 'that which is situated outside the walled enclosure', the untilled, still chaotic part of the world. The contrast between Miðgarðr and Útgarðr finds a parallel in the distinction made in Scandinavian law between two categories of land – 'within the enclosure' (*innangarðz*) and 'outside the enclosure' (*útangarðz*). On this contrast turned the basic concepts of law (individual and collective use of land) and the main structural concept of the cosmos: the human world, the farmstead, the Christian enclosure is a copy of, and finds its divine sanction in, Ásgarðr (Asgard), the enclosure of the gods, the Aesir; but this human world is threatened on all sides by the dark, unknown world of terrors and dangers.[4]

It is interesting to note that the Scandinavians saw their own inhabited places as centres, round whose periphery the rest of the world was distributed. This is clear from the names given to these inhabited places: Meðalhus, Meðalland, Meðalfell, Miðgarðr, Miðhús, Miðá, Miðberg ('Middle Enclosure', 'Middle House', 'Middle Mountain', etc.). No less significant is another series of place-names: Bø, By ('Dwelling', 'Homestead'). The ancient population did not need to give these places more precise names, since for these people only one farmstead really existed – the one they owned and lived in. In Norway there were more than a hundred farmsteads with place-names reflecting the concept of a closed and localised cosmos.

Topography plays a very big part in the ancient Scandinavian mind. The first question one asks a stranger is – what is his name and where does he come from. Accordingly, mention of any person in the sagas, even a minor character or someone only referred to in passing, is always accompanied by information about his provenance: whose son he is, and where he comes from. This does not only apply to people; in tales about gods and giants we are unfailingly told where their farmsteads are situated and what they are called. *Grímnismál* (*The Lay of Grimnir*) – one of the poems in the *Elder Edda* – consists almost entirely of descriptions of the places and farmsteads of the gods and of fallen heroes. At the root of all these accounts lies the firm conviction that both man and god must possess landed property. The site of the dwelling has 'grown together' with its owner so intimately that neither is conceivable without the other. A man's full name consists of his own name and the name of the farmstead in which he lives. The name of the dwelling may be derived from the name of its owner. In other cases there figures in the topographical designation the name of the god who is protector of the settlement, and in some place-names we find words indicative of the well-being and prosperity which rule – or perhaps, more accurately, ought to rule – there. The essential point is this: the name of the farmstead was not a trivial matter for the inhabitants and the course of their lives. It was the name of their patrimony, their home: for the allod or *oðal* was not only the inalienable inherited property of the family but also 'home'. We can say that just as the man possessed the farmstead, so it in turn 'possessed' him and put its own stamp on his personality.

In Scandinavian mythology, the world is this totality of farmsteads owned by people, gods, giants, dwarfs. As long as primordial chaos reigned, the world was formless: there were no settlements. The process of ordering the world – the separation of the sky from the earth, the creation of time, of day and night, of the sun, the moon and the stars – was also the process of settlement, the founding of farmsteads, the creation of the well-ordered topography of the world, once and for always. At each nodal point of the world – at its centre, on the ground, in the skies, at the place where the rainbow begins, leading from earth to heaven, and at the point where the earth meets the skies – at all these places there are settlements, farmsteads, burgs.

Scandinavian topography is not based on purely geographical coordinates: it is saturated in emotional and religious significance, and geographical space represents at the same time religious-mythological space. The one passes effortlessly into the other. Chaos, which preceded the creation of the world and its people, was called *Ginnungagap*, 'the great void'; but here 'void' is not so much a negative concept, not simply the opposite of 'fullness' but is felt rather as some sort of potentiality: a state which is the precondition of the subsequent creation of the world, and permeated with magical power.[5] But in the early Middle Ages the Scandinavians placed Ginnungagap in the north, as an ocean covered with ice. Midgardr in mythology was the world of people, created by gods, a fortress protecting men from attack by the giants. But in actual Scandinavian topography this word was, as we have seen, used as a name for farmsteads and settlements.

In so far as space is mythological, it is of course inevitably lacking in any sort of topographical precision. At the beginning of the thirteenth century, the Icelandic writer Snorri Sturluson mentions more than once in the *Younger Edda* (his work on Scandinavian mythology) that the farmsteads of the gods are situated in heaven. Sometimes, however, these statements are self-contradictory. Thus, Ásgardr is said to be situated in heaven and on earth. Valhalla is apparently in heaven – but then it is also to be found where Ásgardr is. Nevertheless, at the beginning of his account, Snorri tells the story of the journey of King Gulfi to Ásgardr, whither he repairs in order to gain wisdom and knowledge. The obstacles which he overcomes on the way from Sweden to Ásgardr are not connected with his having to leave earth; they lie in dreams and visions sent to him by the gods (Aesir). Further on, Snorri tells us that Ásgardr was built 'in the centre of the earth'; 'at that time it was called Troy', and with this identification of Ásgardr with Troy, the abode of the gods makes landfall on earth. Of the 'House of Gladness' (Gladsheim) erected in the middle of Ásgardr, Snorri tells us that this was the 'largest and best dwelling on earth'.[6] Confirming that Baldr's estate, Breidablik, is in heaven, Snorri quotes a fragment from *Grímnismál*:

> There where Baldr
> has built his dwellings
> they call it Breiðablik;
> *in that land*
> where I know
> there are fewest evil things.[7]

Strangely enough, Snorri does not seem to see the contradiction between his own words and the unambiguous specification of location given in *Grímnismál*.

In the *Ynglinga saga* we are told of the legendary 'Great Sweden' lying in Eastern Europe. This was the 'Abode of the Gods', and beside it was the 'Abode of Men'. The 'Abode of the Gods' was in its turn divided into two parts, the kingdoms of the Aesir and of the Vanir.[8] Leaving the abode of the Aesir, Thor proceeded eastwards to do battle with the monsters and giants who were the enemies of both gods and men. In general, Ásgarðr is very similar to Miðgarðr; it too is a farmstead surrounded by fortifications, in which people live, and it is distinguished from other farmsteads only by virtue of its size and wealth. In later sagas and tales by the same Snorri, the pagan gods have been transformed into the ancestors of the royal dynasties of Sweden and Norway, and figure as the first representatives of these dynasties. That is to say, the pagan gods have been demoted. But there are no grounds for assuming that the ancient Scandinavians ever imagined their gods as dwelling in some sort of higher sphere.

The contradiction in the siting of Ásgarðr, which, according to Snorri, lies either in the region of the Don (Tanais), that is, in Middle Earth, or in heaven, reflects not only the kind of geographical imprecision inherent in myth, but also the effect of the clash between two religions with their own very different notions of space. It should not be forgotten that Old Scandinavian mythology is preserved for us in manuscripts dating from no earlier than the thirteenth century. There is no gainsaying the influence of Christianity in these manuscripts, though the extent to which Christianity deformed the pagan beliefs of the Scandinavians is open to question. Recasting of the old myths involved a reinterpretation of the spatial categories. Describing the death of Oðinn and the burning of his body on the funeral pyre according to pagan rites, Snorri writes: 'It was people's belief that the higher the smoke rose into the sky, the more elevated in heaven would he be who was cremated, and therefore a man was considered the nobler, the more possessions were burned with him.'[9] Here, the influence of Christian beliefs is obvious. The 'lines of force' leading from on high downwards, which Snorri mentions, seem to be of Christian provenance.

Parts of the world are connected with definite mythological concepts: thus, the domain of the evil spirits is located in the north and east, where lie the 'fields of darkness' (*Nidavellir*) and the kingdom of the dead – *Hel* (though, according to other accounts, *Hel* is below the earth). The general shape of the world as imagined by the Scandinavians was the 'earthly circle' (*kringla heimsins*). A colourful and vivid description of it is given by the legal formula in verse, according to which he who breaks a treaty of conciliation will be outside the law:

A vagabond he shall be and a wolf in places where
Christians pray and where heathens worship, where fire
burneth, where the earth bringeth forth, where the child
lispeth the name of mother, where mother beareth a
son, where men kindle fire, where the ship saileth, where
shields blink, sun shineth, snow lieth, Finn glideth, fir-
tree groweth, falcon flieth the live-long day and the fair
wind bloweth straight under both her wings – where
Heaven rolleth and earth is tilled, where the breezes waft
mists to the sea, where corn is sown. . . .[10]

The earthly circle below the dome of heaven – this is the world of men and gods in the age of paganism. The image of the 'rounded earth' is found in Snorri, both in the *Younger Edda* and in the sagas of the Norse kings, which were given the general designation of *Heimskringla* from the first words of the *Ynglinga saga* (*kringla heimsins*).

Man's intimate contiguity with the world surrounding him

ruled out any possibility of an aesthetic relationship with nature, or 'disinterested' admiration of it. Being himself an organic part of the world subject to the rhythms of nature, man was hardly able to take a detached view of nature. In the poetry of the barbarians the manifestations of nature are seen as active agents. Sea, rocks, fish, wild animals, birds, are all equally warranted partners in the world drama, on an equal footing with fantastic beings, gods and their servants, the Valkyries, and with man, the being who is implicated in all of these. The scant references in the artistic output of the Germanic tribes to the beauties of nature belong to a different order of feeling, and bespeak a more complex and undifferentiated relationship with the world than aesthetic perception thereof in the exact sense of the term. The Icelandic sagas are exceptionally precise in detailing all the adventures befalling their heroes, but ignore completely any trait of nature that goes beyond the minimum required for scene-setting. Is this assertion not perhaps contradicted by the well-known passage in *Njáls saga* in which we are told how Gunnar, sentenced to three years of exile from Iceland for committing murder, leaves his home?

> They rode down towards Markar River. Just then Gunnar's horse stumbled and he had to leap from the saddle. He happened to glance up towards his home and the slopes of Hlidarend. 'How lovely the slopes are,' he said, 'more lovely than they have ever seemed to me before, golden cornfields and new-mown hay. I am going back home, and I will not go away.'[11]

It was a decision that was to cost him his life, for he perished at the hands of his enemies. But Gunnar's words – 'perhaps the only example of an emotional relationship with nature to be found in the Icelandic sagas'[12] – are more readily explained, in my opinion, in terms of Gunnar's attachment to his native soil, his farm and his house, his reluctance to give in to his enemies, his readiness to accept whatever fate had in store for him, than as an example of admiration for the beauties of nature.

The cosmic world-view of the Germanic tribes, which

shared many common features with that of other barbarian peoples, differed strikingly in some respects from the Christian world-view. Nevertheless, the more we find out about the perception of space in the Christian Middle Ages, the more clearly can we identify therein traits deriving from the 'world model' of the barbarians.

Here too, at the outset of the Christian Middle Ages, human life did no more than flicker fitfully in corners of a nature hardly as yet animated by the activity of men. The peasant in the early Middle Ages was acquainted with a limited number of people residing either with him or close by. The network of social relationships into which he had to fit was simple and durable. All the greater was the role which his relationship with nature played in his life.

Man's partial separation from nature was to last as long as the great mass of people went on leading a life based on natural husbandry, with nature as the main source of supply for all their basic needs. Bound up with this undifferentiated relationship between people, both individuals and groups, and the earth, is the image of the 'grotesque body' which finds exaggerated expression in the graphic arts, in literature and in folklore, as well as in the mass festivals and carnivals of the Middle Ages and the Renaissance. Man was frequently depicted as part of nature: images of animal-men and plant-men, trees with human heads, anthropomorphic mountains, beings with many hands and many legs, recur over and over again all through antiquity and the Middle Ages, and find their most complete expression in the works of Brueghel and Bosch.[13]

M. M. Bakhtin refers to various characteristics of the 'grotesque body', e.g. the predominance therein of a 'somatic fundament' of protuberances and orifices which cancel its localisation and limitation and link it with the rest of nature: exaggeration of the anal-erotic and gastric functions, emphasis on the metamorphoses of birth and death, aging and rejuvenation, and on aspects of fertility, the productive forces of nature. All of this meant the demotion of what was lofty and ideal to what was earthy and material. The grotesque body was represented as non-individualised, incomplete and constantly intertwined with the earth which gives it birth and swallows it up again. The eternally renewed generic body was cosmic, universal and immortal – in sharp contrast to the circumscribed, strictly limited and individualised body canonised in modern art and literature. If in itself the grotesque body exemplified cosmic elements, in the folk legends of the Middle Ages, on the other hand, the wide earth itself took on somatic form and was thought of as a grotesque body. The levelling of all barriers between the body and the world, the fluidity of transition between them – these are characteristic traits of the medieval popular culture, and, accordingly, of the popular imagination.[14]

This world picture was engendered by man's relationship with nature as an extension of his ego, and was very closely bound up also with the similar organic unity of the individual with the social group. It is an attitude which gradually evaporates *pari passu* with the transition to modern times, when the development of industry creates the conditions for man to make a new approach to nature as the object of his technical pressure. In the Middle Ages, such a subject–object relationship between man and the surrounding world was simply impossible. What was missing was the intermediary link which enables man to use nature and at the same time excludes him from her embrace – the artificial provision of whole new systems of complicated and self-diversifying tools, which are the necessary intermediaries between man and nature. Medieval agricultural implements did not replace man's muscular strength; they merely complemented it. Accordingly, medieval man did not set himself the task of transforming nature. His aims *vis-à-vis* nature were those of the consumer.

Of course, man's relationship with nature in the Middle Ages cannot be seen in the same light as primitive man's relationship with nature. Medieval man no longer merges into nature, even if he does not yet stand in conscious opposition to it. He confronts the rest of the world which he measures according to his own yardstick – a measure which he finds in his own body and in his own actions.

In these conditions nothing could be more natural than to measure space by means of the human body and its movements, by man's capacity of acting upon matter. Here man was physically 'the measure of all things' and, above all, of the earth. Length, breadth and area were not determined by means of any absolute measures or standards in abstraction from the actual concrete situation. Distance was measured by the number of steps one took to traverse it (hence 'foot'). Square measure had very little meaning for farmers who knew nothing of geometry. The elbow, the span, the finger – these were the most natural and the most widespread units of measure. The time taken to do a job was measured on the basis of the worker's assessment of the amount of land tilled. Arable land was measured in morgens – that is, the area of land which could be tilled in one day. These measures of area not only varied from one place to another; it never entered anyone's head to suppose that a relatively more accurate system of measuring land might be required. The accepted and universally widespread system of land measurement was completely satisfactory; it was the only possible, indeed only conceivable one, for the people of the Middle Ages.

This is, incidentally, of great importance for historians who are trying to determine the area of landed estates and farms in the Middle Ages: the numerical data contained in feudal estate inventories and governmental registers seem ready-made to be set out as statistical tables, but incautious use of them can simply create an illusion of accuracy, since the components underlying these cadastral data vary very widely in dimensions. Medieval measures – especially land measures – were variable, and here lies the main difference from modern usage. As the English historian F. W. Maitland aptly remarks, 'If we go back to an earlier time the less we think of "superficial measure", the better.'[15] And as another specialist admits, medieval agrarian measures are the despair of modern statisticians.[16]

In documents of the period, the usual way of specifying the 'size' of an estate is to state the income yielded by it, the number of ploughs necessary to cultivate it (or the number of oxen to be yoked), or the amount of seed necessary to sow the ground. We may find rather detailed descriptions of the boundaries of an estate with an inventory of all its assets (streams, ditches, hills, bushes, trees, roads, crosses on the crossroads, etc.) and information about neighbouring estates – but nowhere in medieval documents do we find an *exact* measure of land area expressed in commensurate and generally applicable units. Every medieval land measure is specific to the plot of land in question. The same thing can be seen in the process of taking over a new plot of land. So much land may be enclosed as a man can circumambulate between sunrise and sunset. Often the settler had to carry torches with him and light bonfires along the boundary of his claim; this consecrated his claim and made it inviolable. In Icelandic law, a woman could stake a claim to as much ground as she could circumambulate in a day, leading a cow on a rope. In Norway, it was permissible for the individual to claim for himself from common land that plot on to which he had thrown a knife or which he had scythed. At the root of these conventions lies the principle of labour outlay: the dimensions of the portion of land which a man may claim for himself are determined by the work he can apply to it, by his own physical contact, that is, with the earth.

It is not only medieval notions of space that are characterised by imprecision and approximation. As we shall see, time was measured in an even more capricious way. In general, with regard to quantitative terms – measures of weight, capacity, numbers of people, dates, etc. – arbitrariness and imprecision were the norm. The general attitude to numbers was a contributory factor: medieval man was disposed to see in numbers, not primarily a means of reckoning, but rather a revelation of the divine harmony that ruled the world, and hence a form of magic.

So, medieval man's relationship with nature was not that of subject to object. Rather, it was a discovery of himself in the external world, combined with a perception of the cosmos as subject. In the universe, man saw the same forces at work as he was aware of in himself. No clear boundaries separated man from the world: finding in the world an extension of himself, he discovers in himself an analogue of the universe. The one mirrors the other.

Just as there was no basic opposition between man and his natural surroundings, so there was no opposition between nature and culture. In modern times, nature has come to be construed as the empirical world, as an extra-human datum, an element that human culture can manipulate; but in the Middle Ages no clear boundary was recognised between the two, or, at best, it was vague and movable. Hence, even the word *natura* cannot be adequately translated as 'nature' in the present-day meaning of the term. Nature as the medieval mind understood it was God's creation. The personification of Nature found in the twelfth-century philosophical allegories is the handmaiden of God, the incarnation of his thoughts and designs in the material world. For medieval man, nature was a 'great reservoir of symbols'.[17]

A clearer idea of world and space perception in epochs remote from ours may be gained from a study of the categories of microcosm and macrocosm (or megacosm) prevalent in these civilisations.[18] The microcosm is not simply a small part of the whole, it is not just an element of the universe, but a miniature replica of it, as it were, reproducing it in its entirety. Theologians and poets aver that the microcosm is as complete and perfect in itself as is the larger world we live in. The microcosm was conceived in the form of man, who could be understood only within the framework of the parallelism between the 'small' and the 'great' universe. This theme, which is found in the ancient East and in classical Greece, enjoyed enormous popularity in the Middle Ages, especially from the twelfth century onwards. The elements of the human body were identical, it was held, with the elements forming the universe. Man's flesh was of the earth, his blood of water, his breath of air and his warmth of fire. Each part of the human body corresponded to a part of the universe: the head to the skies, the breast to the air, the stomach to the sea, the feet to the earth; the bones corresponded to the rocks, the veins to the branches of the trees, the hair to the grass, and man's feelings to the animals. But it is not only his sharing the same constituent elements that links man to the rest of the world. Medieval descriptions of the ways in which the microcosm and macrocosm are ordered, turn on one basic principle: the laws of creation are to be found in analogy. The effort to grasp the world as a single unified whole runs through all the medieval *summae*, the encyclopaedias and the etymologies; everything was seen thus, from God, the Bible and the liturgy downwards through man, beasts and plants, to cooking, yoking oxen and ploughing the land.

But if we are to grasp the exact meaning of the concept 'microcosm', we have to take into account the changes which the concept of 'cosmos' underwent in its transition from the ancient world to the world of the Middle Ages. Antiquity saw the world as complete and harmonious; medieval man saw it as dualistic. The ancient cosmos comprised the beauty, the orderliness and the dignity of nature. These qualities were lost in the Christian view of the world, which came to mean the 'human world' (*mundus* in the Middle Ages means 'humanity') and no longer carried a lofty ethical and aesthetic connotation. The world of Christianity was no longer one of 'beauty', for the world was sinful and subject to the judgment of God, and Christian asceticism rejected it altogether. Truth, according to Augustine, must be sought not in the external world but in the spirit of man itself. God's most wondrous works are to be seen not in the creation of the world but in its redemption, and in life eternal. Christ alone saved the world from the world ('Christus mundum de mundo liberavit'). As a result of this transformation the concept of 'cosmos' broke up into two diametrically opposed concepts: *civitas Dei* and *civitas terrena*, with the latter closely bordering on the concept of *civitas diaboli*. Man stands on a path which leads both to the Holy City of the spirit, the heavenly Jerusalem or Zion, and to the city of Antichrist.

From antiquity the concept of the cosmos retained its sense of 'order', and it was especially in the teaching of Pseudo-Dionysius the Areopagite that the hierarchical ordering of the world was stressed. But this world was a mystical one, and its hierarchy was one of sacred spiritual ranks. In such circumstances the visible world can hardly have an independent role. The beauty of the old Hellenic cosmos withers and fades before the radiance of the church.[19]

'Rehabilitation' of the world and of nature does not really begin until the twelfth century. Better able as he then was to act on and manipulate the world he lived in than he had been in the early Middle Ages, man began to pay rather more attention to his surroundings, and interest in the study and the elucidation of nature grew steadily. But this interest was not in nature *as such* – nature is not independent, but a creation of God whose glory it declares. The philosophers of the twelfth century speak of the necessity of studying nature; for in the cognition of nature in all her depths, man finds himself, and by means of this knowledge he draws closer to an understanding of the divine order of things and indeed of God himself. Underlying these arguments and images is a confident belief in the unity and the beauty of the world, and also the conviction that the central place in the world which God has created belongs to man.

Repeatedly, medieval thinkers strove to embody the idea of the microcosm and macrocosm in graphic illustrative form. In the allegorical drawings illustrating the works of the Abbess Hildegard of Bingen, the macrocosm is represented in the shape of the symbol of eternity – a circle, which Nature holds in her hands, while she in her turn is crowned by divine Wisdom. Within the circle is placed the human form – the microcosm. He bears within himself heaven and earth, says Hildegard, and in him are concealed all things.[20] In one of the miniatures decorating the works of the Alsatian Abbess Herrad of Landsberg, man-microcosm is surrounded by the planets and the four cosmic elements – fire, water, earth and air. The analogy between microcosm and macrocosm lies at the very root of medieval symbolism, for nature was conceived of as a mirror in which man can contemplate the image of God.[21] But if all the basic traits of the universe can be found in man, Nature herself is at the same time imagined in human form. The twelfth-century poet Alan of Lille imagined Nature in the form of a woman in a diadem bearing the zodiacal constellations and clad in garments decorated with pictures of birds, plants, animals and other creatures, all arranged in the order of their creation by the Lord. Human heads and figures served as allegories of the winds, and the earth was depicted in the form of a woman. Into the mouth of Nature, Alan puts words concerning man's similarity to her.[22] In a drawing illustrating the *Key to the Understanding of Nature* (*Clavis physicae*) by Honorius Augustodunensis (Honorius of Autun), the cosmic powers, the world elements and even the concepts of cause and effect are personified in human figures and bodies. Space and time are also given human shape: *tempus* is an old man, *locus* is a female figure. Allegorical images such as these in no way prevent the philosopher from discoursing on the incorporeality and intelligibility of space and time.[23]

The image of the 'world tree' is widespread among many people in an archaic stage of development. The tree played an important part in their cosmic representations and was the main structural factor in the organisation of their mythological space. Sets of opposites, such as up–down, right–left, sky–earth, clean–unclean, male–female and so on, were connected in the human mind with the idea of the 'world tree'. We find an interesting metamorphosis of this image in the works of medieval writers, many of whom describe the 'inverted tree' (*arbor inversa*) growing from heaven down to earth, with its roots in heaven and its branches on earth. In this form, the tree served as a symbol of faith and insight, and embodied the image of Christ. But at the same time the tree preserved a more archaic significance – that of man-microcosm and world-macrocosm.[24]

The medieval symbol expressed the unseen and the ideal through the visible and the material. The visible world is in harmony with its archetype, the world of the highest supreme essences (*archetypus mundus*). Because of this relationship, it was held possible to get beyond the literal, factual meaning of this or that event or object, and discern the symbolical or mystic meaning, i.e. gain access to the secrets of the faith. This system of symbolical interpretation and allegorical simile served as a means of drawing up a general system of classification for the widest possible range of things and events, and their correlation with eternity.

The persistence with which the poets, the artists and the theologians of the Middle Ages return again and again to the theme of anthropomorphic nature and cosmic man is neither a traditional pose nor a conventionality; it reflects a special relationship between man and nature, one which was to be lost in subsequent ages. Man was aware in himself of the analogy, or rather the kinship, between the structure of the cosmos and of his own being. In nature he saw a book from which wisdom could be learned, and at the same time, a mirror which reflected man. 'All created things', wrote Alan of Lille, 'exist for us as a book, a picture and a mirror.'[25] Man accounted himself the crown of creation, made in the image and likeness of God; and all other things were made for his sake. But this apotheosis of man is very different from that of the Renaissance; in the cosmological world-view of medieval Christianity man has not yet gained *independent* significance; in and by his being he declares the glory of God.

The unity of man with the universe is revealed in the harmony interpenetrating them. Both man and world are governed by the cosmic music which expresses the harmony of the whole with its parts and which permeates all, from the heavenly spheres to man. *Musica humana* is in perfect concord with *musica mundana*. Everything that is measured by time is bound up with music. Music is subordinate to number. Therefore both macrocosm and man-microcosm are ruled by numbers which define their structure and determine their motion.[26] Both world and man can be represented with the help of the same geometrical figures, symbolising the perfection of God's creation. It is in these numbers that the secret of the beauty of the world lies; for the medieval mind the concepts 'beauty', 'orderliness', 'harmony', 'proportion', 'comeliness', and 'propriety' were very close to each other, if not identical.

The orderliness of the world extended also to the political sphere. As in antiquity, the state was held to be similar to an organism; the citizens were its limbs (John of Salisbury). The organic unity of the body politic required the coopera-tion and collaboration of all the strata composing it. As medieval thinkers saw it, discord and strife among them threatened the integrity of the whole world-order.

It is not infrequently asserted that medieval people were deficient in the 'aesthetic' enjoyment of nature, which they were unable to 'admire'; they were incapable of selecting certain aspects of nature for admiration to the exclusion of others, and nature itself was not an object of contemplation. In support of this thesis, the story is told of Bernard of Clairvaux, who walked for a whole day along the shores of

[61]

Lake Geneva without noticing the lake, such was the extent
to which inner contemplation of God could draw medieval
man's attention away from the world surrounding him. But
an argument based on Bernard of Clairvaux is not very
convincing, for we can hardly judge the average man of the
period by the standards of this fanatical champion of the
faith and ardent advocate of withdrawal from the world.
However influential Bernard and other ascetics and church
reformers were, they were hardly in a position to dictate the
attitude to the world, and especially to nature, generally
prevalent in the Middle Ages.[27] But other arguments can be
adduced in support of this thesis. When the medieval author
writes about nature, his description has no touches of local
colour; it is conventional and cliché-ridden. This is very
much the case in the epic. For example, in the *Chanson de
Roland* nature plays no independent role. Such mention as
there is of stars, the sun, daylight, dawn is no more than a
string of clichés. Meadows, grass, trees, rocks, ravines are
mentioned exclusively in connection with the deeds of the
paladins; dire meteorological phenomena (cloudbursts,
thunder, whirlwinds, hail, lightning, darkness) are seen as
signs presaging political upheavals, or expressions of nature's
grief over Roland's death in battle. The heroes of the knightly
epic are 'figures in empty space'.[28]

It is well known how abstract the landscape is in medieval
paintings. In the opinion of the German scholar O. Lauffer,
people in the early Middle Ages were so taken up with their
immediate particular surroundings, for example animals, that
they were less aware of the landscape and could have no keen
feeling for nature.[29] A. Biese thinks that the feeling for nature
really was less intense in this period than in antiquity or in
modern times; people were less given to personal observation
of the external world, preferring their flights of fancy. But
as poetry sought to express the deep experiences and feelings
of the inner life, an interest in nature was awakened; and the
natural scene became a symbol of man's spiritual life. This
is especially characteristic of the Provençal troubadours, who
are skilful at linking their state of mind with the world
surrounding them. Even here, however, description of nature

consists mainly of simple enumeration of phenomena. Thus, for example, Bertran de Born:

> If April, and flowers, and verdure,
> Beautiful dawns and bright evenings
> Do not bring me that great joy for which I pant,
> If love, and the nightingale, whose song I hear,
> And the pleasant young green time,
> Which brings joy and sweetness,
> And the burgeoning festival of Easter
> Do not give courage to my lady
> And do not diminish her fears,
> My happiness will hardly come.[30]

Medieval literature offers us no individual appreciation of landscape; the natural scene as represented remains a series of stereotyped arabesques intertwined with the lyrical feelings of the author. The joyful awakening of nature and of our feelings in the spring, the comparison of a beautiful woman to the beauties of May, sorrow compared to autumn or winter in nature – these are the predominant motives in poetry, and they soon became stereotypes. According to A. Biese, not even the most gifted of the troubadour poets or the *Minnesänger* was able to go further than this. Thus, in itself, as an independent value, nature has no place either in medieval literature or in medieval painting.[31]

However, several Lives of the Saints and various chronicles afford evidence that medieval man was indeed capable of admiring the beauty of trees and forests and of finding solace therein. G. Stockmayer quotes a story about Bishop Otto of Bamberg, the 'Apostle of Pomerania', who ordered a certain spruce tree in Stettin to be cut down, because the pagans believed their gods dwelt in it and made obeisance to it as they passed. The people begged the bishop not to have the tree felled, promising on oath never again to do pagan homage to it: they liked the tree for its beauty and the shade which it gave. Stockmayer claims that medieval people also recognised the beauty of flowers but turned their eyes away from them, fearing to endanger their souls by idle attachment to earthly things. Sites for monasteries were chosen not only because of their solitude but also because the monks were attracted by their natural beauty. The anonymous author of a biography of the Emperor Henry IV includes in his work a short story containing a description of nature. Stockmayer says that the authors of imaginative literature were well able to grasp a landscape as a whole, though it was more difficult to reproduce this in painting. In her view, the people of the early medieval period were no less able to appreciate nature than those of later times. It is another matter that medieval man was not 'passionately drawn' towards nature – after all, he was not remote from it but lived in its midst. Nostalgia for nature makes its first appearance in the great cities of the modern age.[32]

Criticising the approach of his predecessors to the question of 'feeling for nature in the Middle Ages', W. Ganzenmüller has shown that the way to solve this problem is not by comparing the Middle Ages with antiquity or with modern times, but by seeking to identify the inner factors which made medieval people react to nature in the way they did. Their attitude to nature was determined first and foremost by their religiosity, the basic component in the medieval world-view. For the people of the Middle Ages, God and the human soul were the absolute values; nature had only relative value. In so far as nature did not contribute to know-ledge of God, it was devoid of value; if it hindered man from drawing near to God, then it was seen as evil, a manifestation of satanic powers. A subjective reaction to nature on the part of medieval man would be bound to collide with a way of thinking geared exclusively to Holy Scripture. Hence there arose a more or less identical way of perceiving and repro-ducing nature. Formally, most ways of reproducing nature in art and literature had been inherited from antiquity. Nature was seen as a symbol of the deity, and its manifesta-tions were perceived and apprehended, not directly for them-selves, but as material for allegory or moral sermonising. 'Transcendental' experience of nature is most fully expressed in the works of the great mystics of the twelfth and thirteenth centuries, especially of St Francis of Assisi. The immediacy of St Francis's relationship with nature, his seeing in all creatures his brothers and sisters, must not blind us to his deeply religious experience of the world; even for him, nature was not a value in itself – what he sought in it was the 'image of God'.[33]

Before we can get to grips with the question of exactly how medieval man apprehended nature, we must first of all be clear as to what we mean by an 'aesthetic' relationship with nature. Let us start from our thesis of the close bond between medieval man's picture of the world on the one hand and of himself on the other – seeing himself in nature as in a mirror and at the same time finding nature within himself. This non-differentiation in his relationship with his natural surroundings does not exclude the possibility of admiring nature and artistically representing it. On the contrary, it presupposes this, not indeed as a completely isolated and conscious aesthetic standpoint, but rather as one aspect of a more intricate and manifold relationship with the world. Only as this relationship disintegrates can use value and aesthetic value emerge in relative distinction from each other; in the medieval world-view they are as yet co-extensive. So, nature could awaken in medieval man feelings of admiration, fear or other emotions, which could hardly, however, be separated from his efforts to satisfy his purely practical needs at her expense.[34] It has been said of savages that 'they do not pick flowers' (to make bouquets). But the Andaman islanders, for example, have a calendar based on the scents of flowers, since different kinds of flowers bloom at different times of the year.

Whenever we come across something in medieval texts that seems to point to an aesthetic relationship with nature, we have to ponder very carefully the specific complex of ideas and feelings underlying the case in point. Without denying medieval man's capacity to admire the beauties of nature, we must not forget that nature herself could not be the ultimate object of his admiration. For nature was the symbol of the world invisible. Contemplation of the visible world served to reveal a world of essences, on another and higher plane, which it was impossible to approach directly: the way to their apprehension led from the visible to the invisible (*per visibilia ad invisibilia*). The human mind, the theologians taught, is unable to grasp the truth except through the intermediaries of material things and images. On the façade of the abbey church of Saint-Denis, built under his direction, the Abbot Suger had the following inscription placed: '. . . through sensual beauty the soul is elevated to true beauty, and from earth . . . it is raised to the heavens. . . .' Such an understanding of the visible world heightened its value, in that it related finite things to imperishable essences, and at the same time prevented these things from being mistaken for something valuable in itself and possessing a significance not dependent on transcendental categories. This dual attitude to nature lays bare the limits within which a knowledge of nature, whether scientific or artistic, was possible in the Middle Ages.

Further, we must always bear in mind the difference between 'a feeling for nature' and the *expression* of this feeling in literature and art.[35] Medieval aesthetic principles served as a sort of filter through which the more immediate expression of human emotions could hardly penetrate into poetry or painting. The representation of nature in medieval poetry is usually subject to the canons of convention. The rhetorical, conventional depicting of landscape, which has its origins in antiquity, runs right through medieval literature. In medieval poems and romances we meet over and over again with the same series of formal clichés (ideal 'forest', 'garden', 'eternal spring', and so on), by means of which some sort of description of natural phenomena is given. The artistic landscape as a whole is unreal, legendary, though some of its details may be naturalistic.[36] Hence, recent works devoted to the analysis of the representation of nature and space in Western European literature of the Middle Ages concentrate not so much on the way in which writers perceived landscape at that time, as on the symbolic function fulfilled by landscape and natural phenomena in medieval art.[37]

The role of spatial representation in the fabric of poetry is rather peculiar. The medieval poet was not very receptive *vis-à-vis* the actual physical traits and distinctive features of a landscape and limited himself as a rule to the barest of topographical information. Localities are specified in so far as this is necessary to set the scene of action for the dramatis personae. The forest in the courtly romance is simply the

place where the knight wanders; the garden is the scene for
an amorous adventure or a conversation, a field is no more
than the arena for single combat. In itself, the landscape is
of no interest to the author. The way in which spatial relations are depicted is such that the perspective and the scale
used by the author are constantly changing; one has the
impression that the personages of the romance are moving in
space in a series of leaps, like figures on a chess-board. Far-
off things are described as though they were being viewed
from close at hand. The parallel with late medieval painting,
in which distance is rendered as a smaller version of the
foreground, is bound to suggest itself.[38]

Then again, space not only surrounds the hero but is
experienced by him, interlocks with him. The hero in medieval poetry carries with him his own spatial sphere of action,
inherently and existentially his, into which emanate the
powers that stream from him, and which in its turn defines
him in a specific way. The spatial environment and the hero
sojourning therein interpenetrate each other and complement
each other. More, time itself is construed in spatial terms (see
below).[39]

Do these statements not contradict each other? On the one
hand we have the undoubted indifference of the medieval
poet to landscape, upon which he is reluctant to confer any
independent value; and on the other hand, a kind of 'blending' of the dramatis personae with that part of space which
they occupy. Our argument is that here we have two aspects
of that same special way of perceiving nature peculiar to
the Middle Ages which was outlined above. Not entirely
separated from the natural locus, remaining a part of it, man
– precisely for this reason – did not convert nature into the
object of his observation 'from without'; before he could do
that, the distance between him and his natural environment
would have to increase.

The world did not present itself to the medieval beholder
as manifold and heterogeneous; man was content to gauge it
from his own narrow corner. Of the physical world beyond
his immediate ken he could garner at best only haphazard,
fragmentary and often very questionable information.
Merchants' and pilgrims' tales of what they had seen in far-

off countries became encrusted with legends and fancifully inflated. The testimony of eye-witnesses mingled with the accounts of ancient authorities. Since not only man's relations with nature were non-differentiated, but also his conceptions of this world and the world above, the geographical ideas of the age easily accommodated both planes. A description of the 'earthly circle' would include, along with fragments of genuine geographical information, biblical images of paradise as the centre of the earth. The descriptions of animals in 'bestiaries' testify to rather better powers of observation on the part of their authors, but even here there is plenty of evidence that medieval man was not over concerned with drawing a dividing line between his own experience and the marvels recounted in fairytales. More important for him was the symbolical interpretation of natural phenomena and the moral lessons to be learned from them. The 'bestiaries' – handbooks on symbolical zoology[40] – provided an edifying guide to such interpretation.

The propensity to judge the whole world on the evidence of that small part of it known to the writer, to substitute one's micro-world for the macrocosm, is found also in the works of the medieval historians. They set out to write universal histories, but, paradoxically, produced provincial chronicles with very limited horizons. The material they offer, in so far as it is not derived from the Bible or other sources, is mainly concerned with their own country or region. As an example, we may take the well-known French historian of the eleventh century, Raoul Glaber. Glaber reproached his predecessors, Paulus Diaconus and the Venerable Bede, for having written no more than the histories of their own countries, and promised to relate instead, as he put it, 'the events that have taken place in the four corners of the earth'. In fact, Glaber's view of history is that of Cluny in Burgundy, where he spent most of his life. This limited viewpoint is boldly applied to the whole of history. In the same way, another historian, Adhémar of Chabannes, wrote a history of France, which is in fact no more than a chronicle of events in Aquitaine.

As P. M. Bitsilli neatly puts it, the medieval thinkers and artists were 'great provincials', unable to outgrow their

provincial standards and see further than their church bells
sounded. Thus, the universe appeared to them in the guise
of a monastery, a feudal estate, an urban community or a
university. In any case,

> the world of medieval man was small, comprehensible
> and easily surveyed. Everything in this world was
> ordered and properly distributed; each man had his own
> task to perform and each man had his own self-respect.
> There were no empty places, no gaps; nothing was
> superfluous or unnecessary; each voice merged in the
> general harmony, and every creature, even the devil and
> the wicked pagan Mahomet, fulfilled the role preordained
> for them in the design of Providence, and duly discharged
> the duties laid upon them. In this world there were no
> unknown places, heaven was as familiar as earth and there
> was no reason why one should go astray. The traveller
> who wandered from the path fell into the nether regions
> or rose into heaven where he would find familiar places
> and people he knew. It was pleasant and easy to survey
> this world and reproduce it as a whole, without
> remainder, in all its manifestations, with all its 'empires',
> its treasures and its wonders, showing it on 'maps of the
> world' and in encyclopaedias, to sculpt it in thousands
> of little figures huddled up close to the cathedral walls,
> to delineate it in gold and bright colours in frescoes. . . .
> So, much ready-made material is available for a
> preliminary study towards a cultural synthesis of the
> Middle Ages: we know how medieval man imagined the
> world as a whole. This material is not very complicated;
> the medieval cosmos was not only very compact but
> also very homogeneous in spite of the apparent diversity.[41]

A very apt description of the world of medieval man,
which requires, however, one important correction: this spat-
ially small world, which could be viewed and surveyed in its
entirety, was exceptionally densely ordered; along with
earthly beings, objects and phenomena, it included within
itself another world, created by religious belief and religious
superstition. From our standpoint, we could call this world
of medieval man a dual world, though for him it was a unity.

[69]

In volume, medieval man's knowledge of the world was not much less than that of his present-day counterpart, but in content it was radically different. Along with knowledge – albeit limited – of the physical properties of an object, there was another kind of knowledge – knowledge of its symbolical meaning, and of its significance in various aspects of the relationship between the mortal world and the divine world. It is difficult therefore to agree entirely with Bitsilli's assertion concerning the 'simplicity' of the world as perceived by medieval man. On the contrary, the symbolical reduplication of the world made it extremely complex; everything could be, indeed had to be, interpreted and understood in different ways. Beyond the integument it was necessary to 'see' the essence, concealed from physical sight. The world of symbols was inexhaustible.

Again, the 'provincialism' of medieval thinkers can only be accepted with certain reservations. The attempt to unite in one historical frame the annals of a monastery and the progress of the human race from its creation to the impending end of the world, surely goes beyond mere 'provincialism': it was rather an attempt to place particular local events in the light of world history. The particularism of medieval history was indissolubly linked to its universalism.

With the transition from paganism to Christianity, medieval man's conception of space underwent a radical structural transformation. Cosmic space, social space and ideological space were all given hierarchic structure. The earthly feudal system is an isomorph of the hierarchy of God's creatures and the ranks of the angels; and while the lexicon of relations between lord and vassal is permeated with religious terminology, the vocabulary of the theological tracts is not infrequently laced with terms borrowed from feudal and monarchic procedure.[42] All relationships are vertical, running from above to below; all beings are distributed on various planes according to their degree of perfection which depends on their relative proximity to God.

The idea of an angelic hierarchy goes back to Pseudo-Dionysius the Areopagite, whose treatise was translated into Latin by John Scotus Eriugena in the ninth century. The work enjoyed enormous popularity in the high Middle Ages.

God had created a heavenly hierarchy and also an earthly one, distributing specific functions to angels and men. The hierarchical principle informs both earth and heaven. The angelic hierarchy of seraphim, cherubim and thrones, dominions, powers and authorities, principalities, archangels and angels, is the prototype for the earthly hierarchy of clergy and the secular hierarchy of feudal lords and vassals. To this social world of the heavens and the earth corresponds the general structure of the universe.[43]

The symbol of the universe was the cathedral, the structure of which was designed as a replica in every detail of the cosmic order; its interior, with its dome, altar and side-chapels, was meant to give the beholder a complete representation of the structure of the universe. Not only the design as a whole, but every detail, was imbued with symbolical significance. The worshipper in the cathedral could contemplate the beauty and the harmony of God's creation. The lay-out of the royal palace was also linked with this image of the divinely ordered universe: heaven was imagined in the shape of a fortress. In an age when the illiterate masses were very far from thinking in terms of literary abstractions, architectural symbolism provided a natural way of illustrating the structure of the world; the images conveyed a religio-political meaning. The main doors of the cathedrals and churches, the triumphal arches, the entrances to the courts and palaces, were seen as 'the gates of heaven', and the majestic edifices themselves as 'houses of God' or 'cities of God'.[44] The spatial organisation of the cathedral also had a built-in time dimension: the future (the 'end of the world') is already there, for all to see, at the west door; the holy past is preserved in the east.

In the Middle Ages the universe was imagined as a series of concentric spheres. There was some disagreement as to the number of spheres; the Venerable Bede, drawing to some extent on ancient sources, held that the world was surrounded by seven spheres – air, ether, the Olympian, fire, the stellar sphere, the heaven of the angels and the heaven of the Trinity. In the twelfth century, Honorius Augustodunensis drew a distinction between three celestial spheres: the bodily or visible, the spiritual or angelic, and the intellectual, in which the Blessed Elect contemplate the Holy Trinity. The scholastics, also appealing to Aristotle, postulated fifty-five spheres, to which they added yet another – the sphere of God the Prime Mover. In one way or another, however, the earthly world, correlated as it is with the world above, tended to lose its independent value. Graphic evidence of this is forthcoming from the work of medieval painters. Along with figures placed firmly on earth, heavenly powers are usually depicted as well: God the Father, Christ, the Virgin Mary, angels. These two planes of medieval painting are superimposed one upon the other, experienced in parallel, as higher beings are able to come down to earth. Frankish poets of the ninth century depicted God as the ruler of a fortress reminiscent of the palace of the Carolingian kings, with the sole difference that the fortress of God is in the sky.

The paired sets of diametrical opposites into which medieval dualism divided the world were arranged vertically: heaven is opposed to earth, God to the devil, the ruler of the underworld. The concept of 'up' is connected with the concepts of nobility, purity, goodness, while the concept of 'down' is tinged with shades of baseness, coarseness, impurity, evil. The contrast between matter and spirit, between body and soul, also contains the antithesis of up and down. Spatial concepts are indissolubly bound up with religious and moral concepts. The ladder which Jacob saw in a vision with angels flocking up and down it between heaven and earth is a dominant *leitmotif* in the medieval conception of space, and one which finds singularly powerful expression in Dante. It is not only the structure of the other world, in which matter and evil are concentrated in the lower reaches of hell, while spirit and goodness adorn the heavenly heights; the whole movement of the poem is conceived vertically. The cliffs and fissures of the infernal depths, the fall of bodies dragged down by the weight of their sins, the gestures and glances, even Dante's vocabulary – all of this draws attention to the categories of 'up' and 'down', to the diametrical opposition between the lofty and the base. These are indeed the determining coordinates of the medieval world-view.

The religious and moral interpretation of the universe tends to render spatial relationships on earth very imprecise. In the 'Christian topographies' factual geographical information is mixed up with biblical references. Positive knowledge is saturated with a moral and symbolical content; earthly paths merge, as it were, with ways to God, and religious and ethical values are superimposed on and overrule the purely cognitive values; as far as medieval man was concerned, knowledge of the earth's surface could hardly be compared with knowledge that would save his soul. 'Christian topographies' transported man with ease from his earthly settlement to the banks of the four rivers that ran through paradise. As it was written in the Old Testament book of the prophet Ezekiel (5:5): 'Thus saith the Lord God, This is Jerusalem; I have set it in the midst of the nations and countries that are round about her.' Accordingly, Jerusalem was moved in medieval maps to the centre of the earth, and was accounted the 'hub of the universe'. Items of geographical information inherited from antiquity were interwoven with biblical symbols and with fantastic descriptions of exotic countries where Christian custom and prescription were not observed, where polygamy was permitted and cannibalism flourished, where human sacrifice was practised and where wondrous beings, half-human, half-animal, lived.

While the geography of the classical world and its medieval heirs (the Venerable Bede, Adam of Bremen, William of Conches, Lambert of Saint-Omer) acknowledged the sphericity of the earth, other authors, worried by this contradiction with the biblical account, preferred the hypothesis that the earth was a flat disc (Cassiodorus, Isidore of Seville) or tried to combine both views (St Basil and others). In Isidore's view, the round earth is washed on all sides by the ocean, and the earthly disc itself is divided by the T-shaped Mediterranean into three parts – Asia (the 'Land of Shem'), Europe (the 'Land of Japhet') and Africa (the 'Land of Ham'). Cosmas Indicopleustes, the author of a *Christian Topography* which enjoyed great popularity in the Middle Ages, set himself the task of disproving the 'heresy' that the earth was a globe, and not flat as taught in Holy Scripture. These 'Christian topographies' were a retrograde step in comparison with classical cosmography, but they fulfilled medieval man's

[73]

deep need for information about 'the divine cosmos' and ways of saving his soul.[45] Pilgrimage – widespread in the Middle Ages and the most worthy form of travel – was seen not simply as a physical journey to the holy places, but as a spiritual way to God, as an 'imitation of Christ'. According to Tauler, *homo viator* proceeds from the 'humanity' of Christ to his 'divinity', finding on the way 'rich pastures' of truth. The 'way' was understood as a spiritual quest.[46]

The contrasted pair 'earth/sky' had religious and ethical significance for medieval man. The sky was the seat of higher, eternal, ideal life, while the earth, in contrast, was the vale of tears, where sinful man eked out his earthly span. The world beyond the grave was imagined as being just as substantial as the earthly world – more so, indeed, since it was imperishable. Losing one's way on earth could lead to this other world; thus Dante finds himself at the gates of hell, having wandered from the path in the dark wood. On earth there were holy places, righteous places, and there were sinful places. Travel in the Middle Ages mainly took the form of pilgrimage to the Holy Places, understood as a progress away from places of sin. Striving to perfect oneself morally involved topographical displacement: one left the 'world' to sojourn in the wilderness or enter a monastery. Attainment of a holy or sanctified state was also understood as movement in space: the saint could be taken up into paradise, just as the sinner could be thrown into hell. The locus occupied by a man had to conform to his moral status. In the medieval mind, this world and the world beyond were continually intermingled.[47] Not only the individual man bent on his salvation but Christ's church in its entirety was imagined in the shape of a female pilgrim pursued by the devil.

Study of Western European literature of the Middle Ages enables us to identify two stages in the development of the conception of movement as the simultaneous embodiment of spatial displacement and a shift in man's inner condition. In the early Middle Ages, man was usually seen as a being beset on all sides by temptation and the forces of evil. Under this threat he fled the world, left friends and family. In this stage there is little trace of the search for new experience, for adventure, which is a commonplace in literature from the twelfth century onwards. In this second stage, the idea of transition, of displacement in space, thrills the imagination of the authors of romances about King Arthur and the Knights of the Round Table, allegories of love and descriptions of the ascent of the soul to God. And of course spatial displacement took on a new dimension at the time of the Crusades. When they came to any European town, the ordinary folk who took part in the First Crusade used to ask, 'Is this Jerusalem?' For them, Jerusalem was not a geographical point whose actual position was unknown to them, but the scene of Christ's Passion: and Christ could be found everywhere. All that was needed was to attain to the requisite stage of holiness.[48]

The religious conception of space in the Middle Ages also finds expression in the division of the world into the Christian world on the one hand and the non-Christian world, the world of the infidel on the other. By virtue of its teaching that henceforth there was no Greek and no Jew, Christianity represented a major advance on earlier conceptions of man, which had been restricted to the tribe (among the barbarians), a chosen people (the Jews) or a single and unique political formation (the Romans). Nevertheless, medieval anthropology excluded all non-Christians and, partially at least, heretical Christians or schismatics also, from the ranks of those entitled to full human status. Only in so far as it was graced by the Christian faith and subjected to the church could the world be described as a cultured, well-ordered world in which God's blessings could proliferate. Beyond the limits of this Christian world, space lost its positive qualities; there began the forests and the wastelands of the barbarians to which God's peace and human institutions neither extended nor applied. Such a division of the world by a religious criterion determined the behaviour of crusaders in the territory of the infidel; methods and means which were impermissible in Christian lands were legitimate in the crusade against the heathen. In so far as Christ had died for all, however – including the infidels – the church regarded it as an important part of its mission to convert non-Christians to the truth, even against their own will – *compelle intrare*. Hence, the frontier between the Christian and the non-Christian worlds was movable. Medieval Christianity was a religion of the 'open' missionary type. Thanks to the church's efforts and its militant servants, Christian space was extended *pari passu* with the moral and religious transformation of space wrested from the forces of evil.

Parts of space were differentiated according to the degree of their sanctity. Holy places – churches, chapels, crucifixes at major road-junctions – were under divine protection, and crimes committed in them or near them were punished with particular severity. A place could be not only more or less holy; like man himself, it could be endowed with nobility and enjoy special privileges. Just as people were divided into nobles, free-born and bondmen, so earthly domains acquired similar juridical status and could even ennoble their possessors. Domicile on 'free' ground could alleviate the condition or change the status of the serf. Thus, a place, like a man, had rights. The community, the state, the empire consisted of people and lands.

With the Christian Middle Ages came a certain change in the way people saw the relationship between their local surroundings and the rest of the world. As before, most people still lived in relative isolation, but nevertheless they were beginning to have some notion of the larger world beyond their horizons. This was the Christian world, the sphere over which the church universal held sway, uniting its many scattered units both ideologically and organisationally. The ecumenical concept of the unity of the Christian world was a necessary correlative of the economic and feudal particularism and separatism of the Middle Ages. In this context, it is instructive to compare the treatment of space in the epic and in the courtly romances. The world of the *Chanson de Roland* is homogeneous, sketchily localised, well known to the heroic protagonists. The paladins who act within the framework of this strictly delimited world – the western parts of France – have grown up with the notions of faithful service to their lord and devotion to the Christian religion, and they are fighting a precisely delimited enemy – the Saracens. Quite another world appears in the romances about the 'Knights of the Round Table'. Here danger lurks everywhere over the whole wide world stretching from

England to Constantinople. This is a protean and mysterious world in which the lovelorn hero performs feats of arms in his quest for the beloved.[49] Geographical space expands and increases in complexity, and at the same time there is a progressive annexation of the inner space of the human soul, revealing hitherto unsuspected riches.

Our efforts to clarify medieval man's conceptions of space have led us further afield into a circle of problems which, it might seem, have little to do with the category of space. This is because there was no such thing as 'space' in the abstract, nor was space itself equal in status at all points or susceptible of commensurate partition. Medieval conceptions of space are indivisible from medieval cognition of nature, with which man stood in specific intimate relationships and *vis-à-vis* which he was not yet able to adopt a clearly detached stance. Ascribing to nature his own traits and qualities, he also imagined himself as similar to nature in every detail. Man was aware of his inner links with the particular part of space which he happened to own and/or which was his 'home'. We saw above that the Germanic tribes regarded inherited landed property as 'homeland' or 'fatherland'. This 'localised microcosm' was related in Germanic belief to a world picture built up on the basis of this model. On these barbarian notions was imposed a Christian teaching which had amalgamated earthly ways with heavenly ways, and which had made possible the fusion on one plane of this world and the world beyond, the local and the biblical.

It will be seen from all this that medieval man's ideas of space were in a very high degree symbolical in nature; ideas of life and death, good and evil, right and wrong, sacred and secular, were united with concepts of up and down, with the cardinal points of the world and with parts of the spatial universe; they had topographical coordinates. But the symbolism of medieval concepts of space is not limited to the moral-religious aspects; it also possessed other specific characteristics. The symbol was not simply a sign or marker signifying and denoting a real object or an idea. The symbol not only stood for the reality but at the same time attached itself, as it were, to it. When a land deal was being concluded, it was not enough to draw up the requisite documentation;

there was also a ceremony consisting in the public presentation of a piece of turf by the former owner to the new one. This piece of turf symbolised the whole property, and handing it over signified that the land was being transferred literally 'from hand to hand'. When a painter depicted a church or monastery held in the hands of the saint who was its patron, neither the painter nor the beholder saw in this a mere convention: the image participated in the prototype. In some measure, the symbol took on the qualities of what was symbolised, to which again the properties of the symbol were transferred. To the medieval mind, the image was inwardly united with what was imaged, material qualities were ascribed to the spiritual, and the part could stand for the whole.

The specific quality of medieval symbolism is immediately connected with medieval ways of perceiving space. A plot of land lies within certain limits, but at the same time it can fit, as it were, into a piece of turf handed over in court from one owner to another. The situation of a church is well known as are its dimensions and its capacity – but at the same time this church lies in the hands of the patron saint to whom it is dedicated. These examples are heterogeneous, in that they draw upon two quite different sources of medieval symbolism. The first (the transfer of landed property by means of the handing over of a piece of turf) originates in the symbolism of the barbarians. The second example (the image of the church in the hands of the patron saint) comes from the world of Christian symbolism. Let us look more closely at these forms of the symbolical perception of space.

The art of the Germanic tribes was symbolical and conventional through and through. The animal style of the Germanic peoples in the first millennium AD was very far from being a naturalistic representation of animals. The images of wild animals carved in stone, wood, metal and bone are totally fantastic. These animals belong to the world of fairytale and in no way resemble real living animals, although it goes without saying that the people who carved these images were far from lacking in powers of observation. One of the most characteristic traits of these images is the total absence of any common scale. The limbs of an animal are treated separately, independently of each other. This freedom of choice in the matter of scale generates a confusion of large with small, of the part with the whole, of the primary with the secondary. The head of the animal is too big for the trunk, the extremities are not proportional to the body. What is so striking is that the separate components are treated naturalistically while the animal as a whole is grotesque and fanciful. The image appears unnatural and strained.

The same element of the fantastic and the capricious treatment of the relationship between the whole and the parts appears in Old Scandinavian poetry. The Icelandic or Norwegian skald does not pay equal attention to all the events related in his poem, nor to the whole personality of the protagonist – he concentrates entirely on the intensive isolation of one detail, one particularity, some single characteristic of the hero, or a single episode of the action; and this singularity has to represent the whole. In both the art and the poetry of the barbarians, the part symbolises the whole, acts as a substitute for it; representation of the part is more than sufficient to evoke in the beholder's mind the whole. It seems as though the part can have the same spatial coordinates as the whole. The principle of the spatial incompatibility of whole and part was not self-evident to the barbarian mind.

The barbarian mind divided the world up in a special way, very different from the way our minds work today. What appears to us to be contradictory was not necessarily so for the barbarians, and vice versa. Nature, living and dead, people and animals, or birds, sea and earth, and so on – for us, these are different orders. To the barbarians, however, they did not seem so very different from each other; things were, it seems, classified according to criteria quite different from ours. Hence, in the skaldic kennings – the specific symbolical designations with which skalds filled their songs and poetry – the sea is regularly identified with the land ('land of fish', 'land of seals', 'land of salmon') and the land with the sea ('sea of deer', 'lake of spruce', 'fjord of bushes'); the house is identified with a 'ship', the fish is the 'serpent of the sea'. In the poetry of the skalds, as in barbarian ornamentation, proportions are confused; in the kenning, large is equated with small, the particular with the general, the immovable is compared with what moves. The mythological associations in the kennings give the impression that the poets using them perceived the world in a largely undifferentiated form. But it is fairer to say that what we have here is a different taxonomy of reality; it is strange to us simply because it is so different from our own method of classifying the external world.

The skaldic kennings contain no abstract or general concepts, but give concrete definitions, 'here and now' images. The only way in which the skald can make an artistic generalisation is by way of linking the particular case with the mythical image. The kenning puts the microcosm in the place of the macrocosm, and as a result, in the imagination of the listener to skaldic songs (they were composed and performed orally, and written down only several centuries later) there arose, along with real people and actual events, the whole world of gods and giants, the wars of the gods with monsters; and in this context the facts of earthly life acquired an additional resonance, they took on a heroic, indeed a mythological, dimension. The hero's struggle with his enemies blended with cosmic collisions in which gods and other supernatural forces took part. People were participants in this struggle, which assumed in its skaldic presentation the dimensions of world catastrophe.

These traits of the graphic and poetic arts of the Scandinavians in the early Middle Ages seem to me to reflect certain special features of barbarian symbolism which go back to the very ancient past. We may note parallel linguistic features in Old Norse which appear to date from a very archaic cognitive stratum. I refer to the so-called partitive attributes, in which the part is defined by the whole, or the whole by the part. These designations consist of proper names and certain personal pronouns in apposition either complete or partial: that is, partition and participation are not clearly demarcated. In the songs of the *Elder Edda* and in the sagas, examples are frequent: e.g. *vit Gunnar*; *þeir þóri*. Such expressions cannot be translated literally as 'we – Gunnar', 'they – Thorir', which would be meaningless in English. We have to fill in the meaning as 'both I and Gunnar', 'Thorir and his people'. In constructions of this type, the proper name serves as a grammatical attribute whose purpose is to pinpoint the collective, which is inadequately defined by the pronoun. Akin to this is the practice of designating family groups by compounds containing the denomination of a member of the group: *feðgin* (father and mother), *feðgar* (father and son, father and sons), *maeðgin* (mother and sons), *maeðgur* (mother and daughter(s)), *sys(t)kin* (brothers and sisters). Here, family relationships are expressed unilaterally: the parents by the father, father and sons by the father, mother and sons/daughters by the mother, brothers and sisters by the sister.

In the opinion of S. D. Katznelson, constructions of the type *þeir Egill* indicated not chance assemblies of people but quantitatively determined stable formations. The form was used to designate groups which were seen as indivisible units: the conjugal couple, parents with their children, relatives, the family with its retainers, the leader with his armed followers, companions on a march or on a voyage – in short, social collectives. The fact that such a collective was always united round the person of its senior member – king, father, navigator, etc., made it possible for the group to be identified by his name: the idea of the collective taking precedence over its several parts. It is always assumed that the collective as determined is known to the listener or reader.[50] Outside of the context of the saga or song in which it occurs, translation of such a term is usually impossible. Thus for example, *vit Guðmundr* in the context of the saga means 'Guðmundr and Skapti', and *vit Broddi* means 'Broddi and þorsteinn'.[51] Relationships within the boundaries of such a group were so close-knit in the minds of its contemporaries that it was enough to mention the name of its head member for the group as a whole to be identified. It would seem that individuals belonging to such a collective always thought of themselves in relation to it, never in isolation from it.

The special interest of these old partitive constructions, according to Katznelson, lies in the fact that the *part* does not feature in them as the direct subject or object of a specific action: the action is ascribed to the *whole* as agent, and this whole alone can take a predicate. In other words, outside the boundaries of the quantitatively determined set, the part is not conceived either as an independent unit or as something which can enter into relationship with other sets. The attributes proper to its several parts are transferred to the whole set and, vice versa, the attributes inherent in the plurality as a whole are transferred to the component parts.

This elliptical use of the pronoun in association with a proper name is peculiar to Old Icelandic, and is virtually unknown in other Germanic languages. As for the peculiarities of Scandinavian art and poetry which we mentioned above – the combination of the whole with the part, taking the part as representative of the whole – parallels to these are found among other peoples in a comparable stage of development. But this sort of symbolism does not die out with Old Scandinavian culture; it is not difficult to trace it in medieval society as well. The intricate and extensive system of rituals, formulae, ceremonials, judicial procedures, solemn occasions, which regulated and shaped the whole tenor of social existence in the Middle Ages and informed all artistic and literary production, absorbed much symbolism going back in many cases to the barbarian past.

A second source of the symbolic perception and interpretation of space in the Middle Ages was Christian Neo-Platonism, which saw genuine reality, not in earthly things and manifestations, but in their divine and heavenly prototypes, as whose replicas and symbols they were accounted.

Christian symbolism 'doubled' the world by giving space an additional dimension, invisible to the eye, but accessible via a whole series of interpretative insights. These polysemantic interpretations derived from the words of St Paul: 'The letter killeth but the spirit giveth life' (Second Epistle to the Corinthians 3:6). Accordingly, each text of the Scriptures was interpreted both literally and spiritually or mystically; and the mystic interpretation was, in its turn, threefold. In all, then, a text was susceptible of four interpretations. First, it had to be understood factually (the 'historical' interpretation). Secondly, the fact could be seen as the analogue of some other event. Thus, the events related in the Old Testament had, over and above their own immediate sense, another meaning – a veiled, allegorical meaning, indicative of the events related in the New Testament (the 'allegorical' meaning). For example, the biblical story of the sale of Joseph by his brothers, his imprisonment and his subsequent advancement, had to be understood as an allegory of Christ, betrayed and deserted by his disciples, crucified and resurrected. Thirdly, there was the moral interpretation: an event could be seen as a lesson in moral behaviour (the 'tropological' interpretation). The good Samaritan who succoured the man attacked by robbers, and the recalcitrant Absalom, were held up as examples of how Christians should and should not behave. Fourthly, in any event there lay concealed a sacramental, religious truth (the 'anagogic', that is, higher or spiritual interpretation). Rest on the seventh day, prescribed by the Mosaic law, was interpreted in conformity with Christian belief, as eternal repose in heavenly peace. The four interpretations are summed up in the couplet:

> Littera gesta docet, quid credes allegoria,
> Moralis quod agas, quo tendas, anagogia.

('The literal meaning teaches you about what has happened; the allegorical meaning teaches you about what you believe in; the moral meaning teaches you how to behave; the anagogical meaning reveals your aspirations.') Comparing the human soul to a building, Hrabanus Maurus wrote that 'history' – the literal understanding – provides the foundations, while the other three interpretations are the walls, the roof, and the internal furnishings of the building. In his work *Allegoriae in Universam Sacram Scripturam* ('Allegory on the Whole of Holy Scripture'), this theologian of the Carolingian period gives an extensive list of the terms occurring in the Old and New Testaments, deriving their allegorical, tropological ('changing the direction of the discourse') and anagogical interpretations.[52] One and the same concept can be interpreted in all four senses. Jerusalem in the literal sense is a town on earth; in the allegorical sense, it is the church; in the tropological sense, it is the righteous soul; in the anagogical sense, it is the heavenly home. Duly interpreted, the whole of the Old Testament can be seen as a proclamation and prefiguring of the birth of Christ and his mission as saviour.

[83]

The theologians applied this method of interpretation only to Holy Scripture, and rejected the possibility of interpreting secular texts in similar fashion. But there was nevertheless a tendency to extend 'fourfold interpretation' to works of literature. In the letter to Can Grande della Scala, Dante says that the *Divina Commedia* has to be understood as 'polisemos': 'nam primus sensus est qui habetur per litteram, alius est qui habetur per significata per litteram' ('one meaning is the literal meaning, another meaning is that of the entities signified by the letter'). In illustration of this method of interpretation, Dante takes a section from the Book of Psalms (114:1–2): 'When Israel went out of Egypt, the house of Jacob from a people of strange language; Judah was his sanctuary, and Israel his dominion.' Dante comments on this text as follows:

Now, if we look only at the letter, what is related here is the exodus of the Children of Israel from Egypt in the days of Moses; allegorically interpreted, we are told of the salvation which is ours through Christ; the moral sense reveals to us the conversion of the soul from the grief and burden of sin to a state of grace; the anagogical interpretation shows us the passage of the sacred soul from the servitude of its present state of corruption to the freedom of eternal glory. And although these mystical meanings are called by various names, they may all be called the allegorical interpretation, since they all differ in this from the literal and historical meaning.[53]

If the symbolical interpretation of the Scriptures was beset with difficulty for laymen, and remained to a large extent the 'food of the theologians', yet the symbolism of churches, their structure and lay-out, every detail in a cathedral, and the religious ceremonies which took place therein – all of this was addressed to all Christians, and was designed to edify them in the mysteries of the faith.[54]

Medieval realism – especially if we consider it, not as interpreted by theologians and philosophers, but in the vulga-rised forms that appealed to the 'average man' – was a debased form of Platonism, to which it bore only a superficial resemblance. Medieval man was much given to blending the spiritual with the physical order of events, and was also inclined to interpret the ideal as material. His mind did not grasp the abstract as such, as something beyond the visible concrete embodiment. Spiritual essences and their earthly symbols and reflections were objectivised and comprehended as things, which it was accordingly equally permissible to collate and represent with the same degree of precision and naturalism.

Such quantitative factors as the extent and location of earthly things and the distance between them lost all precision when the centre of gravity moved from them to the world of essence. Medieval man assumed that it was possible to cover enormous distances in the twinkling of an eye. The saint was able to do a thirty-day journey in three days. Saint Bridget covered the distance from Ireland to Italy in the time it took her to wink her eye once, while Saint Aidan went from England to Rome and back in twenty-four hours.[55] Sacchetti credited the 'great magician' Abelard with being able to get from Rome to Babylon in one hour. Spirits issuing from the body 'run so quickly, that if one soul left the body in Valencia and entered into [another body] in some village in the county of Foix, and heavy rain was falling all the way between the two places, scarcely three drops would fall upon that soul'.[56] Souls, like angels, are at one and the same time in space and outside it. There is nothing inherently improbable about falling into hell while wandering on earth. For the world beyond the grave is at once far-off and close about you; in fact, the concepts of 'near' and 'far' in the sense of spatial separation are here strictly inapplicable. The medieval world is equipped with certain 'lines of force'; when a man finds himself in their field of action he is, as it were, liberated from the power of earthly laws, including those of space and time. Much of what medieval man perceived via his senses and his consciousness and much of what he imagined cannot be localised in space at all.

Man's way of seeing the universe also reflects his way of seeing himself. Hence, man's perception of space is bound up with his own self-evaluation. What place does he occupy in space? In this space what can be taken as a point of reference? It is well known that in the Renaissance, when the

[85]

human personality broke free from its traditional corporative and conventional bonds and asserted itself as a free agent, conceptions of space changed; the individual came to be aware of himself as the central point round which the rest of the world turned. The principle of perspective rediscovered by the artists of the Renaissance assumes the presence of an observer viewing all the parts of the picture from one single immovable point, each part being then seen at a specific angle. It is precisely the presence of this putative viewer that is the binding and integrating factor for all the details of the picture, and, accordingly, for the reality depicted in it. The elements of the cosmos are imagined as seen by this beholder at a given moment in time; they are related to him as to a central point, acting as a dimensional point of reference for the limitless and endless space beheld through the foreground of the picture (Alberti's *fenestra aperta*).

This subjective-anthropocentric position, this rationalising of the visual and optic impressions, is alien to the man of the Middle Ages. In his case, one should rather speak of a theocentric 'world model'. But God is not only the centre of the world, which he orders and apportions around him and in dependence on him. He is immanent in everything and everywhere, in all his creatures. The circle was seen as the symbol of completion, perfection; and the idea of the circle and sphere served as an image of God and the world. For Dante and for St Thomas Aquinas, for the poet and the theologian alike, the cosmos was spherical. Among the definitions of God included in an anonymous manuscript of the twelfth century is the following: 'God is an intelligible sphere whose centre is everywhere and whose circumference is nowhere' ('Deus est sphaera intelligibilis, cuius centrum ubique, circumferentia nusquam').[57]

The representations of space corresponding to this theocentric 'world model' are clearly distinguishable throughout the course of medieval graphic art. Painting of this period eschews linear perspective. The separate sections of the picture, each with its own degree of foreshortening, are not related to each other in terms of perspective; while the picture as a whole lacks depth, and its content seems to be entirely distributed on one plane. This monoplanar image presents an opaque surface veiling the inner space of the image. The medieval painter is not disturbed by the palpable lack of proportion in his work: trees and mountains can be the same size as human figures; a house is shown disproportionately small so that all its constructional detail can be accommodated in the framework of the picture. Key figures are always given in full. Often they stand out of their setting, which turns into a general decorative background. Obviously non-related areas of space are placed collaterally in one plane. Medieval aesthetics required the painter to provide not an illusion of the visible world but, in accordance with the teaching of Neo-Platonism, a divulging of 'intellectual vision'.[58] To such a vision much is accessible that is not perceivable by the eye. Hence, medieval painting places the beholder in a special situation which might be described as the 'drama of the meeting of two worlds'. The palpable and physically visible world is contiguous here with the suprasensual world. The medieval beholder of a painting, an icon, a sculpture, was aware of nothing to prevent free passage from one plane to the other.[59]

We can hardly doubt that, like ourselves, medieval man was able to distinguish between close and distant objects and was aware of their real dimensions. But these purely empirical observations were not transferred to painting, and no aesthetic value was placed upon them. God was the centre round which the world imaged by medieval painters turned. Since the truly significant was not that which was seen by physical sight but that which was apprehended by the spiritual eye, medieval painting took the visible world not as independent but as subject to higher, suprasensual powers, and worked on the premise that the human, earthly way of seeing things is unreliable. The beholder of a medieval painting does not represent a centre from which a section of reality can be contemplated. The picture assumes the presence not of one but of some or many observation points. This is the reason for the 'deployment' of images, the lack of proportion, the 'inverse perspective'. The picture may collocate images belonging to two or more stages of the narrative. As a whole, the picture is organised not by the rules of unity but on an associative basis. Space is neither articulated nor is it measured by the perceptions of the individual. The overall result is that the picture does not draw the spectator into it; it 'expels' him from it.[60]

These peculiarities of medieval painting, however, are not to be taken as showing that the painters of the period 'abolished' or 'eliminated' space. On the contrary, a comparison of ancient classical art with medieval art will provide evidence of a new conception of space in the latter. The art of classical antiquity knew perspective,[61] but was not concerned with the communication of unity as the inner bond binding the elements of the picture or the plastic relief together. According to E. Panofsky, classical art was characterised, not by systematic space as in modern art, but by aggregate space; a feeling for space, it would seem, not requiring that images should be systematically related therein.[62] The transition from antiquity to the Middle Ages saw the collapse of the old artistic forms and canons. Artists think only in terms of the plane. Connection between figures becomes insubstantial, being based on a rhythmic fluctuation of colours in a painting, and on alternation of light and shade in a relief. This representational principle has its analogue in Neo-Platonic philosophy: 'Space is nothing more than the brightest of lights' (Proclus). In Romanesque art, both bodies and space are reduced to planes, with the result that both the real world and artistic space are understood as a continuum. Making no effort to create the illusion of space, the artist aims at making artistic space homogeneous by means of its properties of light.[63]

A new stage in the artistic mastery of space came with the Gothic style. As the 'bearer of an idea', the space of the Gothic cathedral is dematerialised and 'spiritualised'; it is infinite, but at the same time organised and rhythmically articulated. While the ancient statue stands independently in temple or forum, wherever convenient, medieval sculpture links separate figures organically in a harmonious ensemble; they are components of an indissoluble whole – the cosmos of the Gothic cathedral. Between the figures and their spatial environment there exists an inner unity. The Gothic statue has to be sited in a niche, under a canopy; the sculptural relief is provided with an arch-shaped covering – these are means of correlating them with the mass of the cathedral, a means of delimiting and articulating free space. But, within this delimited space, the plastic elements of Gothic represent something else – they are elements of an unlimited, an infinite world. E. Panofsky[64] draws a parallel between Gothic architecture and scholastic philosophy, which had reinterpreted Aristotle's theory of space: the finite, empirical cosmos is included in the infinity of the divine essence.[65] Like the numerous all-embracing encyclopaedic constructions of 'high' scholasticism (the *summa* as the totality, the universal theory of the world), the Gothic cathedral embodied the entire system of Christian knowledge and expressed the 'visible logic' of the cosmos. In each of its parts the whole was reproduced, so that each detail was in its own way a miniature replica of the cathedral – just as the scholastic treatise was built up on the principle of a 'system of like parts and parts of these parts'.

The space within the Gothic cathedral gives the impression of movement; it is not static, but appears to be, as it were, in constant genesis: emergence and change. The whole experience is informed by the fluidity and the richness of meaningful forms, a source of inexhaustible creative fantasy on the part of the medieval master craftsmen who built the cathedrals, and carved and sculpted them. Space and body are apprehended by them as a unity, united in essence, for this complex representation is not as yet susceptible of clear logical expression or of ordered presentation in conceptual form. Space was apprehended as a reality which possessed its own structure and ordering. From this derives the inner unity of the Gothic cathedral. Space in the Middle Ages was understood in a special way – this is attested by the fact that the very concept as we understand it did not exist; the word *spatium* meant 'extent', 'interval', while *locus* meant the place occupied by a particular body, not the abstract notion of space in general. The abstraction makes its appearance only in the new physics of Gassendi and Newton.[66]

At least in part, the artistic thinking of the medieval craftsmen and the scholastic reasoning of the philosophers reflected the general world-view of medieval people. This general world-view was based on a 'world model' which architects and painters, poets and philosophers, might render more or less clearly, fully or systematically, but whose elements were common property.

So we see that space as perceived by medieval man was neither abstract nor homogeneous, but individual and qualitatively heterogeneous. It is not conceived as a form prior to matter; space is just as real as the rest of God's creatures. Space as apprehended in the Middle Ages is a closed system with sacral centres and an earthly periphery. The cosmos of Neo-Platonic Christianity is graduated and hierarchical. The experience of space is tinged with religious and moral overtones. Space is symbolical. For a long time, apprehension of space remained anthropomorphic, reflecting the specifically close relationship between man and nature which characterised pre-industrial society.

With the development of an urban population with a new, more rationalistic way of thinking, this traditional way of apprehending nature began to change. As man's practical activity became more and more complex and his effect on nature more direct and purposeful, thanks to the development of new tools and the invention of machinery which came to adopt an intermediary position between man and his natural surroundings, he found himself confronted with problems of a new type. Before man's inquisitive and searching intelligence, nature begins to be desacralised and secularised. Certain philosophers advocate a combination of religion with understanding of the natural world, decrying those who 'like peasants' are content with nothing more than faith, and fail to use their powers of reasoning.[67]

The rise of industry generates the need for a more precise and standardised method of measuring bodies and areas. Commercial activity confers a new importance on the speed with which one can travel between trading centres. As urban civilisation takes shape around him, man is less and less susceptible to the rhythms of nature; he detaches himself more and more from her and begins to look upon her as an object to be utilised. His horizons widen.

The mastery and reorganisation of space in this historical epoch spreads into the realm of socio-political relations. Social bonds, which in the earlier period had been more personal in character, now become 'earthed' – transposed from the person to the earth. In particular, the feudal state, which in the early Middle Ages had been a relatively loose and fluid system of personal relations between lord and subjects, a system without clearly drawn boundaries, now acquires firmer outlines. A parallel process to this takes place in the inner annexation of political space by the authority of the king, which introduces throughout the territories it administers a unified legislature and judiciary, a common coinage and a unified system of taxation.[68]

As the transition to the Renaissance proceeds, a new 'world model' begins to take shape in Western European thinking, a model in which a homogeneous space organised on new lines plays an important part.[69] But it is, of course, not just space that is apprehended afresh, but all the basic components of this model, particularly the one which is most closely connected with space – time.

CHAPTER IV

What is time?

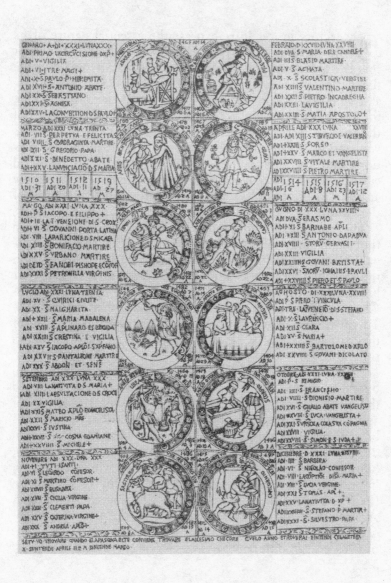

Few factors in a culture express the essential nature of its world picture so clearly as its way of reckoning time: for this has a determining influence on the way people behave, the way they think, the rhythm of their lives and the relationships between them and things. It is sufficient to compare the cyclical conception of time dominating the civilisations of the ancient East and of classical antiquity with the apocalyptic conception of the world's evolution from creation to destruction, and the merging of time and eternity in medieval culture, for us to recognise the radical difference between the attitude to life found in ancient cultures and that typical of the culture of the Middle Ages.

The comparison underlines the importance of making a thorough study of the problem of time in the historico-cultural plane; but it does nothing to help us to understand the category of time as apprehended by medieval man. For his attitude to time was shaped not only by the Judaeo-Christian conception but also by several other antecedents. To get to grips with this, we have to go back to the age of the barbarians and see how they perceived and reacted to time.

In an agrarian community, time was determined above all by the rhythms of nature. The peasant's calendar reflected the alternation of the time of year, and the succession of agricultural seasons. Among the Germanic tribes, the months bore names indicative of the agricultural and other tasks then due: 'month of fallow' (June), 'month of mowing' (July), 'month of sowing' (September), 'month of wine' (October), 'month of threshing' (January), 'month of branches' (February); 'month of grass' (April). In Charlemagne's time, an attempt to introduce these names into the official calendar came to naught as these names did not always mean the same time of year in different parts of Germany: 'month of tilling'

[94]

was August in some places and March or April in others.[1]
Among the Scandinavians, May was called the 'time of
gathering eggs', and also the 'time when sheep and calves are
rounded up'; June was the 'sunny month', the 'time for
going up to summer pasture', October was the 'month for
slaughtering cattle' (this is retained in Swedish), and
December was the 'month of sheep' or the 'month for mating
cattle'.[2] Summer was called the time 'between ploughing and
stacking'.[3]

Among the Germanic tribes the words *tíð* and *tími* were
not used in any precise sense. They merely indicated times
of the year, periods of indefinite duration and of more or
less significance. Sometimes, though rarely, they were used
with reference to shorter periods of time – the hours. The
word *ár* had two basic meanings: 'year' and 'harvest' or
'abundance'. The year – indeed, time in general – was not
construed simply as duration, but rather as a plenitude of
some concrete content, a content which is always specific
and determinate. It is significant that these concepts did not
reflect a linear flow of time (from the past via the present
into the future), but rather a rotation of time: *tíð* (cf. English
'tide') meant the tidal rise and fall, or the weather; while
ár (English 'year', German *Jahr*) meant 'harvest', and was
therefore clearly tied to a periodically repeated activity.

The barbarians apprehended time in anthropomorphic
fashion, and the extent to which it was 'filled' determined its
apparent duration. In this connection, analysis of the Old
Icelandic word *öld* is instructive. Its primary meaning is
'time', 'age'. But this is not a chronological age comprising a
definite number of commensurate temporal sections. An age
is characterised by its content: it has a moral character. In
the Icelandic Eddic lay *The Song of the Sybil* (*Vǫlospá*), which
paints a mythological picture of the origin and the history of
the world, it is prophesied that before the end of the world

> Brothers will fight
> and kill each other,
> siblings
> do incest;
> men will know misery,

adulteries be multiplied,
an axe-age, a sword-age,
shields will be cloven,
a wind-age, a wolf-age,
before the world's ruin.[4]

This time of moral decay and collapse is characterised by the terms *sceggiöld* ('time of axes'), *scálmöld* ('time of swords'), *vindöld* ('time of storms'), and *vargöld* ('time of wolves'). But the word *öld* in the lays of the *Elder Edda* has another meaning as well: that of 'human world' or 'people'. In *The Song of the Sybil*, the list of dwarfs ends with the words 'this list . . . will abide for ever, as long as people are alive' (*meðan öld lifir*).[5] In the same way, in *The Words of the High One* (*Hávamál*), in *The Words of Atli* (*Atlamál*) and in other Eddic lays the term *öld* means 'people'. The word *öld* (English 'old', German *alt*) is probably connected with *ala* (Latin *alere*) 'to rear', 'to give birth to', and this again points to the close connection between the two concepts – that of time and that of organic life.

It would seem that originally the concepts of 'age' and 'human world' were closely related, as the old Scandinavians believed that time does not flow outside of the human world and is permeated with human content. This is evident from the prologue to the *Heimskringla* of Snorri Sturluson. The Icelandic historian speaks of the replacement of one age by another in the early days of the Scandinavian world, when it was ruled by the dynasty of the Ynglings, who traced their line back to Óðinn. The first of these ages was the 'Age of Cremation' (*brunaöld*), in which the dead were burned on funeral pyres along with their goods, and memorial stones were raised in their memory. This age was succeeded by the new age – 'the Age of the Burial Mounds' (*haugsöld*). 'However, the Age of Cremation persisted for a long time among Swedes and Norwegians', adds Snorri.[6] In this strange relationship between two ages, when the new age collides with the old, and the two go on coexisting side by side, we can discern the true meaning of the word *öld*; this 'age' is not a chronological stretch of time but a qualitatively determined condition of human existence. Hence, even the change from one age to another depends on human actions. In *Sverris saga* – the story of the Norwegian royal usurper who lived at the turn of the twelfth–thirteenth centuries – we find words addressed by him to his comrades-in-arms, the 'Birchlegs': 'A great and wondrous change of ages has come about (*alldascipti mikit oc undarliga*) when one man takes up the place of three, those of king, jarl and archbishop: I am that man.'[7]

The close connection in the barbarian mind between the concepts of time and of the human race can be seen also in the etymology of the word *veröld* (English 'world' from Old English *weoruld*) which is a compound of *verr* (man) and *öld*. The world is the 'age of men'. Here, the concepts of time and life are united in one word. For the ancient Scandinavians time was not an empty form but always had its own, invariably concrete, qualitative content. The time in which one Norwegian king rules is good, there are bountiful harvests, peace reigns, cattle multiply and fish are caught; the time of another reign is bad, there is dissension in the land, hunger and poor harvests. In order to bring about fertility and good harvests, sacrifices have to be made to the gods and libations poured out at feasts in their honour. According to a legend which has parallels in the folklore of many peoples, when things were going particularly badly for the ancient Swedes, they even sacrificed their leader.[8] It is possible that the original meaning of the sacrifice made by the king *til árs* was not simply to ensure a good harvest; without this ritual influencing of the future, the new year could not begin; the leader was seen as the creator of the new year.[9]

Evidence as to the ways, according to old Scandinavian belief, in which time could be influenced is to be found in Snorri's story of King Aun, who extended his own life by sacrificing his sons to Óđinn: each son secured for him ten additional years of life.[10] The Goddess Iđunn kept an apple in a dish; when the aesir began to grow old they ate a piece of it, and were promptly rejuvenated, 'and so it will continue up to Ragnarök' (the 'Twilight of the Gods').[11]

In an agrarian society the regulation of time by natural cycles determined not only man's dependence on the succession of seasons, but also the specific structure of his awareness. In nature there is no development, or at least it was not obvious to the people of this society. What they saw in nature was a regular repetition, rhythmic and circular, which they were in no position to control; and this eternal return was bound to take a central place in the minds of men, both in antiquity and in the Middle Ages. Repetition not change was the crucial factor governing their awareness and their behaviour. For them, the unique and the unprecedented had no independent value – the only truly real acts were those sanctified by tradition and regularly recurrent.[12] Archaic society rejected individuality and innovatory behaviour. The normal, indeed the virtuous, thing to do was to behave like others and like those who had gone before. Such traditional behaviour alone had moral force and value. Hence, life for a man in a traditional society consists of a continuous series of repeated actions which his forefathers performed in the same way. Inevitably, a standard way of doing things and behaving crystallises, which is ascribed to the progenitors of the race, to the gods or to a 'cultural hero'. The repetition by people of acts which can be traced back to a divine prototype connects them with the divinity, and confers reality upon them and upon what they do. All human activity, productive, social, family, intimate, becomes significant and is endorsed in so far as it participates in the sacral order, and follows the ritual established 'at the beginning of time'. Thus, mundane time is deprived of its own value and autonomy, and man projects himself into mythological time. This is especially obvious at times of festival and ceremonials which set up a direct link with the myth and embody the behavioural model. The myth was not simply retold but re-enacted as a ritual drama, and was accordingly re-experienced in all its lofty reality and tension. Re-enactment of the myth 'cut off' mundane time and reinstated mythological time.[13]

The 'archaic' way of thinking is anti-historical. The collective memory of events that have really taken place is transformed, as time goes by, into myth, depriving these events of their individual features and retaining only those which fit into the model imposed by the myth; events are reduced to categories, and individuals to archetypes. Novelty is of no interest to this way of thinking; what matters is repetition of what has already been, of that which goes back to the beginnings of time. What has to be recognised in this way of apprehending time is its 'extra-temporality'. There is no sharp division between past and present, for the past is for ever being born anew and returns to form a real part of the present. Against the loss of independent value of the present must be set its gain in depth and in the acquisition of a nontemporal, non-transient character, since it is now directly correlated with the mythical past, which is apprehended not simply as past and gone, but as eternally enduring. Life loses its fortuitousness and transience; it partakes of eternity.

An essential aspect of temporal reckoning lay in keeping account of generations. By determining which generation a person belonged to, and by establishing the sequence of generations, one could get quite a satisfactory idea of the sequence of events, the way things had happened, and one could substantiate claims in law. The concept of the generation produced a feeling of a living continuity of organic human groups into which the individual fitted as the real bearer of links connecting the present with the past, and transmitting both into the future. It was a feeling invested with far more significance and value than the mere identification of a point on an abstract chronological scale. But keeping account of generation is a form of local calculation of time. Such calculations were made in the shape of genealogies, ancestral tales and sagas. Listing and enumerating ancestors clarified not the general chronology of the people, the tribe, or the state, but the successive links within the confines of the kin, the family; and it was by no means customary to try to correlate these with the passage of time outside the limits of the circle of kinship.

The significance of this form of relationship with time – a form which we might call 'ancestral' or 'family' time – was shaped by the largely introvert character of the family or clan groups, leading isolated lives and only superficially connected among themselves. In each farmstead or community, time passed in subordination to the rhythmic change of generations and to the few monotonous events which made any impression on the life of the group.[14] There is plenty of evidence for this in the Icelandic sagas. Chronological guidelines are given in these by preference in the form of *lang-fedgatal* – enumeration of ancestors. Sometimes this enumeration comprises several generations in a family tree, but in other cases the author limits himself to references to the father or to father and grandfather. Assertions that the events described in the saga took place in the reign of a specific Norwegian king are associated with the desire to give the narration a precise date, thus attaching it chronologically to the events of 'great history'. Even such an 'unhistorical' saga as *Hrafnkels saga* begins with a dating of the settlement in Iceland of Hrafnkel's father at the time of the Norwegian king Harald Fairhair, and the author takes the opportunity to set out the genealogy of Harald over five generations although this was familiar to everyone and there was no need at all to reiterate it in the context of the saga. Elsewhere, when a king is referred to, the intention is to show the influence of historical events on the dramatis personae in the saga (for example, the uniting of Norway by Harald, and the emigration of the ancestors of the saga's heroes, or Christianisation and the way it involved certain Icelanders in dispute and conflict). In addition, the saga writers did not limit themselves in their choice of temporal guidelines to the political events in the country's history; local events were also used – things that happened on the level of 'ancestral' or 'family' time (see above), and which had made an impression on people's minds (blood-feud between families, the murder of an Icelander, a stormy session in the Althing, etc.).

The ancestral cult, which played an enormous part in the lives of the Germanic peoples, was closely connected with their awareness of time. The ancestor could, as it were, be born anew in one of his descendants; within the family, names were inherited and along with them the personal qualities of their bearers.[15] The past was restored, personified in the man who repeated the character and re-enacted the deeds of his ancestor. This was why the graves and burial mounds of ancestors were sited alongside the settlements of the living; these were not two different worlds, but one single world in which past, present and future were seen to be adjacent and effectively co-existent. Hence also the belief, which we have

[100]

just mentioned, that it is possible to influence the course of time – not just present time but also future time. In a certain sense, only present time exists for the barbarian, but this is a very broad and very capacious present, which cannot be reduced to the single moment of the mathematical present; it includes the past and the future, and there is no sharp cleavage between it and either of them. In fact, if time is cyclical and the past is reiterated, then future time is nothing more than an ever-renewed present or past. The 'spatial' understanding of time[16] found expression in the older strata of many languages, and indeed most concepts of time were in their origins of a spatial nature.[17]

The ability to return to the past and to influence the future course of events can be achieved through magic. It is possible to forecast the future (as the Sibyl-Vǫlva did, for example, in the most renowned of the lays of the *Elder Edda*, forecasting the end and renewal of the world) and to see it in dreams (prophetic dreams play a major part in the sagas). For, as we have already stressed, to the barbarian mind time was not simply an abstract linear duration; it was people's lives, and it changed qualitatively as these lives changed. Time was the togetherness of human generations, succeeding each other and renewing each other like the seasons of the year. Future time is also fate. Urd (Urðr), one of the three Norns living at the root of the world-tree Yggdrasill, is the personification of fate, of the future, of that which must be (cf. Saxon *wurth*, Anglo-Saxon *wyrd*, English 'weird').[18]

Time is just as real and substantial as the rest of the world. Therefore, time can be ordered and divided, which is what the gods did when they were creating the world; having created heaven and earth, they divided time up and fixed the way it should be reckoned.[19] Time can be foretold, and its content can be changed. Hence, time for the man of the archaic age was something totally different from what we mean by it; it was not simply a mode of the world's existence, abstracted from things, but a concrete, objectively existing element, a web on the loom of the gods; the Norns cut the threads – which are human lives.[20]

The above-mentioned 'extra-temporality' of the barbarian perception of time (extra-temporality from the point of view of modern attitudes to time, which are characterised by an awareness of its swift and irreversible onward flow and by the identification of only one present – the 'instant' moment) reflected an inherent feeling for the fullness of existence. Being had not yet been dismembered by analytical thought into separate categories, abstracted from any concrete content. Time and space as apprehended by the Germanic peoples were not *a priori* concepts, existing outside and before experience; they were given only in experience itself, of which they formed an indissoluble part, which could not be detached from the living fabric. That is to say, time was not so much apprehended as experienced.

We see then that time for these peoples is always concrete in content and integrated with life. There are no instruments for determining the course of a day and night; it is enough to know the position of the sun in the sky. The ancient Icelandic code of laws, *Grágás* ('Grey Goose'), lays down that a lawsuit should begin to be heard in the Althing when the sun fully illuminates the yard of the *thing*; the judges must ascend the 'Law Rock' while the rays of the sun fall on the western part of the ravine. The day's activities are halted when the sun begins to incline towards the horizon – or, to be more accurate, when it appears to be a spear-length from the horizon, the spear being placed at the 'middle mark of sea-swell' (between high and low water mark).[21]

The length of a journey is measured in time (the number of days spent at sea or travelling on dry land). There was no need for anything more precise. It occurred to no one to imagine a journey between two points, in abstraction from the traveller making that journey. When measurements of distance are mentioned, it turns out that these measurements do not correspond to any sort of fixed or standard units. Thus, *röst*, which is sometimes translated as 'mile', really indicates the distance between two halting places (cf. English 'rest'). Obviously, the actual length of a *röst* varied in accordance with many conditions. The variation factor was so great indeed that the Scandinavians distinguished between 'short' and 'long' *rastir*. Thus, for the ancient Scandinavians, a journey was not simply an empty length, but always concrete space; or, to put it more accurately, it was a movement of

people in concrete, tangible space. Speaking of the distance
between two points, a man would imagine himself making
the journey in time. When the Norwegian Óttarr, who
visited England at the end of the ninth century, was telling
the English king, Alfred, about distances in Scandinavia, he
gave them in terms of the number of days it took to sail from
one point to another with a favourable wind.[22]

The mythological (or mythopoetic) conception of the
world is characterised by non-homogeneity of both space
and time; just as certain areas of space are sacral, under the
special protection of the gods – temples, burial places,
meeting places, farmsteads dedicated to a god – so the course
of ordinary, everyday time is broken by moments of sacral
or festive time.

Time in archaic society is not something outside people,
unrelated to their lives and doings. On the contrary, it is
something within them, and therefore it is possible to
influence its course and even its quality. Time is a chain of
human generations. There was one word for both 'age' and
'human kind', since age is exactly that – the life of generations
of people. As a concept, eternity was, it would seem, alien
to the barbarians, who were introduced to it only through
Christianity.[23]

This lack of any precise way of reckoning time went hand
in hand with great interest in establishing the facts about
earlier happenings and the order in which they had taken
place. It is symptomatic that the beginnings of Scandinavian
literature are in the shape of historiography; the earliest
Icelandic and Norwegian books are also works of a historical
character. Thus, the *Íslendingabók* (*Book of the Icelanders*)
by the earliest Icelandic historian, Ari Þorgilsson, is full of
references to the events of European history, to which he
tries to relate the known facts of the early history of Iceland.
Together with the Christian reckoning of time from the birth
of Christ, Ari takes as his starting-point the murder of St
Edmund, and he also refers to the reigns of various popes,
to the rule of the crusading King Baldwin, to kings of
Norway and Sweden, to the Byzantine emperors and to the
Patriarch of Jerusalem. Further chronological landmarks are
provided by the lists of Icelandic bishops and 'law-speakers'.

Wishing to establish his own genealogy, Ari traces his line back to the Ynglings, the dynasty of ancient Swedish and Norwegian kings, and to their founders – the heathen gods Njǫrđr and Freyr. The *Íslendingabók* is permeated with a concern for chronological trustworthiness.[24] A special chapter is devoted to the reform of the Icelandic calendar. Ari tells us that when this reform was introduced in the Althing, the Icelanders present showed enormous interest.[25] And yet with all Ari's lively interest for questions of chronology, we have to admit that he relies mainly on his own memory and on the reminiscences of his predecessors. Of þorkell Gellisson, to whom he appeals as an authority on the date of the beginning of the colonisation of Iceland, Ari says: 'He could remember a long way back.'

In the family sagas of Iceland there are also many references to time and chronological sequence. Almost always, however, there is a lack of indisputable data on the duration of the events described. Usually, duration is indefinite, and it is impossible to say how many years separate one event from another. The authors of the sagas may appear to have a developed sense of time, but in fact the measurement of time in the sagas is imprecise and confusing.[26]

The transition from paganism to Christianity was accompanied by a radical restructuring of temporal concepts in medieval Europe. But the older way of apprehending time was not so much eradicated as pushed into the background, there to persist as a 'lower' stratum of folk consciousness. For example, the pagan calendar which reflected the seasonal changes of the year was adapted to the needs of the Christian liturgy. The church festivals, marking the turning-points of the annual cycle, go back to pagan times; agrarian time was also liturgical time. The year was divided up by festivals recalling events in the life of Christ, and by holy days. In different countries, the year began at different times – at the time of the birth of Christ, at Holy Week, or at the Annunciation. Accordingly, time was measured by the number of weeks 'until Christmas', 'since Christmas', and so on. For a long time theologians opposed the fixing of 1 January as the beginning of the year, on the grounds that this was a pagan festival; but 1 January was also the day on which Christ was circumcised.

The twenty-four-hour period was divided, not into hours of equal length, but into hours of day, from sunrise to sunset, and hours of night, from sunset to sunrise. That is to say, in summer, the hours of day were longer than the hours of night; in winter, vice versa. Until the thirteenth and fourteenth centuries, instruments for measuring time were rare objects of luxury. Even scholars did not always possess such things. Walcher, the Englishman engaged in studying the movements of the heavenly bodies, complained that the accuracy of his observations of a lunar eclipse in 1091 was impaired by his lack of a clock.[27] The most usual form of clock in medieval Europe was the sundial (the Greek gnomon), the sand-clock or the clepsydra (water-clock). The sundial was, of course, of no use in dull weather, and the clepsydra was more of a rare luxury than an instrument for the accurate measurement of time. If it was absolutely necessary to know the time at some point after sunset, it was measured by the burning down of a torch, of a candle or of oil in a sanctuary-lamp. Just how slow progress was in finding some means of measuring time can be seen from the fact that the use of candles for the purpose, adopted by Alfred the Great at the end of the ninth century (when journeying through his country he took with him candles of the same length which were lit one after another), was still being observed in France under Louis IX (thirteenth century) and Charles V (fourteenth century). Monks reckoned by the number of pages of holy scripture they had read, or by the number of psalms they had sung between two observations of the sky. For every hour of the day and night there were special prayers and invocations. For the mass of the people, the main time signal was the sound of the church bells, calling them regularly to morning prayers or other religious services. The twenty-four-hour period was divided into a series of sections – the canonical hours (*horae canonicae*), of which there were normally seven; these were signalled by the striking of the church clock.[28] In this way, the recorded passage of time was controlled by the clergy. The etymology of the word *campana* (bell) given by John of Garland at the begin-

ning of the thirteenth century is fantastic in the true spirit of
the Middle Ages, but also in its own way significant:
'Campane were given this name by the peasants living in the
country (*in campo*) who cannot tell the time except with the
help of the bells (*per campanas*).'[29] It was mainly by ear that
medieval people knew the time, not by eye.

Local life was entirely regulated by the sound of the bells:
'harvest bell', 'curfew bell' and 'pasture bell', chiming regularly in rhythm with the liturgical year. We gain some idea
of how approximate measurement of time was in the Middle
Ages if we recall something that happened in Mons at the
end of the twelfth century. As the chronicler tells us, a
judicial trial by single combat was scheduled for sunrise one
morning, but only one of the contestants turned up. Having
waited in vain for his opponent, he appealed to the judge to
declare him the victor, as his adversary had failed to present
himself at the set time. For this, it was necessary to establish
that it was indeed past nine o'clock, and the court officials
had to appeal to the priest, the man best able to cope with
such matters.[30]

In as much as the tempo of life and of the basic occupations
of the people depended on the rhythm of the seasons, there
was no reason why it should ever be necessary to know the
exact time, and the customary division of the day into broad
sectors was quite sufficient. The minute as a division of time
or as an integral part of an hour did not exist. Even after the
invention of the mechanical clock and its spread in Europe,
it was a long time before it had a minute hand.

In paradoxical contrast to the imprecision in the measurement of time and to medieval man's inability to detect relatively small intervals in its flow, there were purely intellectual
exercises in the graduation of time, completely devoid of any
factual or experimental basis. These were due to the urge for
complete systemisation and for exaggerated detail which is so
typical of scholasticism. Honorius Augustodunensis (twelfth
century) divides the hour up into extremely fine components:
it consists of 4 'points', 10 'minutes', 15 'parts', 40
'moments', 60 'signs' and 22,560 'atoms'. And although he
regards the minute as 'a small interval in the hour' (*minutus*
also means 'reduced', 'small'), Honorius, following Isidore

of Seville, agrees that the hour is the 'term of all things' ('Hora est terminus cujusque rei').[31] This sort of 'atomisation' of time, which goes back to Lucretius, is bound up with the conception of time as a reality homogeneous with things: medieval authors likened the 'atoms of time' to the 'atoms of the body' and the 'atoms of number'; and the comparison of the flow of time to the flow of water was not simply for them, as it is for us, a metaphor. But the basic temporal categories of the Middle Ages were the year, the season, the month, the day – not the hour, let alone the minute. Medieval time is protracted, slow and epic.

The agricultural calendar and the division of the twenty-four-hour period varied, as one might expect, from one area to another. It is hardly necessary to point out that medieval man's time was essentially local time, varying from one locality to another and independently observed in each.

Agricultural time is natural time, not occasional or eventful time; hence it does not need to be exactly measured, nor indeed is it susceptible of exact measurement. It is the time of people who do not run nature, but who are subject to its rhythms. The contrasts peculiar to the medieval mind are also shown in the way the twenty-four-hour cycle was divided up. Night was the time of danger and terrors, of the supernatural, of demons and of other dark and mysterious forces. Night was particularly significant for the Germanic tribes, who reckoned time by the number of nights. Crimes committed under cover of night were punished with special severity. Christianity tried to combat and overcome the conception of night as the time when the devil ruled. Christ, it was taught, was born at night so as to bring the light of truth to those wandering in the night of their error. The light of day was seen as scattering the terrors engendered by the darkness of night. Despite this, throughout the whole of the medieval period, night remained the symbol of evil and sin, and if the Christian Vespers were designed to inspire the soul of the believer with tranquillity and the awareness of the nearness of God, the devil was still closer at hand and more dangerous under the cover of darkness. The contrast between day and night is the contrast between life and death; 'The Lord gave day to the living, and night to the dead,' said Thietmar of

Merseburg. The contrast between summer and winter was seen in the same light. And all of these contrasted pairs had ethical and sacral significance.

There were days that were regarded as favourable for this or that enterprise and days that were unfavourable: lucky days and unlucky days. Right up to our times people clung to the belief in the connection between man's fate and the signs of the Zodiac, upon whose position in the firmament the character of the time depended. A knowledge of the lunar calendar was necessary for successful dealings with magic.

The calendar which is so frequently portrayed throughout the Middle Ages in miniatures, in carvings on the walls of churches and cathedrals, in frescoes, in learned treatises and in poetry, is primarily the agricultural calendar, in which each month is indicated by particular agricultural occupations. This type of calendar was borrowed by the Middle Ages from antiquity, but did not follow its original model in all respects. In the classical models the months are represented by astronomical symbols combined with passive human figures; but in Western Europe of the early Middle Ages, a system of personifying the monthly tasks, showing real people hard at work, was elaborated. These are no longer abstract allegorical figures but the 'labours' of the months.[32] As a result there arose a significantly new genre in which man's earthly activity is shown as taking place under the gaze of heaven, and forming part, as it were, of one single harmonious rhythm of nature as medieval Christianity understood it.

The collection of feudal rents and the performance of feudal duties by the peasants were of course, also, regulated by the agrarian calendars. Land surveys for tax purposes, cartularies, and estate cadastres continually mention the most important festivals marking the beginning or ending of payment of quit-rent, pasturage and harvest. In the minds of the peasants and landowners these occasions had an absolutely clear social content; they mark in fact the reification of the production relations of feudal exploitation.

The family time (time reckoned in terms of generations) of the barbarian epoch continued to be of use in the developing feudal society. Feudal lords were deeply interested in genealogies, by means of which they traced their pedigrees back to distant, often legendary or semi-legendary princely ancestors. This way of securing the family's prestige by means of an appeal to the length of its genealogical tree exhibits the ruling class's attitude to time: the powerful, noble, influential man in the Middle Ages is the man with many generations behind him, the man in whom family time – and therefore historical time – has condensed. History in the Middle Ages remained the history of the old feudal families and dynasties. It was not for nothing that the medieval French word *geste* meant both 'history' (history of feats and exploits) and 'noble kin', 'heroic family'.

Unconcerned as they were about the exact measurement of time, the people of the Middle Ages showed rather more interest in questions of chronology. The basic genre of historical narration in the Middle Ages is represented by annals, chronicles, annual registers of historical events which (from their standpoint, at least) merited attention. Chroniclers sought to arrive among themselves at some agreement on dates for kings and popes. Many works were published on ways of calculating historical periods, and many chroniclers saw themselves as specialists in the precise dating of kings and bishops, and of important events in the past. In the works of Isidore of Seville (*Etymologies*) and of the Venerable Bede (*On the Times* and *On the Reckoning of Time*) all the units of time are considered, from the hour and the day to the year and the world eras (*aetates mundi*). This interest in time and its reckoning is also shown by the early medieval attempts to draw up paschal tables (together with the permanent calendar reckoned in relation to Christmas, there was also the calendar of the movable church feasts, which were determined according to the date on which Easter fell). At the same time, an enormous mass of documents of this period contain no dates at all, and historians are often hard put to it to assign any approximate time to their compilation.

The time in which earthly kingdoms exist and in which earthly events succeed each other was not apprehended either as the only time or as the true time. Together with earthly and secular time there existed sacral time, which alone possessed true reality. The category of the divine archetype which determines the minds and the behaviour of people in archaic societies, continues to be central to the world-view of medieval Christianity. The personages and the events recorded in the Old and New Testaments are endowed with reality of a very special nature. Biblical time is not transient; it represents an absolute value. With Christ's act of redemption, time acquires a special duality: 'the time' is at hand, or already 'fulfilled', time has reached its 'fullness', the 'last times' are at hand, it is the 'end of time': the kingdom of God exists already, but earthly time is not yet concluded, and the kingdom of God remains the final end, the aim towards which all must strive.

The time scale of Christian myth differs very widely from that of pagan myth. Pagan time, it would seem, was apprehended exclusively in the forms of myth, ritual, seasonal change and the succession of generations, while in medieval society the category of mythological, sacral time ('history of revelation') coexists with the category of secular, worldly time; and both of these categories are united in the category of historical time ('history of salvation'). Historical time is subordinate to sacral time, but is not dissolved in it: the Christian myth gives a *sui generis* criterion for defining historical time and evaluating its meaning.

Having broken with the cyclic world-view of the pagan world, Christianity took from the Old Testament the experiencing of time as an eschatological process, a process of tense expectation of that supreme event which would crown history and explain it: the coming of the Messiah. But while sharing the eschatology of the Old Testament, New Testament teaching recast it and introduced an entirely new conception of time.

First of all, in the Christian world-view the concept of time was detached from the concept of eternity, which in other ancient cosmological systems had absorbed and subjected secular time. Eternity is not measurable in temporal units or components. Eternity is an attribute of God; time is created and has a beginning and an end, which circumscribe the duration of human history. Secular time is correlated with eternity, and at certain crucial moments human history 'breaks through' into eternity. The Christian strives to pass from the time of the earthly vale of tears into the abode of eternal bliss enjoyed by God's elect.

Secondly, historical time acquires a definite structure, being divided both quantitatively and qualitatively into two main epochs: up to the birth of Christ and after the birth of Christ. History moves from the act of divine creation to the Day of Judgment. In the centre of this process is the decisive sacramental fact, which determines its direction, giving it a new meaning and predetermining all subsequent developments – the coming of Christ and his death. Old Testament history is seen as the epoch of preparation for the coming of Christ; subsequent history is the result of his Incarnation and his Passion. This event is once and for all, non-repeatable, and unique in its significance.[33]

Thus, the new conception of time is based on three decisive factors: the beginning, the culmination and the end of the existence of mankind. Time becomes linear and irreversible. The Christian orientation of time differs both from the orientation of classical antiquity, directed towards the past alone, and from the messianic, prophetic fixation on the future, which is characteristic of the Judaic conception of time found in the Old Testament. The Christian conception of time gives due importance to the past, since the New Testament tragedy has already taken place, and to the future, since this will bring judgment, recompense and retribution.

The presence of these nodal points of reference has a profound effect on time: time is 'straightened out', 'stretched' and vectorially directed; their presence engenders a tension field between the ages, proclaiming – in the shape of history – the immanent and harmonious grand design which will bring about the resolution of these tensions. It is worth noting, however, that, for all its insistence on the linear nature of time, Christianity did not entirely jettison the cyclic concept; fundamentally, all that happened was that the cyclic concept was construed in different fashion. In fact, in so far as time was separated from eternity, it appeared to man, when he contemplated the ages of history, as a linear sequence; but this same earthly history, taken as a whole, in the framework formed by the creation and the end of the world, also appears as a complete cycle: man and his world return to the Creator, time returns to eternity.

In Christianity, historical time takes the form of a drama. The beginning of the drama is man's first free act – Adam's fall. Intimately connected with this is the coming of Christ, sent by God to save mankind. Judgment follows at the close of man's earthly existence. The interpretation of earthly history as the history of the salvation of mankind gave it a new dimension. The life of man unfolds on two temporal planes at once: on the empirical and transient plane of earthly existence, and on the plane of the realisation of God's predestined plan. Man is a protagonist in a cosmo-historical drama, in the course of which the fate of the world and the fate of his own individual soul are decided. It was this awareness that gave a special and distinctive character to the world-view of medieval people, who felt their personal involvement in history.

The Christian awareness of time as a drama is based on a dualistic relationship with the world and its history. Earthly life and the whole of history are seen as the arena of a struggle between good and evil. These are not impersonal cosmic forces; on the contrary they are rooted in man himself, and if good is to emerge victorious in history and in his own soul, man's free will and goodwill are necessary. From the recognition of man's internal freedom of choice there follows the central drama of the Christian view of time and history. Earthly life with its transient joys and sorrows is not self-sufficient and acquires its true sense only when it is incorporated in the sacramental history of the salvation of mankind. Thus, past and future are of greater significance and value than the present, which is fleeting. A similar attitude to the current events of the present inheres in the mythological world-view which sees in them no more than the reflection of the original forms, a repetition of the divine archetype. The Christian myth, however, differs radically from the pagan 'nature' mythologies, in that the Christian myth is a *historical* myth; earthly history is not left to the whim of supernatural beings, but is cast in a specifically dualistic mould from the fusion of sacral and secular elements. Hence, within the framework of the Christian world-view a philosophy of

[112]

history becomes feasible, as does the construing of time as an irreversible historical sequence.

At the fountainhead of the Christian philosophy of history stands St Augustine. Promulgating a new conception of time, Augustine rejected the cyclicism of the ancients. The Hellenic perception of time does not attribute absolute meaning to 'before' and 'after': all will be reiterated in the 'great year' of the Pythagoreans. Plato taught his disciples in the Academy in Athens in a certain year, and an incalculable number of years previously the same Plato taught in the same Academy in the same Athens. The cyclic view excludes the notion of directed time and knows nothing of a final end to history. It was Old Testament eschatology that laid the groundwork for the Christian understanding of time, which is based on the idea of the uniqueness and the irreversibility of events. The teaching that time is circular is 'false' and alien to Christian belief, since it denies the uniqueness of the revelation of the Son of God, and makes the final salvation of man impossible. Here, Augustine is referring mainly to the teaching of the early Christian thinker Origen, who tried to combine the Christian world-view with the ancient belief in repeated reiteration of what has already been (the so-called '*apokatastasis*'). To this hypothesis 'of the impious', Augustine opposes the 'true and straight way' of God. With God's help, 'sound reason has broken out of these self-repeating circles'.[34]

'What is time?' This is the question over which he racks his brains. We think we know what is meant when we speak of it, or hear others speak of it. 'If nobody asks me, I know: but if I were desirous to explain it to one that should ask me, plainly I know not.'[35] The secret of time is ineffable; we can but pray to God to give us understanding of these matters, which are on the one hand the most ordinary, but which are, on the other hand, not only incomprehensible but *essentially* inaccessible to us. 'And we talk of "time and time" [*tempus et tempus*], "times and times" [*tempora et tempora*] . . . most manifest and ordinary they are, and yet the self-same things are too deeply hidden: yea, the finding out of them is new to meditation.'[36] Time has extent but it cannot be measured by the movements of the heavenly bodies: it is vain to attempt to do so, for did not God at Joshua's request stop the sun, so that the battle could be finished on the same day: time was extended. So time is not the movement of bodies though bodies do move in time.

The ability to measure the duration of time-flow is given to the human spirit, and it is in the soul alone that the forms of perception of time past, present and future inhere: these forms do not subsist in objective reality. ' 'Tis in thee, O my soul, that I measure my times . . . the impression which things passing by cause in thee and remains even when the things are gone, that is it, which being still present, I do measure.'[37] We perceive the past through memory; the present through sight, and the future through expectation.[38]

Augustine does not share Aristotle's view of the objectivity of time as a measure of movement. Human time differs radically from the succession of moments which constitutes physical time. Anthropological time, according to Augustine, is an inner reality, and the spirit alone perceives it. Comprehending the future by means of premonition, and the past by memory, and by including both in man's present life, the soul 'enlarges itself', 'plenishes itself'. But this is not a quantitative enlargement; *distentio* is a vital activity of the human spirit.

The world of ephemeral objects is extended in time. God is far above all times, and exists outside time in eternity, in comparison with which even protracted time is insignificant.[39] It is difficult to explain the relationship between time and eternity, since man tends to think about eternity in temporal categories, whereas in eternity there is no temporal succession. Eternity precedes time as its cause. Time and space are properties of the created world. This point of view was adopted by all the thinkers of the Middle Ages. Following John Scotus Eriugena, Honorius Augustodunensis divides nature into four aspects: the first is 'Nature which creates and is not created' ('Natura quae creat et non creatur'), which is God; the second is 'Nature which creates and is created' ('Natura quae et creatur et creat'), consisting in the Ideas, the primordial causes (*praedestinationes*); the third, 'Nature which is created and does not create' ('Natura quae creatur et non creat'), consists of temporally delimited objects, cognised in space and time ('generatio temporalium, quae locis et temporibus cognoscitur'); the fourth aspect is 'Nature which neither creates nor is created' ('Natura quae nec creat nec creatur') which is the term and end of all things – God, to whom all things return and in whom all is completed.[40] Thus, time and space characterise the earthly world and are themselves created by God; they have transient nature, for, as Augustine says, the Holy Trinity, itself not characterised by space or time, moves its creations in space and time. We have to distinguish (in the Neo-Platonic sense) between (a) intelligible Time and Space, pre-existent (immanent) in the Word of God until it realises them in the created world, and (b) the transient time and space of the world.

Augustine's views on time differ not only from those of Aristotle, but also from Plato's conception of time. According to Plato, time is never-ending and similar therefore in this respect to eternity; hence, time itself leads man to eternity. But Augustine, by converting the Platonic ideas into the thoughts of God, clearly distinguishes the time of events as experienced on earth, from divine eternity. Augustine's view is rather closer to Neo-Platonism. Plotinus taught that man must raise himself from time to eternity. But time was construed by Plotinus as substantial and metaphysical, while Augustine makes the concept of time an inner psychological state of man.[41]

Putting, as it did, the life of the soul and its salvation in the foreground, nothing could have corresponded better to the general requirements of Christianity than the Augustinian philosophy of time. Earthly time as perceived and experienced by the human spirit appears in Augustine's teaching as a necessary parameter of the soul. Emphasising the swiftness and irreversibility of secular time, against a background of suprasensible eternity Augustine sets the philosophical scene for his reading of human history. In opposition to the supporters of the idea of progress in earthly history (Tertullian, Origen, Eusebius), who held that the creation and spread of the Pax Romana prepared the ground for the victory of Christ, Augustine formulates the doctrine of the unbridgeable gap between the City of God and the City of Earth. The City of God is the invisible spiritual community

[115]

of all Christians, the visible embodiment of which is the church; the City of God is eternal. The City of Earth is the state; it is transient and doomed to destruction. Both cities go their own way, and if progress in the Civitas Dei consists in the gradual discovery of divine truth, in human affairs there is no progress at all. In the present, as in the past and as it will be in the future, men experience calamities and disasters. This thesis was further developed by Augustine's pupil Orosius, who collected in his *History* numerous examples of the wars, epidemics, famines, earthquakes, murders, crimes which fill the pages of history. In Augustine's doctrine, the pessimism aroused by contemplation of the ephemeral and corruptible life on earth is blended with optimism, justification for which is seen in our expectation of heavenly felicity. This ineradicable dualism arises from the very nature of the forces which determine the course of history: 'But in this rushing stream of human life two currents . . . flow together: the evil, derived from Adam, and the good bestowed by the Creator.'[42] It is this ambivalence of time – as it passes, mankind's sins multiply but our knowledge of God is enhanced – that gives history its tragic character. It is not given to men to know when history will come to an end, but 'if the judge delays our salvation, it is out of love, not out of indifference, out of care for us, and not out of incompetence; he could, if he so wished, appear at the present moment, but he waits until our number is fulfilled to the last man.'[43]

In contradistinction to the early Christian apologists, who interpreted the Gospel, the Apocalypse and the apostolic writings as pointing to the imminent Second Coming of the Saviour and, consequently, the consummation of history and the time process, Augustine reminds us that it is impossible for man to lay down time limits for the Divine Reason, and emphasises that it is up to every Christian to conduct himself in such a way that he is ready at any moment to appear before the Last Judgment. It is on the great drama of salvation that the minds of the faithful must concentrate.

Augustine it was, again, who laid down the foundations of the teleological philosophy of history. Every act of divine intervention in the lives of men constitutes a fact of history;

and historical facts have a religious value. The meaning of history lies in the discovery of God. Thus, having taken over from Judaism the conception of a linear time which continues without interruption, Christianity gave it its own structure by relating it to the central events in history. History is divided into two ages: up to the Incarnation and the Passion of Christ, and thereafter.

By subordinating earthly history to the history of salvation, Augustine saw unity in the movement of the human race in time. History took on a universal dimension; it was informed by one single meaning and guided by one transcendental design. The traditional form of historiography in the Middle Ages was the universal chronicle, beginning with a retelling of the Book of Genesis. This traditional form gave the chronicler the chance of tacking the history of his own time on to a world-historical whole.[44] But historians did not always restrict their account to the contemporary events known to them; this would be to leave history unfinished, with its meaning not entirely revealed. Otto of Freising, having brought his account down to the middle of the twelfth century, adds a description of the Last Judgment. Real history unfolded itself 'in the shadow of the future', to quote Augustine.[45]

Augustine's ideas governed historiography for much of the Middle Ages. It was not so much a question of finding a causal explanation for events as of fitting them into the universal historical scheme of man's transit through the ages, from Adam to the coming of Antichrist. The medieval historians saw the succession of events and things *sub specie aeternitatis*. History – the eternal struggle between good and evil – goes on, on the earth and in the heavens, in time and outside of it.[46]

Over the centuries, history remained very largely church history, and it was usually clerics who wrote it. There was, however, a deeper reason for this predominant interest in the history of the church. The church was the earthly embodiment of the City of God; and it was thanks to the church that man's salvation was assured. Thus, the history of the church was regarded as the core of the whole historical process, and it was through its prism that history in general was viewed.

So it is with the *Ecclesiastical History of the English People* by one of the greatest historians of the early Middle Ages – the Venerable Bede. He recognises two epochs: the epoch of those events which he relates in the history of England and of the English church, and the epoch of the Bible, these epochs being hardly divisible. The historian perceives his own epoch in biblical categories, and looks upon the world around him as though it were the world of the Bible. Bede's world is 'open to the past', his sense of time is anachronistic: history is apprehended by this Anglo-Saxon monk as some-thing outside time, as a process in which the same patterns are repeated, and in which there is no true development. Bede does not compare the biblical epoch with his own; for such a comparison to be made there would have to be some clear distinction between the two as a basis. For Bede, biblical events which happened at some time or other in the past, continue into his time.[47] Bede is a typical example of that sort of thinking which was prevalent among theologians and historians in the early Middle Ages. Earlier Gregory of Tours had also interpreted the history of the Franks in the 'biblical perspective'.[48]

Comparison of medieval Christian historiography with that of the ancients will soon reveal the former as a retrograde step in the development of historical awareness. As Alois Dempf puts it, in the Middle Ages philosophy and the symbolic theology of history left no time for the study of history proper, and historiography was nothing more than the application of the scholastic method to history.[49] But comparison with classical historiography does little to help us to understand the specific features of the medieval attitude to history. The historians of the Middle Ages knew the ancient authors and evaluated them in their own way, but this did not deter them from working out their own attitude to history in keeping with their world-view and sense of time.

The temporal aspect of this way of thinking is marked by the use of such categories as 'eternity' (*aeternitas*), 'age' (*aevum*) and the 'time' of human life (*tempus*). These categories are distinguished not merely by difference in their duration, but by their totally disparate inner value. Eternity is an attribute of God; it is outside time. In comparison with eternity the 'time' of human existence is insignificant, and acquires some meaning only in so far as it can be seen as a preparatory step towards transition into eternal life. As for *aevum*, this is an intermediary concept between eternity and time; it is 'created eternity'. Eternity has neither beginning nor end, whereas *aevum* has a beginning but no end. Time has both a beginning and an end.[50] According to Thomas Aquinas *aevum*, like *aeternitas*, is given 'all at once' (*totum simul*) but it also has sequence.

Honorius Augustodunensis gives a somewhat different interpretation of the temporal concepts. *Aevum*, according to him, is eternity, existing 'before the world, with the world and after the world' ('Aevum est ante mundum, cum mundo, post mundum'); it belongs to the one God, who was not, neither will be, but who always is ('non fuit, nec erit, sed semper est'). The world of ideas or of the archetypes of the world, and also of the angels, is characterised by 'eternal times' (*tempora aeterna*) – a concept with a subordinate meaning to that of 'eternity'. 'Earthly time is the shadow of eternity' ('Tempus autem mundi est umbra aevi'). Time began with the world and will end with it. Time is measurable, and, probably therefore, Honorius derives the word *tempus* from *temperamentum* ('proportionality', 'correlation'). 'Time,' he writes, 'is nothing more than the sequence of things [events]' (*vicissitudo rerum*).[51]

A typical and instructive medieval way of representing the concept of time is the image of a rope stretching from east to west and showing signs of wear from its daily winding and unwinding, (Honorius Augustodunensis).[52] That time was apprehended as substantial is also shown by its equation with the world, with humankind (*mundus – saeculum*). Time like the world is corruptible (Ordericus Vitalis).[53] Its flow does not mean that mankind is progressing; if those living at a later date know more and see farther than their predecessors, this is because they are like dwarfs standing on the shoulders of giants – it does not mean thay have better eyesight (Bernard of Chartres, John of Salisbury, Peter of Blois).[54]

In the thirteenth century, philosophical and theological

interest in the study of the problem of time was stimulated anew by the ideas of Aristotle as, thanks to the Arabs, they became known in the West. In part, Thomas Aquinas shares Aristotle's view that time is a measure of movement.[55] But if his contemporary, St Bonaventura, accepted the Aristotelian cosmology and tried to construct a 'Christian Aristotelianism',[56] St Thomas combined it rather with Neo-Platonism. According to Aristotle, only gods and eternal beings are outside time, but St Thomas asserted that in a certain sense all substance – including created substance – exists outside time. Considered with regard to its substance, a being cannot be measured by time, since substance has no sequential succession, and corresponds not to time but to the present moment (*nunc temporis*); when it is observed in motion, however, a being changes on the time scale. A being, subject to change, moves further away from eternity, and this mutability affords evidence that creation is incomplete.[57] In contrast to Augustine and his pessimistic contemplation of the *malignum saeculum*, Thomas Aquinas claimed that the eternal salvation of mankind is being realised in the historical process.[58]

Common both to mythological time and to the time-form known to the medieval historians is the assertion that earthly time is in a certain sense illusory, since only time as construed in Christian belief has total reality. The time scale inherent in the Christian myth is not limited to one linear sequence. In St John's Gospel (8:58) Jesus says: 'Verily, verily, I say unto you: before Abraham was, I am.' The present as apprehended by the people of the Christian Middle Ages was not so much pregnant with the future as burdened with the past. In comparison with 'original time' – the time of the Bible, immutable, eternally enduring Time – earthly time, current time, was perishable. This is the 'time of phenomena', not 'essential time', and therefore it is not independent. Time is merely an external variation on the ground-theme of its immovable world. 'Times change, words change, but the faith is unchanging', for 'that which was true once, will always be true.' Therefore it was believed that 'Christ will be born, is being born and has been born' (Peter Lombard).[59] The truth is not subject to time, is not amplified in its course.

But this meant that man's historicity did not partake of truth, and earthly history was no more than a shadow, devoid of independent value and authenticity. Its interpretation reduced to the deduction of the meaning of separate events from the ideal conception of history.[60]

The periods used for measuring the swift-flowing time of earthly existence acquire quite another duration and density when they are used for measuring events in the Bible. The six days of creation represent a whole epoch, incommensurate with earthly 'days'. It is impossible even to imagine, wrote Augustine of the six days of creation, what these days were like; this is one of the great secrets of God.[61] In his *Elucidarium* Honorius Augustodunensis answers the question – how long did Adam and Eve stay in the Garden of Eden? Seven hours is the answer. 'Why not longer? Because immediately after the woman was created she betrayed her creator. At the third hour after his creation man named the animals, at the sixth hour the woman, only just created, ate of the forbidden fruit and gave of it to the man, who ate of it out of love for her, and then, at the ninth hour, God expelled them from the Garden.'[62] So man's innocence lasted a few hours of one day! But these were hours spent in paradise, and to them the Christian mind ascribed a content that would fill earthly years.

The concept of historical time is realised in the anthropomorphic categories typical of the medieval mind. Particularly popular in medieval historiography and philosophy was the concept of universal-historical epochs conceived in terms of human age. In II Peter 3:8, it is said that 'one day is with the Lord as a thousand years, and a thousand years as one day'. Taking this text and the early Christian commentaries upon it as his basis, Augustine equated each day of creation to a thousand years of time, and tried to compute the duration of the history of mankind, seeing in the days of creation symbolical prototypes of the ages through which history is to proceed. According to Augustine there are six historical epochs: from the creation of Adam to the Flood, from the Flood to Abraham, from Abraham to David, from David to the Babylonian captivity, from the captivity to the birth of Christ, and, finally, from the birth of Christ to the end of the world. These six universal-historical ages correspond to the six ages of man: infancy, childhood, adolescence, youth, maturity, old age. In the same way, Isidore of Seville interprets the concept of *aetas* in two ways: as the age of a human being, and as an age of the world.[63]

Taking the longevity of the biblical patriarchs as his starting-point, Augustine reckoned that in the course of each of the first two 'ages' – *infantia* and *pueritia* – there were ten generations, each having a life-span of a hundred years. The following three ages (*adolescentia, iuventus, aetas senior*) each had forty generations. The sixth and last historical period (*senectus*), which began with Christ, is now proceeding and may not be measured in terms of generations, since, as it is said in the Acts of the Apostles (1:7), 'It is not for you to know the times or the seasons which the Father hath put in his own power.' So Augustine dismisses any possibility of computing how much time we have left.[64]

Nevertheless, several medieval writers did try to work out the duration of this sixth and last period. Bede announced that the end of the world would come in the year 1000; and this date figured very largely in the forecasts of would-be prophets in the tenth century. The legends concerning the spread of mass psychoses in Europe as the year 1000 approached, took shape at the end of the fifteenth century when people were really afraid that the end of the world was imminent.[65] At a later time, there were not-infrequent attempts to compute the date of the coming of Antichrist and the end of the sixth period of mankind's life on earth.

Another parallel was drawn between the ages of man and the hours of the day: thus in the morning Abel toiled, at the third hour came Noah, the ninth hour was that of Moses the law-giver, the eleventh hour brought the birth of Christ.

Here, in the doctrine of the six ages of mankind, the usual medieval liking for the symbolical interpretation of anything and everything carries a tinge of historical pessimism; for are we not in the last, the sixth age of world history, the age of caducity? As early as St Paul's First Epistle to the Corinthians (10:11) there is reference to 'the end of the ages' having come upon mankind. A little more than a thousand years later, Dante – also living in expectation of the end of the world – hears Beatrice tell him that in the Celestial Rose the 'thrones are nigh complete' and that only a few places are vacant, awaiting the remainder of God's elect.[66] A pessimistic attitude to the times was widespread in the Middle Ages: the good and happy times of man's existence lay far behind him and the world was approaching its end in a state of moral decay. Formerly, people had been strapping and healthy, now they were undersized and puny; in olden times women had been faithful to their husbands, and vassals to their lords; now things were very different. From the doctrine of the analogue between microcosm and macrocosm was inferred a parallel between the aging of the world and the aging of man. An Anglo-Saxon poet calls all living men old because the world has reached its sixth and final age.[67]

'*Mundus senescit*' – 'the world is growing old'. What has become of the great figures of the distant past – the biblical personages and the heroes of antiquity? In one of the songs in the *Carmina Burana* cycle, among the complaints, part serious and part ironic, about the general decline and corruption of the world, there is mention of the fathers of the church – some of them in the almshouse, some of them on trial, and some of them in the fish market. 'Mary is no longer attracted by the religious life, nor Martha by an active life, Leah is barren and Rachel has runny eyes, Cato's taken to the bottle, and Lucretia's a tart'.[68] A ribald joke in *Carmina Burana*, as in many other medieval works, has a double meaning as well as ideological overtones, and therefore cannot be taken simply as a joke. Historians bewail the corruption of the world in the same way. 'How has everything changed!' wrote Ordericus Vitalis, the Norman historian of the twelfth century; 'love has grown cold, evil waxes strong. The wonders which were formerly a token of holiness have ceased to be, and all that the historian can do is record crimes and more crimes. . . . The hour of Antichrist is at hand.'[69]

It is a curious paradox: a society obsessed with its vision of the aging, putrefying world, and revering biblical patriarchs and grey-beard prophets, was in fact a society run largely by young people. People died young in the Middle Ages. We have no sort of general representative data on this question, but it is well known that not only many rulers ascending the throne by birth-right, but also popes and other church dignitaries, rose to their high office while still young men, and died before reaching old age. Abelard and St Thomas Aquinas were professors before they were thirty. Two men who in Catholic eyes personify medieval Christianity – St Thomas Aquinas and St Francis of Assisi – were respectively forty-nine and forty-four when they died. In general, people in their forties were regarded as elderly. The ideal age was held to be thirty-five – the age at which Christ 'wished to consummate his earthly life'. Following ancient and medieval authorities, Dante asserted that youth lasts till twenty-five years of age, and maturity ends at forty-five, after which old age begins.[70]

It was widely believed in the Middle Ages that all change inevitably involved deterioration. 'Whatever changes, loses its value,' we read in a poem of the twelfth century. The terms *modernus, novus* and words derived from these were derogatory rather than temporal in meaning. Their positive meaning was retained during the first centuries of Christianity, when 'new' meant Christian, and 'old' pagan. But at a later period, when genuine antiquity had been virtually completely forgotten, the term *antiquus* acquired a positive sense and came to be synonymous with 'authoritative'. Novelties, said John of Salisbury, often turn out to be things well known to the ancients. Truth does not change with time. Another writer admitted that everyone was afraid of novelty and innovation.[71] 'All despise their own time,' wrote the English historian Walter Map, 'and each age prefers its predecessor.'[72] And yet, counter to tradition, he himself saw antiquity as 'the age of copper', and his own age as 'the age of gold'! To the medieval ear, the term *modernitas* tended to have an abusive, derogatory meaning; anything new, unhallowed by time and tradition, was viewed with suspicion. Accusations of 'unheard-of innovations', of 'new fashions', were brought primarily against heretics (*novi doctores*) and were a lethal means of casting social aspersion. Value belonged exclusively to what was old. In point of fact, a few thinkers recognised that what was old and revered had once been new, and that therefore, as Anselm of Havelberg wrote, we have to distinguish between good and bad in both old and new; he adds, however, that in the realm of the spirit no change takes place ('unus et idem spiritus').[73]

The words of William of Conches throw the contrast between medieval and modern values into sharp relief: 'We recount and expound the ancients, we do not invent new things' ('Sumus relatores et expositores veterum, non inventores novorum'), since 'the ancients were much superior to our contemporaries' ('Antiqui multo meliores fuerunt modernis').[74] *Antiquitas* is synonymous with such concepts as *auctoritas* (authority), *gravitas* (dignity), *majestas* (greatness). In the medieval world, originality of thought counted for nothing, and plagiarism was not considered a sin.[75]

It was not only the past, however, that dominated medieval thought. History, as seen through the prism of Christianity, has direction; it develops and resolves itself according to a predestined plan and moves towards a consummation in which earthly life fuses with the life beyond. This conception of the apotheosis of history in God could not but act as a counter-balance to historical pessimism. Fear of the Last Judgment mingled and blended with hopes of salvation and attaining the kingdom of heaven.

The belief that the world was in the final stage of history was not without influence on political thought as well. In the struggle between empire and papacy this line of thought was used by protagonists of the imperial power to endorse and justify their universal claims. The argument that after the 'Roman Empire' of Frederick Barbarossa and Frederick II there could be no other, and that the kingdom of Antichrist would ensue, had immediate political cogency.[76]

The concept of the aging world and the imminent final catastrophe was an integral part of medieval thinking. Precisely because of these ideas, however, a knowledge of history was held to be necessary. History played an important educational part, providing men with examples of more than transient significance:

> For if books conceal the works of past ages,
> Then, I ask, whom shall posterity follow?
> People, like cattle, would be deprived of reason,
> If they were not informed of the times of the six ages

wrote Bishop Benzo of Alba in the eleventh century.[77]

It would not be true to say that there was no feeling for history in the Middle Ages. Such rudimentary knowledge as was available concerning the history of peoples and states was in the hands of the small number of scholars. And yet Christianity implied a specific historicism; and the main literary output throughout the period consists of books on ancient and modern history and on the Bible. The medieval mind was dominated by its awareness of those historical events round which all previous history centred: the birth of Christ and his death on the cross. Medieval society was placed thereby in a definite historical setting linking the past with the future. Since both the beginning and the end of history were known, its content was intelligible to man. The secret meaning of the whole historical process was, of course, known only to the Creator; but every event in it had to have cogent meaning, since every event was subject to the general law governing the whole.

The Christian philosophy of history endorsed a belief in progress, in contradistinction to the radical pessimism with which antiquity had viewed history. But 'progress' in this medieval context – in so far as it can be applied at all to the medieval view of history – had its special peculiarities. In the first place, it referred only to the spiritual life: in the course of history men draw near to a knowledge of God, as his truth penetrates them. The City of God moves towards its full realisation. As for earthly history, medieval historians had neither the words nor the concepts to express the continuity of the historical process (excluding the metaphysical concept of *translatio*, on which more below); they liked to write chronicles, annals, 'lives', 'acts', 'antiquities' and finally 'stories', but not history as the record of the continuous and coherent development of mankind or of a single nation. Secondly, the 'progress' recognised by teleological philosophy is not unlimited. History proceeds towards a predestined goal, and is therefore a process within definite limits.[78] It is the realisation of the divine plan.

The theological view of history of Joachim of Floris is more consistent and affords a new perspective on eschatological history. In his *Eternal Gospel* Joachim describes three great historical epochs, each of which is dominated in turn by one member of the Holy Trinity: at the close of the Old

Testament epoch of God the Father there ensued the epoch of the divine Son; and this in its turn is replaced by the epoch of the Holy Ghost. Each period embodies a historical revelation of one aspect of the Godhead, thus making possible the progressive perfection of mankind which will attain in the third epoch to absolute spiritual freedom. This third and last period is to begin in 1260; religion will be revived and people born anew, and spiritual freedom will enable them to understand the true meaning of the Gospel. Thus, according to Joachim, time in its courses brings ever-new revelations and each stage of human development is furnished with its own imperatives and its own truth as revealed in time.

As Augustine saw it, the truth of history was revealed once and for all in a single unique event – the incarnation of the Word; for Joachim, truth is revealed in a cumulative succession of states, in each of which its successors are latently present. 'The time that passed before the Law, the time that passed under the sign of the Law, the time that passed under the sign of Grace – these times were necessary; and we must recognise another period of time as just as necessary,'[79] wrote Joachim, referring to the ideal era of justice. In the Old Testament, the New Testament is already symbolically present; and in the same way, the New Testament itself is the prototype of the full revelation of the truth. If the traditional pessimistic view of the world as condemned to decay and destruction runs from Augustine through the Middle Ages ('there is nothing stable on earth'), for Joachim, on the other hand, all is transformed and reborn, man and society, the church and its teaching. Yet progress as construed by Joachim of Floris is not an inner florescence of truth, since the world-stages he postulates are already contained in the prefigured divine plan. The views of Joachim were condemned by the church. Bonaventura objected: 'After the New Testament there can be nothing else.'[80] St Thomas Aquinas also defended the view that history can be divided into two epochs only – those of the Old and the New Testaments – and there is no possibility of a third epoch in the future. In this context, he takes up the question of the relationship between tradition and progress; the latter is limited by the former, since with the passage of time all that is possible is a clearer and more detailed understanding of the true teaching as originally given, whose inmost secrets the apostles understood more deeply and more fully than subsequent generations of men.[81] But the very fact that such a theory as Joachim's could be elaborated at all goes to show that, in the Middle Ages, historical time was not necessarily viewed in a purely pessimistic light. Rather we have here an ambivalent hope for salvation mixed up with fear of the end of the world, for not only heaven awaits man but hellfire as well.

The key factor which gives shape to concepts and organises perception into a coherent world picture is language. Language is not just a system of signs; it incorporates a determinate system of values and conceptions. Latin, as the language of culture in Western and Central Europe in the Middle Ages, was an important unifying factor for cultural development in the Babel of fluctuating and unstable languages and dialects spoken by the numerous tribes and nationalities.[82] To educated people – mainly the clergy – Latin seemed for a long time the only civilised language. As they saw it, even the birds sang 'in their Latin'. But Latin had taken shape in a completely different epoch; words used in antiquity and in the Middle Ages had changed in meaning, while the language itself had remained outwardly the same. There is no doubt that Latin was a contributory factor in blinding medieval people to the distance that separated their own time from that of the ancient authors whom they prized so highly; Latin concealed from them the qualitative turning-point in the development of the world which is marked by the period of transition from Roman times to the Middle Ages.

The gulf between past and present was also obscured by the practice, widely prevalent in literature, of borrowing from classical authors. The biographer of Charlemagne, Einhard, could borrow widely from Suetonius on the lives of the Caesars, on the ground that this was the best way of describing the Frankish empire, which for him and his contemporaries did not just imitate the Roman empire but was in fact identical with it.

We have to agree, however, with the scholars in the field of medieval historiography who point out that quotations and borrowings, set phrases and clichés, were a natural way of expressing oneself in an age when authority was everything and originality nothing. A ready mastery of commonplaces – *topoi* – in literature was seen as the author's special way of putting his own thoughts – with the help of references to authorities, a practice which did not exactly encourage individuality.[83] As a rule, the historian saw himself as continuing the work of his predecessors; since, strictly speaking, there is only one universal history which cannot be rewritten anew: it can only be continued.[84]

In the Middle Ages, the world was not perceived as being in flux; it was stable and immovable on its foundations. Change affected only the surface of the system established by God. The concept of historical time imported by Christianity could not overcome this basic conviction. As a result, even the historical consciousness – if one can speak of such a thing in connection with the Middle Ages – remained essentially anti-historical. Anachronism is an inseparable feature of medieval historiography. The past is described in the same categories as the present. Ancient heroes think along the same lines as the chronicler's contemporaries. There is no trace of a sense for local or historical colour, either in the medieval poets or in the arts. Biblical and classical personages appear in contemporary dress and strike attitudes customary for Europeans. The artist, the sculptor, the author of the romance, or the historian, is certainly not intrigued by the thought that in other places and at other times customs, morals, nature, dress, buildings, ways of life, were quite different from what he sees around him. The anonymous moralist who wrote a poem on *La Morale de l'Histoire* does not hesitate to impute the specifically knightly virtue of *courtoisie* to the ancient Romans.[85]

Differences between epochs were not worthy of notice, with the exception of the one great and crucial difference – that between history before the coming of Christ and history thereafter. But the epochs of the Old and the New Testaments were held to be associated in something more than simple temporal sequence: history before the Incarnation of Christ and history thereafter are symmetrical. To each event and each person in the Old Testament there is an analogue in the New; and between them there exists an inner sacra-

[129]

mental and symbolical union imbued with the most profound significance. To medieval man it was perfectly natural and not at all incongruous to see Old Testament kings and patriarchs on cathedral portals, side by side with the wise men of antiquity and characters from the Gospels; and this perhaps more than anything else underlines the anachronistic view of history which is typical of the Middle Ages. These representations are distributed according to a definite scheme; they are correlated in symbolic fashion, forming ordered harmonious series. Contemplating them, medieval man was aware of history in its fullness, its coherence and its unity, its immutability and the continuation of time past in time present.

The principle of analogous correlation between the Old and New Testaments was used as a basis which medieval historians used in attempts to discover a symbolical sense in earthly history. To the Old Testament history of the temple of Jerusalem there corresponded as analogue the history of the church – the mystic 'body of Christ'. The destruction of the temple was paralleled by the persecution of the Christian martyrs. Similar parallels were found in contemporary history: the struggle between Emperor Henry IV and Pope Gregory VII was correlated with the struggle between Judas Maccabaeus and King Antiochus IV. By means of such comparisons the symbolical historians organised the matter of history into a static system of analogues.[86]

Man's nature itself is viewed anachronistically. All people in all generations bear responsibility for the original sin committed by Adam and Eve, just as all Jews are guilty of the crucifixion of Christ; for these events – the Fall and the Passion – are not simply events in the past, but persist eternally and are eternally present. The Crusaders at the end of the eleventh century were convinced that they were punishing, not the descendants of Christ's executioners, but the executioners themselves. The centuries that had elapsed in between meant nothing to them.

Nor was there any genuine development in secular history either. The theory of four earthly kingdoms elaborated by St Jerome (on the basis of the prophecies in the Book of Daniel) – the Assyro-Babylonian, the Medo-Persian, the Graeco-Macedonian and the Roman – meant no more than the transit and succession of empire from one dynasty to another. The idea of monarchy itself remained unchanged. The transmission of power (*translatio imperii*) continues into the Middle Ages. According to Otto of Freising, power passed from the Romans to the Greeks (Byzantines), from the Greeks to the Franks, from the Franks to the Lombards, and from the Lombards to the Germans.[87] In his list of the Roman emperors, Otto includes as a matter of course the German rulers down to his contemporaries. Charlemagne is sixty-ninth in the list of emperors, Otto the Great is seventy-seventh, and Otto III is eighty-sixth. French historians and poets saw the *translatio imperii* as leading to the ascendancy and aggrandisement of the Franks, while their English counterparts transferred it to the Britons.

The concept of *translatio imperii* was combined with that of *translatio studii* – the transmission of knowledge, the migration of culture. In both cases, the political and the spiritual, the emphasis was on the universal-historical significance of tradition, of continuity. In the second half of the twelfth century, the poet Chrétien de Troyes wrote that chivalry and priesthood first arose in Greece; chivalry and learning then migrated to Rome, and now they flourish in France, whence, God willing, they will never depart.[88] Together with these nationalist interpretations there was also a general Western European attitude: 'All power and human wisdom arose in the East and have come to fruition in the West' (Otto of Freising). But this movement in time is characteristic only of ephemeral secular formations. The transient nature, instability and mutability (*mutabilitas*) of earthly kingdoms is in sharp contrast with the eternity and stability (*stabilitas*) of the City of God.[89] In the light of this contrast between earthly history and heavenly permanence, time appears as an imperfect element, as something that really should not exist at all.

Like Jerome's conception of the four kingdoms, Augustine's doctrine of the six ages of mankind depends on the premise that divine providence has laid down from the beginning the design and the sequential continuity of world history. In world history there is no spontaneous development; there is only the working out of an original prefigured plan, the visible embodiment of the divine symbols. The ruling class of feudal society, the clergy and the knights, saw in themselves the meaning and the fulfilment of history. The concept of history as open to the future, rich in new possibilities, was totally alien to the minds of medieval people.

The fourth monarchy does not allow for the appearance of a fifth, and the sixth age of mankind excludes the possibility of a seventh. Historians who attached great significance to the facts of political history divided it up into successive monarchies: for example, the histories by Hermann of Reichenau, Sigebert of Gembloux and Otto of Freising. Those historians for whom events on the earthly plane were functions of the transcendental order rather than concrete realities (e.g. Isidore of Seville, the Venerable Bede, Regino von Prüm, etc.) preferred the theory of the six ages of mankind.

Efforts to overcome the transience of time and to see it in the light of eternity are especially associated with the mystics. In the visions of Hildegard of Bingen, history, in which the events of the Old and New Testaments are correlated, appears in the form of a city with four walls which face different parts of the world. In the south stretches a wall which symbolises the time of Adam; the eastern wall embodies the time from Adam to Noah, the north represents the history of the people of Abraham and Moses, while the west represents time since the birth of Christ.[90] In the revelations of Hildegard, the epochs of the past take on, as do the present and the future, that visual and spatial dimension which was characteristic of the perception of temporal categories in the Middle Ages.

The inability of medieval man to apprehend the world and society as being in a process of development, is the obverse side of his attitude to himself and to his inner world. As member of a group, as bearer of an allotted function or service, the individual strove to correspond as closely as possible to the type in which he was cast, and to do his duty before God. The course of his life was laid down for him, programmed, as it were, by his earthly calling. Hence, inner development of the individual was excluded. In the biographical genre which is the most widespread and most characteristic of the Middle Ages – the Lives of the Saints – there is scarcely ever any mention of *how* they became saints. They are either suddenly reborn, instantly and without any preparatory transition from one state (sinfulness) to another (saintliness), or saintliness is conferred upon them at birth, and has only to be gradually revealed. Failing to comprehend his own inner being in terms of development, man naturally failed to see or relate with the world in terms of process.[91] Individual man and the universe are alike static, such changes as occur being superficial and subordinate to divine providence. In such a system, the individual is as little of a psychological problem as society is a historical one.

No less significant is the long absence of the portrait in medieval painting. Artists must have noticed individual traits in human faces and were certainly able to reproduce them.[92] It was not 'inability' or 'lack of observation' that prevented artists from achieving natural likeness in portraiture, but the effort to bring out the general and suprasensual at the expense of the unique and real features of personality. The absence of portraiture is directly linked with the desire to embody eternal truths and permanent values, and throws additional light on the perception of time in the Middle Ages. Deconcretisation is the other side of atemporality. Man did not feel himself to be existent in time; 'to be' for him meant 'to abide', not 'to be in the process of becoming'.[93] A portrait, however, fixes one of the many states of a man in a spatial-temporal continuum. Again, it was up to the artist to show not only earthly life but also the reality of another, higher plane, bearing in mind that the former was qualitatively derived from the latter. Thus, the aesthetic ideals of the Middle Ages, formed under the direct influence of the ruling ideology, did not favour the development of interest in the artistic portrayal of the human personality – whose existence was in any case still hardly, if at all, grasped. Medieval man 'was afraid of being himself, he was afraid of originality'.[94]

Medieval man's ways of experiencing the passage of time in his own life and in history might be clarified by an examination of 'artistic time'. But in research on the literatures of the Middle Ages very little attention indeed has been paid to the question of time. Some scholars state that in the Middle Ages the subjective aspect of time had simply not been recognised. Others hold that it is possible to speak of subjective, psychological time, time as experienced, in the courtly romance and in lyric poetry.[95] As far as the epic is concerned, the temporal categories are of little significance. In the epic, no contradiction is felt in the discrepancies between the way time passes in ordinary life and the way it passes in narrative. No one is in the least put off by the discovery that the hero, who has spent three years in the antipodes and twelve years on the way back, without stopping anywhere, has in fact been wandering for *thirty* years; and no one is surprised to find that a saint can make the day longer. For quite a long time, past historical events continued to be staged in extra-temporal mythological settings, but the epic had already ceased to 'work over', to embellish, contemporary events. For example, the historical events of the Crusades lost nothing of their spatio-temporal actuality under the pen of the chronicler.

Nevertheless traces of mytho-poetic time are found in the courtly romance as well. Its heroes do not grow old. Lancelot, Perceval and other heroes of this type are ageless beings moving in a biographical vacuum; they remain ever young and manly, ever ready to perform deeds of derring-do. One of them lands in a place where 'all summer and all winter flowers bloom and fruit trees are laden'. The Dark Island in *Erec* is not subject to the seasonal changes of earth; it exists outside of time. The strength of Sir Gawain in the Arthurian cycle varies according to a twenty-four-hour pattern. Time in a courtly romance does not limit the life-span of its personages. The mytho-poetic attitude to time in the romance also allows people belonging to different epochs to appear as contemporaries: for Chrétien de Troyes, King Arthur is a twelfth-century hero.

Two different ways of perceiving time run through the courtly romance and the lyric poetry of the Middle Ages. The first of these is a static time, in which reposes a stylised and enhanced contemporaneity, which knows neither becoming nor change; it is an 'eternal day'. The second is a dynamic conception: time brings change and serves as a transitional stage towards eternity.[96] In this second mood, poetic narration is shot through with a painful awareness of fleeting time which never returns, which passes so swiftly that the mind can scarcely grasp it. In the *Roman de la Rose*, Guillaume de Lorris writes of Time 'which moves by day and by night, without pause or respite, which runs by and leaves us, so imperceptibly that it seems as though it did not move at all; it does not pause for a moment but speeds uninterruptedly onwards, so that it is impossible to grasp what the present moment consists of, even if we ask learned clerics about this; for, before you can think about it, three times as much time has passed; Time, which cannot stop, but always goes on, never returns, like falling water, flowing away to the last drop; Time, before which nothing can stand, neither iron nor the hardest of things, since it eats away and corrodes all things; Time, which changes all things, makes things to grow and nourishes them, wears them out and leads them to destruction; Time, which ages our fathers, and kings and emperors, and which will age us all unless death forestalls our hour. . . .'[97] This gloomy verdict on time is connected in the poem with the author's thoughts on Old Age, whose image he contemplates.

In the heroes of the courtly romances the awareness of swiftly flowing and irreversible time arouses feelings of impatience, a sense of urgency not to 'lose' time, to fill it with deeds befitting the high calling of a knight.

In his studies on the problem of time in the romances of Chrétien de Troyes, Ph. Ménard[98] comes to the conclusion that in them the perception and the experiencing of time are dependent on the characters' way of life. There is no such thing as general time; for each man it passes in specific fashion. For the swineherd nothing changes, he lives in torpor, and time drags oppressively for the unfree artisans; but knights looking for adventure in a spirit of derring-do live, as it were, in an entirely different time. The time of heroic exploit 'breaks into' the course of ordinary time in the courtly romance; the moment of the adventure is not repeatable, it is the time in which the hero has his sole chance to prove himself. Although the past plays a very big part in the minds of the knightly heroes (for example, Perceval finds his own past in the search for the Grail which embodies his future) and the very notion of the knight errant implies an orientation towards the future, the heroes of Chrétien de Troyes stand face to face with the present. This lies at the root of Ménard's disagreement with the traditional view of the medieval 'indifference to time'; flying to the opposite extreme, he asserts that the heroes of the courtly romances had 'dominion over time'. This seems to be going too far; would it not be fairer to say that they perceived time as an inseparable element of their own mode of life? Chrétien's heroes move in time, but the general time of the romance's *universum* is immovable.

A characteristic trait of courtly poetry is absorption in the present. The time structure of the troubadour's song is the lyric moment, in which the hero's condition is crystallised: a condition defined by a permanently unsatisfied love which knows nothing of past or future except in terms of the present. The grammatical tense of the courtly lyric is the present.[99]

Subjective perception of time could hardly be unknown in medieval literature, if only because from Augustine onwards a distinction was recognised between 'conceivable time' and 'experienced time';[100] though of course, the treatment of subjective time in medieval poetics falls far short of the analytical and experimental preoccupation with it in twentieth-century literature, where it has become perhaps the central issue. In relation to the works of Chrétien, Ménard thinks it justified to speak of 'literary time' and 'experienced time'. In his opinion, ways of experiencing time in the courtly romance are determined primarily by the inner condition of the protagonists. In woe and in transports of passion, the heroes of these poems are oblivious of time; the lover is unable to endure time separated from the beloved.[101]

In the same way, when one of the characters in the *Elder Edda*, burning with impatience to take possession of his bride, cries:

> Long is one night, longer are two,
> Endless the thought of three.
> Many a month has moved more swiftly
> Than this half of a bridal eve.[102]

we are forced to conclude that medieval Scandinavians were well aware that the perception and relative value of time can depend on a man's inner state.

The application of the terms *objective* and *subjective* to the world-view of medieval people is in itself questionable. The contrast implied reflects our modern relationship with the world around us, so clearly and consciously divided off from our inner selves. But, as I said above, medieval man saw in himself the 'microcosm' – the duplicate in miniature of the 'macrocosm', the world reiterated in all things. The individual does not stand in opposition to nature, to the world; he is associated with it as analogue. Here, subjective and objective are blended, or, rather, not yet separated. So it is highly questionable to assert that for the medieval author time 'was not a phenomenon of the human consciousness'.[103] Is it not more accurate to say that time was not only a phenomenon of the human consciousness, but also a cosmic, an 'objective' phenomenon?

Some scholars have pointed out a particularity in the way time is perceived in medieval poetry, especially German, which they call '*punktuelle Zeit*' or '*sprunghafte Zeitlichkeit*', i.e. 'selective time' or 'spasmodic time'. In poetic narration, time is not organised as a process, its individual moments are not coordinated and do not form a sequence; life is understood as a congeries of events with no temporal correlation between them. Thus man, as these poets see him, has no personal past, present or future; he is not a historical being at all. Life disintegrates, as the poet sees it, into separate events, which offer us no 'time fix', and life acquires a meaning only in relation to God.[104] Experiencing his time 'filled' with events, medieval man gave little thought to its 'outer' quantitative side, and in this sense temporal determinants were absent from his perception of the world. Indeed, it was not until the thirteenth century that temporal relationships began to play a leading part in his consciousness.[105]

Before this took place, time itself was very largely perceived in spatial terms. Space, not time, was the organising factor in works of art.[106] As we saw above, the various episodes of a narration were not construed by medieval poets as ordered points in a unified temporal sequence; so these moments in time could be represented by them as collocated events, as parts of one and the same picture. Between earlier and later events there was no ordered succession; they existed, as it were, contemporaneously. Such a view, which ignored development and change, tended to distribute time particles on the spatial plane. Hence, time appears to move by leaps and bounds, and the hero of a courtly romance never ages; in fact, he never seems to change at all. If a medieval author had to portray inner change in one of his characters, this was achieved not in temporal terms but in the form of a path leading the hero through some spatial expanse or other. According to E. Kobel (to whom many of these observations are due) this way of perceiving time followed upon identification of its constituent elements as material and objective entities.[107]

If these observations are valid, we may recall that a similar attitude to time – 'spatialisation', spasmodic movement, vagueness of temporal sequence, materialisation of time, absence of the abstract concept 'time' – is characteristic of 'primitive' art. In the latter, of course, all the characteristics we have mentioned are expressed much more vividly; space and time are experienced as an unbroken unity, and appear as attributes of myth and ritual, shot through with magical elements and indivisibly associated with a scale of values.[108] The main difference between the perception of time in the Middle Ages and in a primitive society lies in the opposition between the cyclic concept of the latter and the linear time of the Christian viewpoint.

But perhaps the most powerful expression of the medieval attitude to time is to be found in Dante. The contrast between the swift-flowing time of earthly existence and eternity, and the ascent from the one to the other, determine the space–time continuum of the *Divina Commedia*. The whole history of mankind is here synchronically present. Time stands still: present, past, future – it is all contemporary. As Osip Mandelstam puts it, history as understood by Dante is 'one synchronic act'. 'The enormous explosive power of the Book of Genesis (the idea of spontaneous generation) fell upon the tiny island of the Sorbonne from all sides, and we will not be mistaken if we say that the men of Dante's age lived in an antiquity which was completely awash in modernity. . . . It is already very difficult for us to imagine how . . . the entire Biblical cosmogony with its Christian appendages could have been accepted by the educated people of that time so literally, as if it were a special edition of the daily newspaper.'[109] Perhaps a partial answer to this question is given by another perceptive reader of the *Commedia*, who has remarked that for Dante 'hell is at the same time Florence'; that 'hell is so full of Florentines that sinners from other parts of the fairly wide medieval world could hardly push their way in', and that the terraces of Dante's hell 'are old but peopled with new-comers'.[110] By peopling hell with his contemporaries Dante achieved the maximum convergence of different time-planes, and, in turn, their convergence with eternity.

The ideological design of the *Commedia* is based on the contrast between 'the life of eternity' and 'ephemeral life'.[111] In comparison with God's eternity the span of man's existence is less 'than one eye-wink' in comparison with the movement of the stellar sphere.[112] Supreme bliss is attained only in paradise, 'where centres every *where* and every *when*', where contemporaneity reigns and there is no before or after, where a moment holds more than twenty-five ages, where time yields to eternity.[113]

But if we look more closely at this fusion of biblical and mundane time – alien as it is to everything we understand by 'history' – do we not find precisely therein evidence of medieval man's inalienable involvement in the historical process? In fact, medieval man feels himself on two temporal planes at once: on the plane of local transient life, and on the plane of those universal-historical events which are of decisive importance for the destinies of the world – the Creation, the birth and the Passion of Christ. The transient and insignificant life of Everyman is played out against the backcloth of the universal-historical drama, into which it is spliced and from which it acquires a new, higher and non-transient meaning. This duality in the perception of time is an indissoluble factor in the medieval mind. Medieval man does not live in one single earthly time, he cannot mentally dissociate himself from sacral history; and this awareness affects him

[139]

as a personality, for the salvation of his soul depends on his integration into sacral history. The global historical battle between good and evil is a personal issue for every believer. This participation in world history is at once historical and anti-historical.

This paradoxical combination of a historical with an anti-historical attitude took different forms in Eastern and Western Christianity. This difference made itself particularly felt in attitudes to biblical history: in the representation of scenes of Christ's sufferings, the Byzantines saw no historical sequence, being guided exclusively by the symbolic meaning of the images, never by the historical, while in the West this sequence was invariably observed.[114] The Orthodox liturgy makes much less of motion in time than does the Catholic one, as is already clear from the two types of psalmody.[115]

The specific medieval attitude to time can be discerned in every sphere of medieval life. It is not difficult to trace it in the juridical practice of the epoch. Legislation normally enacted 'for eternity' remained valid in fact for a limited period only, not surpassing the human life-span, and the formula *ad perpetuum* did not guarantee the permanent validity of measures which stood in need of continual reaffirmation. The privileges given by the ruler were of a personal nature and were renewed with each new ascension to the throne. Grants of land and other assets to churches and monasteries required reaffirmation and renewal, in spite of the fact that conveyance of lands and other property to the clergy was by mortmain and therefore inalienable. The French monarchy was hereditary, but the French kings nevertheless made a practice of proclaiming their sons as co-rulers during their own lifetime. Upon the death of a vassal, his heir had to take the oath of allegiance anew to his feudal lord; while the death of the latter meant that the vassals had to retake the oath of allegiance to the new incumbent. A man could not extend his wishes to a time exceeding his own putative life-span. This inability to enact legislation that would remain juridically binding on all subsequent generations seems to have delayed the practice of making a will or testament, since this is based on the premise that a man's will can remain valid after his death. Hence, donations were made during the lifetime of the donor.[116] A man had no competence with regard to time which he could not live to experience.

A man could not dispose of time, because it was God's property. This was the argument used by the church as a basis for its condemnation of usurious money-lending. The rich lend money at interest, but their debtors have the right to use these assets for a certain period – hence, the profit in interest is connected with an accumulation of time. Trading in time as a commodity or 'in expectation of time' is illegal, since time is given by God and belongs to all beings. The usurer carries on his activity at the cost of God's creatures. By selling time, that is, day and night, the usurer trades in light and rest – for day is the time of light, and night is the time of repose – and must therefore be deprived of eternal light and rest and condemned as a sinner. Similar arguments were used frequently by theologians in the thirteenth and fourteenth centuries. 'The time of the merchants' was seen to be in conflict with 'biblical time'. The former was accounted 'the time of sin', while the latter was 'the time of salvation'. Citizens felt impelled to resolve this conflict, and gradually the church also found its way to a compromise with daily practice.[117] In principle, however, time as construed and used by merchants, usurers, and manufacturers was at odds with the theological conception of time, and could not but lead in the long run to its secularisation and rationalisation.

The types of time perception which we have mentioned – agrarian time, family time (or, genealogical, dynastic time), biblical (or liturgical) time, cyclic time and finally historical time – are not identical, and are, indeed, often contradictory. The cyclic view of life – life determined by natural rhythms, by seasonal change – underlay other systems of reckoning time. The image of time as a self-repeating cycle was retained in the medieval mind in the shape of the Wheel of Fortune.[118] Throughout this whole period imagination turned to Dame Fortune, who 'ruled, rules and will rule' the world. As late as the seventh century Gnostic sects continued to adhere to the Pythagorean doctrine of the transmigration of souls and circular time; and the concept of cyclic time reappeared more than once during the Middle Ages, under the influence of

Neo-Platonism and Averroism. In the thirteenth century, the idea of analogous phases recurrent in human life and in the revolutions of the heavens, was widespread among Averroist circles in Paris; in particular, the concept of the circulation of time in eternity was developed by Siger of Brabant, who thereby incurred the censure of the church.[119]

The concept of cyclic time proved to be durable, not only on the theoretic level among the learned, but first and foremost among the people. An agrarian society lived according to the rhythms inherent in its natural surroundings. As in nature, so too in human life there is a sequence of seasons – birth, growth, ripeness, withering and death – a sequence which regularly repeats itself from generation to generation. The agricultural seasons and the sequence of generations are rings on one and the same tree of life. Reckoning by family time conferred the same sort of anthropomorphic character on the perception of time as made itself felt in the relationship with Christianity. Local religious cults which had been widespread in the pagan period did not all die out as Christianity took over (for example, the cult of saints and relics). These practices reproduced and retained a mythological way of perceiving time tied up with rituals, festivals and sacrifices.

The social and material uncertainty besetting most members of feudal society, an uncertainty which deepened as the internal contradictions of this society grew more acute, was bound to encourage a belief in fate or destiny. Countless illustrations show the wheel of Fortune. She herself sits in the centre, crowned as 'sovereign of the world', and keeps the wheel turning; clinging to the wheel, a youth rises upwards, hopeful and expectant; on top of the wheel, a ruler has enthroned himself in solemn state; further on, we see a man dragged precipitously downwards by the spinning wheel, while under it lies the prostrate figure of a victim of inconstant Fate. The concept of Fate was borrowed by the Middle Ages from antiquity. The Christianisation process made Fate subject to God, who has given into her keeping 'worldly glitter', to use Dante's expression. Fortune or Luck, 'sovereign of fates', 'spins her wheel, gay and blessed' and moves 'at its hour, Vain wealth from race to race, from blood to blood,/Beyond the hindrance of all human wit'.[120] However, the idea of Fate, so often encountered in the poets and philosophers of the Middle Ages, was far from completely assimilated by Christian thought, and met with opposition from such outstanding theologians as Peter Damian, Anselm of Canterbury and St Bernard of Clairvaux.[121]

Having got rid of the mass of disparate time-scales used by countless local and family groups, the church and Christian ideology imposed their conception of time on the Western world: earthly time was subordinated to heavenly eternity. Time as an intellectual and problematic concept existed only for the theologians and the philosophers[122] – as far as the masses were concerned, time was experienced mainly, as we have seen, in the forms of natural and family time. These forms now came under the powerful influence of the Christian concept of time to engender a special relationship with history, a specifically medieval historical perspective relating the mortal human individual with the whole of mankind, and investing life with a new meaning.

As I said above, time for medieval society was a slow-moving, leisurely and protracted affair. It was not something to be rationed. The medieval man felt about time the way the Irish do, according to Heinrich Böll: 'When God made time – the Irish say – he made plenty of it.'[123] In so far as time is cyclic and mythological, it is orientated towards the past. The past, as it were, returns continuously, and this lends solidity, gravity, a non-transient character to the present. In this respect, Christianity represented a new dynamic element. Together with the re-enactment of the biblical past in prayer and sacrament, it also opened up new vistas. The bond between times revealed by Christianity gave history a teleological and apocalyptic meaning. In this new perspective, the present had no independent significance: true, it had its place within the world-historical drama, but it was devalued, as it were, by expectation of the Day of Judgment and fraught with very mixed feelings – hope of salvation and fear of retribution.

We have to agree with J. Le Goff when he points to the absence of a unified concept of time, and to the plurality of times as a reality in medieval thought.[124] However, it is not this plurality of times in itself that sets apart the medieval attitude to time. Social time differs not only for different cultures and societies: it is also differentiated within the framework of each socio-cultural system in accordance with the internal structure of that system. The flow pattern of social time is perceived differently by different classes and groupings, who have their own ways of perceiving and experiencing time, and the rhythm in which these groupings function is peculiar to them. In other words, a society does not exhibit what we might call a 'monolithic' time, but rather a whole spectrum of social rhythms modulated by regularities inherent in the various component processes and by the nature of the various human collectives.[125] But just as the various social forms, institutions and processes are mutually integrated as a whole with the overall specificity of the society, so too do the temporal rhythms of these processes and social forms constitute a hierarchy of social times within the given system. A society cannot exist if it has not attained a certain degree of coordination of the plurality of social rhythms. Thus, it becomes possible to speak of a social time which is prevalent in and dominates the society. In a society divided by antagonisms, the social time of the ruling class naturally prevails as long as this class retains real control over public life and is ideologically dominant. Social time is a valuable component in the mechanism of social control exercised by the ruling class. And, vice versa, one of the signs that go to show that this class is losing control over public life, is a change in the structure of time according to which the society lives.

In the Middle Ages, the church exercised tight control over social time; the clergy determined the tempo and directed the flow of time in feudal society by regulating its component rhythms. All attempts at withdrawing from the ecclesiastical control of time were promptly nipped in the bud: the church forbade people to work on feast-days, the due observance of religious prohibitions being regarded as more important than the extra production which could have been achieved on such days – amounting to more than a third of the year. The church specified the foods which it was permissible to eat at

[144]

this or that time and inflicted severe punishment on anyone who broke fast. It even intervened in sexual life by stipulating when the sexual act was permissible and when it was sinful.[126] Thanks to this sort of detailed and comprehensive control of social time, people were totally subject to the ruling social and ideological system. An individual's time was not his own personal time; it belonged not to him but to a higher power placed over him. Hence, opposition to the ruling class in the Middle Ages often took the form of protest against its control of time; eschatological sects, preaching the imminent end of the world and calling people to repent and turn away from earthly things, cast doubt on the value of the ecclesiastical view of time. Chiliasm is an integral factor in medieval life, the form taken by the social aspirations of the deprived and the oppressed. Sometimes anticipation of the imminent end of the world assumed the proportions of mass panic, accompanied by an epidemic of confession, repentance and flagellation. Chiliasm was a peculiar form of relationship with the future, a way of apprehending time which seemed crucially important to certain groups in society.

The course of history itself was construed by the millenarians in terms very different from the official doctrine of the church. They claimed that the Last Judgment would be preceded by the millennium, the thousand years of Christ's reign on earth, which would see the rejection of all feudal and ecclesiastical institutions, of property and of the social structure. Apocalyptic expectation of the imminent 'end of time' symbolised sectarian hostility to the orthodox conception of time. From the standpoint of the official church the danger of the eschatological sects (and all medieval sects were more or less eschatological in nature) was that, by convincing people of the imminent end of the world, they were annulling the inner justification of an earthly order, which the church declared to be God-given.[127]

For all their unorthodoxy, however, in one essential way the attitude of the sects to the remote past and the remote future coincided with that of the church. Both the remote past and the remote future are seen as absolutes, which are not subordinate to the flow of time. The absolute past – the sacral moments of biblical history – does not recede, and can

[145]

be recapitulated in the liturgy; the absolute future – the end of the world – is not brought nearer by the flow of time, for the kingdom of God can break into the present at any moment. It is not the course of time that leads to its consummation – the advent of Christ – but the divine plan. The sectarians do not urge time onwards; they deny it, and prophesy its imminent cessation. Meanwhile, the mystics were affirming the possibility of overcoming the irreversibility of time: Meister Eckhart claimed that it was possible to return 'in a single instant' to one's original abode in the fellowship of the Holy Trinity, and to recover in that single instant all 'time lost'.[128]

Church time could continue to rule just as long as it corresponded adequately to the slow, measured rhythm of life in feudal society. Keeping a record of generations, of monarchs' reigns, of pontificates, had more meaning for the people of the Middle Ages than the precise measurement of short intervals of time divorced from ecclesiastical or political events. No need was felt in the Middle Ages to value and save time, nor was it necessary to measure it and identify its smaller components. The epic leisureliness of medieval life was conditioned largely by the agrarian nature of feudal society. But concomitantly another way of organising public life was taking root and developing within this society – a way characterised by its own special rhythms and requiring more precise measurement and more economical expense of time: the town.

The output of artisans and craftsmen had its own cyclic patterns, but these were not determined by seasonal change. The farmer was tied to the natural cycle, from which he could only with difficulty escape – and even then not completely; the town-dwelling artisan was connected to nature in more intricate and more contradictory ways. Between him and nature there already existed the artificial means he had created – tools of various kinds, all sorts of appliances and mechanisms, which acted as intermediaries between him and his natural surroundings. People living in a burgeoning urban civilisation were even in its early stages behaving according to patterns set by themselves rather than by nature. They were aware of the division they had created between themselves and nature; for them, nature was an external object.

As the town became the locus of a new way of looking at the world, a new relationship with time was engendered. Clocks made their appearance on town steeples and turrets, exemplifying not only the burghers' pride in their town but also answering a hitherto unheard-of need – to know the right time! The towns saw the growth of a new social sector with a totally different attitude to time from that of the feudal lords or peasants. For merchants, time is money, and the employer needs to have an exact way of measuring the time during which his workshop is functioning. Time thus becomes a measure of work. It is no longer the tolling of the church bells calling to prayer, but the chiming of the town hall clock that regulates the life of the citizens, although for several centuries yet they will go on trying to reconcile traditional 'church time' with the newly discovered worldly time of practical life. Time acquires a new value, turning into a crucially important factor in the production process. The appearance of the mechanical clock was at once a completely logical result and a source of the new temporal orientation. Spengler's assertion that the mechanical clock – 'this awe-inspiring symbol of fleeting time', the *nec plus ultra* of the historical view of the world – was first invented around the year 1000 by Gerbert (who became pope under the title of Sylvester II)[129] is not correct. Gerbert did no more than perfect the water clock, an appliance for measuring time which was well known in antiquity. The mechanical clock was invented towards the end of the thirteenth century, and during the fourteenth and fifteenth centuries the town halls of many European cities were adorned with these new clocks. Inaccurate as they were, and lacking a minute hand, these clocks nevertheless marked a fundamental revolution in the arena of social time. Control over time began to slip from the clutches of the clergy. The town community made itself master of its own time, with its own special rhythm.[130]

If we take a somewhat wider cultural-historical view, however, it is not the emancipation of urban time from ecclesiastical control that emerges as the most significant result of the invention of the clock. The fact that for the greater part of his history man felt no need for the continuous and precise calibration of time, nor for its division into equal segments, cannot be explained simply by the absence of adequate measuring instruments. Where a social need exists, the means are usually forthcoming to satisfy it. Mechanical clocks were installed in European towns when the need to know the right time made itself felt in influential social groups. The change-over was not sudden; but the tendency was for these groups to break, not only with 'biblical time', but with the whole world-view of the traditional agrarian society. As apprehended in this older society, time was not an independent category which could be cognised independently of its real, objective content; it was not a 'form' of existence of the world, it was indivisible from existence itself. Time could not be cognised independently of what was happening *in* time; if represented, it took natural and anthropomorphic forms. Hence time could be qualitatively defined and distinguished: time could be 'good' or 'bad', sacral or mundane. The conception of non-qualitative time (time which is neutral in relation to its content and not dependent on the percipient subjects capable of imparting a specific emotional or axiological complexion to time) was not known to the ancients or to the people of the Middle Ages. Accordingly, the division of time into commensurate and interchangeable units was also unknown. The concrete-material character of the perception of time, an organic component in all 'transient things', militated against the formulation of any such abstract concepts.

Finally the invention of a mechanism for measuring time generated conditions favouring the development of a new attitude to time – time as a homogeneous, uniform stream which can be subdivided into qualitatively neutral units of equal size. For the first time in history, the European town is the setting for something quite new in history – the 'alienation' of time as a pure form from life, whose phenomena can now be timed and measured.

That the invention of a mechanical clock was not in itself the cause of this new attitude, however, can best be shown by the following parallel. On arrival in China, the Europeans, as is well known, took over many ancient Chinese inventions, and in turn acquainted the Chinese with some of their own. And although medieval China cultivated a cavalier disdain of everything foreign, the Chinese emperors were captivated by the mechanical clock – not as an instrument for the precise measurement of time, however, but as a toy![131] Not so in the West. Here the clock, used as it was by the nobility, by rulers and by the municipal patricians as a mark of social prestige, served a practical purpose from the very beginning. European society was gradually moving from the contemplation of the world *sub specie aeternitatis* to an active relationship with it: a relationship measured in time.

Having acquired the means of measuring time accurately and, consequently, of reckoning it in equal intervals, the Europeans were bound sooner or later to grasp and apply the radical possibilities inherent therein – changes prepared by the whole development of society, especially of the towns. Time was at last 'stretched out' in a straight line, proceeding from the past to the future through a point called the present. In preceding epochs the distinctions between past, present and future time had been relative, with no fixed boundaries separating them. (In religious ritual, at the supreme moment of consummation, past and future coalesced in the present to become the non-ephemeral, fulfilling the higher meaning of that moment.) With the triumph of linear time the boundaries became completely clear, and present time 'shrank' to a point continually moving vectorially from the past towards the future, thereby turning the future into the past. Present time became transient, irreversible and elusive. For the first time in his history man came up against the realisation that time, whose course he had been aware of only when something remarkable was happening, did not cease to flow when nothing was happening. So time had to be saved, used prudently, filled with activities useful to man. The regular chimes from the turret of the town hall were a constant reminder that time waits for no man, and a summons to use it profitably, to give it positive content.

The transition to the mechanical reckoning of time emphasised those aspects of time which were bound to appeal to the exponents of the new system of production – the entrepreneurs, manufacturers and merchants. Time was recognised as a commodity of great value and as a source of material gain. It is not difficult to see that this new appreciation of the value of time went hand in hand with the growth in self-consciousness, of awareness of the self not simply as a generic being but as a unique individuality: a personality endowed with real temporal coefficients within which the capabilities of this personality are to be realised. Mechanical reckoning of time proceeds without the direct participation of man, who has to recognise that time is not dependent on him. I said above that the towns became the proprietors of their own time, and this is true in the sense that it was the towns which took time away from ecclesiastical control. But it is also true that it was precisely in the towns that man began to lose his proprietary grip on time altogether; from the realisation that time flowed on regardless of men and events, it was but a short step to man's subordination to the tyranny of time. Time imposes its own rhythm on men, making them work more quickly, hurry; not a moment must be lost. The place of time among the basic human values is cogently summed up by Leone Battista Alberti: 'There are three things which a man may call his own personal property – his soul, his body and . . . the most valuable of all things . . . time.'[132] From being the possession of God, time had become a possession of man.

The alienation of time from its concrete content raised the possibility of viewing it as a pure categorical form, as duration unburdened by matter. Time in the pre-capitalist age was always local time. No unified time-scale was observed regionally or nationally, let alone internationally. The particularism characteristic of public life and institutions appeared also in systems of reckoning time, where it proved to be tenacious; and even after the transition to mechanical methods, each town continued to have its own time. However, the new method of measuring time contained in itself the possibility of unifying it as well, and once the situation had passed under central governmental control, a central time as defined by official clocks was imposed on the public as the sole reliable time. Local time had been divisive, while central time and subsequently zonal time made for cohesion and consolidation of connections and communications. People's minds became adjusted to the concept of unified time.

Thus we see that the value of time rose sharply in urban life in the Middle Ages. However, the not infrequent dismissal by historians of the preceding epoch as 'indifferent to time'[133] cannot be accepted without some qualification. The medieval mind was indeed indifferent to time in our modern sense of the word, but it had its own ways of apprehending and experiencing it. The people of the Middle Ages were not so much indifferent to time as insusceptible to change and development. Stability, tradition, repetition, these were the categories governing their thinking – categories in whose terms real historical development was being conceptualised, although it would be a long time before this development could make itself felt.

CHAPTER V

'The country is built on law . . .'

The position of the individual *vis-à-vis* the society he lives in is defined and regulated primarily by the system of law governing that society; while at the same time, the realities of individual position in that society are reflected in its norms and in the manner of their interpretation. We may say in general that the attitude adopted by a society towards law reveals its attitude towards the individual. Contempt for law, a diminution of the role of law in social relations, imply a society's contempt for the personal rights of its members; a high regard for law, on the other hand, is bound up with the presence of certain safeguards protecting human existence, upon which society can rely.

The absence of precise delimitation in the various fields of social activity in the Middle Ages is well known. Between philosophy, morals, jurisprudence, legislation there was no clear division; they overlapped, forming a system whose parts, while they did not always form a harmonious whole, in practice worked actively together, and which were in greater or lesser degree shot through with religious symbolism and religious significance. All forms of human activity in the Middle Ages were subject to rules and regulations, any departure from which was forbidden. The traditionalism of medieval society and its dependence on religion acted as powerful normative factors on the social behaviour of the individual. In this way, law acquired the status of a universal and all-embracing regulator of social relations.

But this high regard for law in medieval Europe – which took shape long before the bourgeois demand for precise guarantees of personal property and personal liberty had made itself felt within the social framework of feudalism – was in no way characteristic of other medieval civilisations, which were, no less (if no more) than the European model, characterised by traditionalism, a normative orthodoxy and the rule of religion.

In fact, medieval Muslim society was, in many ways, not unlike European feudalism. But in Europe, and in spite of the domination of the church, law retained a relatively independent status (we recall the doctrine of 'the two swords', the ecclesiastical and the temporal, the rivalry and struggle between the papacy and its claim of theocratic dominion on the one hand, and lay power on the other). In the Arab world, law remained an indissoluble part of religion; Muslim law recognises no distinction between canon law and civil law; there is only one law – that of the *shari'a*, of the community of the faithful.[1] In the Muslim world, a criminal is judged as a sinner, liable not only to earthly punishment but also to retribution in the world to come. The Arabs never arrived at the concept of civil law: which meant that, by virtue of its purely sacral nature, law was ill-suited to change, and could only with great difficulty adapt itself to new social conditions. Law is a powerful conservative force in Muslim society, its development having been arrested as far back as the tenth century – at the very moment, that is to say, when medieval European law was just beginning to develop.

Turning to China, we find no such close tie between law and religion as is characteristic of Islam. Nevertheless, the medieval Chinese attitude to law is also totally different from the European concept, exemplifying as it does an essentially Chinese way of looking at things. Law is not construed as the basis of social structure, nor does it seek to regulate individual behaviour; for this there exist special prescriptions governing human behaviour in all of life's contingencies. 'To equality, Confucian Asia prefers the ideal of filial relationships formed by benevolent patronage and respectful subordination.'[2] According to the Chinese conception, law, by virtue of its abstract nature, cannot do justice to the infinite variety of concrete actual situations, and is therefore a force not for good but for evil. The idea of 'subjective rights' engendered by law, runs counter to the natural order of things; something breaks down in society as soon as the individual starts talking about his 'rights': there can be no question of anything beyond the individual's obligations to society. 'To insist on having what is supposed to be due to you is anti-social and in contravention of good manners.'[3] In China, the norms of law did not safeguard the functioning of society and of government. Social well-being, Chinese thinkers believed, depended on people's behaviour, first and foremost on those who governed the state. Hence, the principle of legality, of *lawful* government, has no roots in Chinese civilisation.

These two attitudes to law and its role in the life of society – the Muslim and the Chinese – are poles apart from the concept of law that we find in medieval Europe. Clearly, the profound differences cannot be explained simply by the traditional character of the social orders or the mutual relationship of law and religion; they go much deeper. In my view, the conception of law obtaining in a given society depends in the final analysis on the position of the human being in that society. And it is from the viewpoint of the relationship between the law and the person that I now wish to treat some aspects of medieval European law. In other words, I shall treat law as a socio-cultural category, as an element in which essential aspects of human individuality are displayed, and as one of the forms of human self-knowledge.

As before, we start with the age of barbarism. The life of the traditional barbarian society was subordinated to behavioural norms laid down once and for all. The predominance of the stereotype in the art forms of the Germanic tribes (already discussed) is but one small part of the general all-embracing regimentation. Individual behaviour is in strict conformity with a far-reaching system of prohibitions and incentives. The individual does not stand before a choice; he follows examples sanctioned by religion, by law and by the moral code. But in barbarian society law and the moral code do not exist as different bases and forms of social awareness and of human behaviour. Law and morals coincide or are at least very close to each other, since the precepts of law depend for their effectiveness not simply on outward constraints, on a system of punishments; rather, they represent inner imperatives, invested with moral and religious content. Consequently, barbarian law is similar only in name to contemporary law; in reality, it is far wider in scope and function. To assume that law *formed* social relations in a barbarian society is justified only if we take the word *form* in its original meaning: law gave these relations a generally significant form, outside of which they would be unthinkable. If it is accurate to say that form was the true content of Skaldic poetry,[4] this is very largely true of law also.

The Germanic tribes had arrived at a conception of law as a general bond between people even before the adoption of Christianity, and in this connection it is very instructive to analyse the terms for law in use among the Scandinavians. The term *lag* (*lög*) had a whole series of meanings. In the broad sense, the term *lag* signified a state: order ('to put something in proper order', 'to put in place'), degree (with a corresponding adjective: 'sufficiently long', 'proper', 'fitting', etc.), price, payment (prescribed by someone), musical tune (concord, harmony), metre in poetry. The term *lag* was thus clearly associated with the concept of measure, the observance of due proportions in things and relations. In a more specialised sense, the term was used for various forms of human grouping (a company of people, a partnership, cohabitation of man with woman).

In the plural, the term *lag* (*lög*) denoted 'law, right, statute', literally 'that which is laid down', 'code'. The establishment of law for people meant the creation of a system of ties among them. Law was thus the basis of human society. 'The country is built up on law and goes to ruin in the absence of law' ('*með lögum skal land byggja en með ólögum eyða*') said a proverb which amounted to a legal maxim. At the people's assemblies – the *þings* – the experts 'talked law'. Bringing an action meant 'to get/obtain law', and the pronouncement of sentence in court was known as 'the awarding of law'. Further, the term *lög* was applied to the community in the legal sense, the community of people who lived by a law common to all of them. Hence the possibility of such expressions as 'to be at law with other people' or 'to take someone to law'. Hence also the area or region where customary law was effective was known as *lag*. In Norway, these areas defined by the observance of common law began to take shape even before their union within the kingdom, and for several hundred years in Iceland – until its submission

[157]

to Norwegian rule, in fact – the only form of union was that upon the basis of law. What united the people was not the exercise of force or political dominion but an organ for regulating legal relations.[5] Thus, the totality of meanings of the term *lag* (*lög*) covered every known form of ordered union. Evidently, the positive moral value of such a union was also included in the concept. Law was the basis and an indissoluble component of world order. 'Law and order' and world order were virtually synonymous. Law was a boon which must be preserved and guarded. Clearly, this concept was of fundamental importance in the Old Norse world-view.

The same shades of meaning can be observed in another word used by the Scandinavians to denote law – *réttr*. As an adjective, its range of meaning includes such concepts as 'straight', 'direct', 'precise', 'correct', 'just', 'equitable'. As a noun, *réttr* means 'law', 'right'. Conceptually, *lög* and *réttr* are close, but not identical. Like *lög*, *réttr* can denote the law of the land (*lög og lands réttr*) or ecclesiastical law (*Guðs réttr, Kristins doms réttr*). An improvement or an amendment in law was usually called *réttarbot*, but the Norwegian king Magnus Hakonarson, famed for his law-giving, was given the nickname *Lagabaetir* ('Improver of laws'). More often, however, the term *réttr* did not express the concept of law as the state of people united in a community, but rather summed up the personal rights of the individual – his status. Hence, it also denoted compensation for infringement of these rights: *réttr sinn* meant 'his compensation', *konungs réttr* was 'compensation laid down by the king', and so on. Individual status and compensation for any encroachment thereon were accordingly inseparably bound up with each other in the Scandinavian mind; status was construed as something concrete, immediately bound up with the individual, and, at the same time, as something that could be expressed as a given value. So the difference between the terms *réttr* and *lög* is probably that while *lög* covered the general concept of law and had an abstract and all-embracing significance, *réttr* was understood in a more subjective and concrete sense.

In the Old English legal texts the term *right* (*ryht*)

comprises the notions of law, justice, custom, right – the last
of these in both the wide sense of law in general, and in the
narrower sense of personal rights, the status of the individual.
This is the only indigenous term expressing the concept of
law, as the term *lagu* seems to have entered Old English from
the Scandinavian languages, and in any case does not appear
in the sources until a comparatively late date. There are
grounds therefore for assuming that the Old English term
riht denoted a general bond between people, as did the
Scandinavian term *lög*.

To be declared 'outlawed', outside the law, meant not only
the loss of all the rights enjoyed by a man as long as he was
'inside the law'; it was equivalent to being expelled from the
human community in general. The disgraced man, outcast in
a state of *útlegð*, debarred from living in the community,
took himself off to some uninhabited place (hence his appel-
lation of *skógarmaðr* = 'man of the woods', 'living in the
woods') and was regarded as a werewolf or wolf (*vargr*).[6]
Living 'in the law', or 'according to the law', meant living
with people and maintaining with them relations based on
justice and on mutual respect for personal rights. For this
reason, the barbarian law codes are mainly concerned with
the protection of the personal rights and property rights of
free men, and with the meet punishment for infringement of
these rights.

The words for 'law' which we have considered here refer
mainly to custom, to the ancient order of things inherited
from the tribal ancestors. The Scandinavian term *lög* was
close in meaning to its derivative *örlög*, signifying ancient,
long-established law or 'doom'. The belief in doom or fate
played an enormous part in the Germanic mind, and shaped
its understanding of custom. Custom was that with which
everyone agreed and which everyone voluntarily respected,
since it was not only obligatory but also sound and just.

In barbarian society, a man was born with certain rights
and privileges: either he was from birth of noble stock or he
was born into a family descended from either rank-and-file
freemen or from unfree (i.e. dependent) men. In all cases,
certain rights were his by virtue of his social category. Social
ties were still mainly of a natural, organic character: patri-

monial, family, clan relationships. In so far as the relationship between ruler and ruled obtained in this society (there already existed serfs and other categories of non-free men) these ties also fitted in with the predominant social model and assumed a patriarchal character. In general, the individual could not choose those with whom he was to be grouped: the group was formed from his relatives, and even marriage ties were subordinated to the accepted scheme of things and its limiting constraints. The element of choice in the composition of social groups and networks was either lacking altogether or minimal; at most, it was a factor in the formation of groups centring on leaders and princes.

Membership of a social order or stratum in barbarian society determined the behaviour of the individual in that society. All aspects of his life were regulated: it was known in advance how he was to behave in this or that situation; personal choice hardly entered into it. Each and every action was strictly prescribed by virtue of his belonging to one group or another, and by an awareness of family or clan rather than personal honour. The life of every member of the collective group was programmed by custom and the need to follow the example set by gods, forefathers, elders.

Regulation of individual behaviour in barbarian society assumed ritualistic proportions; in so far as it affected the interests of the group, any important individual undertaking was accompanied by special ceremonies and pronouncement of the due formulas, the absence of which rendered the act or undertaking ineffective, null and void. Not that the member of barbarian society was necessarily a cipher without willpower; but this willpower, instead of being expressed in the free taking of decisions, was primarily directed towards the realisation of aims set before the individual by the group he belonged to. Just as the poet or the sculptor brought a wealth of ingenuity, skill and intelligence to producing works of art that complied with the established canons, original variations on traditional themes, so the individual member of society was obliged to behave and act in all respects in keeping with established ritual and custom; his personal distinction lay in unity with the group.

In these circumstances, morality is not so much a hallmark

of the individual, conditioned by his personal qualities and finding expression in his personal behaviour, as a qualitative system proper to his family, his kin, his social stratum, in the same way as his rights and obligations. In fact, these rights and obligations are inseparable from the ethical evaluation of the individuals who make up the group. The aristocracy are noble and honourable, their behaviour is exemplary, courage and generosity are their natural qualities. Such qualities cannot be expected in persons of ignoble birth. Barbarian society acts upon the conviction that moral qualities are inherited in the same way as physical traits. Beauty, intelligence, honour and magnanimity must be sought among the princes of the land, baser qualities among the unfree and the low-born. The son of a nobleman and a bond-woman cannot be expected to display the same character and bearing as the son of the same nobleman by his legal wife of equal birth. Hence, not only were persons of noble birth far more handsomely compensated for harm done to them; a greater load of responsibility also rested on their shoulders, and, if found guilty of a crime, they were punished far more severely than were rank-and-file freemen.

Thus, legal status was inseparable from its bearer and was an essential attribute of him. High-class people were 'noble', 'better'; low-class people were 'inferior', 'bad', 'base'. Legal status, that is to say, took on a moral complexion; and a person's legal condition both determined and reflected his personal qualities. The legal and moral categories had, in addition, an aesthetic component. Nobility was naturally associated with beauty, just as the concepts of evil and deformity were inseparably linked. In Old English, for example, it was not possible to say of something or someone 'beautiful but bad'. There was no way of expressing a purely aesthetic judgment. 'Beautiful' was a moral evaluation as well as an aesthetic one. Beauty was an expression of personal honour and dignity. In the same way, the intellectual qualities were inseparable from the ethical: 'intelligent' carried the connotation 'honest'.[7]

In barbarian society, law was not something occupying a special compartment of social life. All its facets were regulated by custom. Law and custom provide the element in which society exists, and they are at the same time an indissoluble dimension of the human consciousness.

The conversion of the barbarians to Christianity had a profound effect on their whole way of life, and was in itself a symptom of a transformation in their social structure. Acceptance of the new religion depended on a radical change in the traditional customs and institutions of the Germanic tribes. In the field of law, the church brought far-reaching change; and though morality and law would continue to be closely associated throughout the Middle Ages, they would never again be synonymous. Morality became concerned with man's inner existence, with his conscience and with the exercise of his free will, while law came to be understood as a supra-individual instance which all men were called upon to obey.

The barbarian concept of law was not completely ousted by the new combination of church and the feudal system, but was taken up – albeit in partially revised form – as a constituent part of medieval law. In general, law, like any other facet of medieval life, was throughout the Middle Ages strongly influenced by Christian doctrine.

The church was the bearer of a nomocratic concept of law deriving from the Bible, especially from the Epistles of Paul. His theory of divine law promoted the thesis of the universal rule of law as laid down by God. Baptism – the act whereby natural man becomes a Christian, a faithful member of the church – was seen as a 'rebirth'. The member of society is not *Homo naturalis* but *Homo Christianus*. Baptism was a special means of institutionalising the individual in medieval collectives; upon the individual it laid certain legal obligations which he could not transgress, though he had had no say in their formulation. Law in any case is not established by men but by God; *lex est donum Dei*. The members of the church – the members of the community of the faithful (*universitas fidelium*), which comprised both lay and clergy – were not equal among themselves, the clergy being preferred over the lay members, who again were not equal among themselves, since all had rendered 'service' to God in varying degree, though by nature all men are equal. The hierarchy of merits and services implies that the rights of individuals are not identical. An individual's position in society is based upon his service.

The highest position is occupied by the monarch appointed by God. Just as the world (the macrocosm) is directed by God, and the human body (the microcosm) by the soul, so is the body politic directed by the monarch, whose relation with his subjects might be compared to the relation between the head and the limbs. The power of the monarch does not depend on the will of the subjects. The monarch is subject to one God alone, whom alone he serves (*rex – minister Dei*). The church was, however, at pains to stress that the monarch by divine grace bore a certain responsibility to the church, for the church alone proclaimed God's will. The ruler was bound by no earthly institutions or ordinations. All subjects received the law from their ruler, the divinely anointed one to whom they owed complete and unquestioning obedience. A crime committed against the ruler was both treason and sin, for the criminal was offending against the divine power inherent in the ruler. The ruler's duty was to concern himself with the welfare of his subjects. Not agreement but unconditional obedience and loyalty on the part of the subjects was the basic ingredient of the law. The subjects could have no influence on the law, as they were ill-informed and lacking in understanding. In accordance with this way of thinking, the sovereign enjoyed unlimited unilateral power in relation to his subjects, to whom he was bound by no sort of obligation. He even had dominion (*dominium*) over them with regard to their property, of which he could make such use as seemed appropriate to him in the interests of the community.[8]

Underlying these notions, which are so far removed from political and social reality, is the idea of the priority of the common weal, as represented by the ruler, over the interests of the individual. Law, like the 'communal body', is immortal, while individual man is mortal. What matters is the good of the whole, not the good of an insignificant part of the whole – the individual. In consequence, the individual saw himself in the light of this concept, as completely absorbed in and swallowed up by the community – the great unified organism in which each component member has his calling (*vocatio*) and carries out his allotted function. Accordingly, the individual does not exist simply for himself. What is important is not his 'personality' but the duty that falls to him, the service he discharges.

Thus, law is crystallised in the person of the ruler, the embodiment of the idea of law (*lex animata*), dispensing justice and mindful of the common weal. Only the church is competent to decide in what circumstances the ruler who has abused his power has forfeited his right to be considered God's representative and servant. The church alone is able and entitled to distinguish *tyrannus* from *rex iustus*; and only the church can strip a tyrant of plenipotentiary authority (which becomes a just ruler) and absolve his subjects from the duty to obey him. It is well known how the ideologists of the papal theocracy tried – not always without success – to put these principles into practice: witness the policies of Gregory VII and Innocent III. On the other hand, the protagonists of the doctrine of an all-powerful monarchy by the grace of God, argued that the king, as the earthly embodiment of God, could not be subject to the church. The efforts made by the monarchy to substantiate its links with transcendent reality found a ready echo in the popular mind. The sanctity of imperial and royal power was readily deducible from the premise that the syzygy formed by the people and the lay authority partook of the divine.[9] Christ himself was not infrequently depicted as an earthly ruler. The coronation ceremonies of an earthly ruler were without fail accompanied by religious rituals which visibly and palpably proclaimed the divine nature of his power.[10] Actual events were nearly always in flat contradiction of this pious and theocratic thesis.[11] Nevertheless, the high value placed on law in theocratic doctrine deserves close attention. In idealised form it reflects the truly enormous importance of the role of law in the life of the feudal community. Abstracted from everyday practice and everyday reality as it was – as every ideal must be – the nomocratic theory of divine law nevertheless gave a higher dimension to everyday life.

Passing now from the teachings of theologians, jurists and political theorists to a body of ideas which enjoyed a much wider currency in the Middle Ages – ideas which were not so much expressly formulated as tacitly taken for granted as the indispensable prerequisite for the formulation and application of law – we find both Pauline and anti-Pauline concepts. The belief was widely held that law is an indissoluble element of the world order, as eternal and indestructible as the cosmos itself.[12] The world, whether the human world or the world of nature, is unthinkable without law. Law is the basis of all human society; on law are built up relations between people: 'where there is society there is law' ('ubi societas, ibi jus').[13] All kinds of living beings and indeed all things have their own law, which is an inalienable property of all God's creatures (hence not only men but also animals and even things can be held accountable for transgressions of this in-built law). The way of life and the manner of behaviour of all beings are determined by their status. This is the medieval concept of 'natural law', the universal law of the cosmos as interpreted in theocratic terms.

No one – neither emperor nor any other ruler nor any assembly of lay officials or representatives – worked out or formulated new statutes. In as much as God was seen as the source of the law, it followed that law could not be unjust or bad; it was good in itself, good in essence. Law and justice were synonymous. Injustice could ensue only where law was inadequately applied, misinterpreted or forgotten. Just as evil in the world was explained as the absence of good, so injustice was held to be due to misapplication of law. Law was just because it was reasonable and in keeping with the nature of men. St Thomas Aquinas defined law as 'the establishment of reason for the common good, as promulgated by him who cares for the community of men'. It was essential to observe all these conditions: law must be based on reason, must serve the common good and must be in relation to the competence of the instance which duly and fittingly promulgates it.[14]

Equally inseparable from law was its halo of antiquity. There can be no such thing as innovation in law; law exists from time immemorial, just as eternal justice does. This is not to say that law is in its entirety laid down in law books and legal codes, and needs no further articulation by human

[165]

agency. As a whole, as an idea, law is imprinted on the moral consciousness, and moral norms are drawn from it as circumstances arise which humanity has not yet faced. Law is not remodelled; it is 'sought and found'. What makes the antiquity of law valuable, however, is not so much its chronological age in itself as the fact that this vouches for its incontestability, its essential goodness. Ancient law was good and just.[15] The great legislators of the Middle Ages were not innovators, creators of new laws; they 'found', 'sought out' ancient law and rehabilitated it in the light of its manifest rightness; a process in which previously existent law was not abrogated but was supplemented; a process in which if anything was extirpated it was those distortions of law which people had admitted into the canon.

Thus it is curious, but highly characteristic of the medieval mind, to find the Frisián law books introduced by the assertion that the Frisián people must have that law which God himself laid down when Moses led the children of Israel through the Red Sea. After exposition of the Ten Commandments the prophets and kings are enumerated (beginning with Saul and David), who ruled down to the birth of Christ; and then comes a list of the Roman emperors, including, as one might expect, all the French and German rulers down to the date of the Frisián law books.[16] In this way, the law actually in force among the Frisiáns is presented as part of an unbroken legal chain stretching back to the dawn of mankind. Of the 'history of law' in the proper sense of the words there is no trace.

In the same way, the laws of King Alfred the Great begin with a long introduction expounding the Ten Commandments and other examples of biblical legislation. In addition there is a short account of the history of the Apostles and of the decisions reached by ecclesiastical synods, both ecumenical and English. Alfred is modest about his own role as legislator: 'I have not dared to presume to set down in writing many of my own, for I cannot tell what innovations of mine will meet with the approval of our successors.' But he did select for retention the most just of the laws of his royal predecessors (Ethelbert, Ine, Offa); the rest he rejected. This collection of laws found favour in the eyes of Alfred's counsellors.[17] The legislator's task was held to be not new legislation but the selection and adoption of the wisest and most equitable edicts from ancient law. Anglo-Saxon legislation in the tenth and eleventh centuries consists for the most part of borrowings from earlier codes, interlaced here and there with innovations. Lists of customs and usages are often introduced by a preamble ascribing them to one or another celebrated ruler of earlier times. Many of the Old Norwegian laws are described as 'The Laws of Saint Olaf' although they are really precepts of customary law written down at a considerably later date. The legal code compiled in England in the early twelfth century was entitled 'The Laws of Edward the Confessor', who had in fact nothing at all to do with them. The Lombard king Rothari saw it as his duty not to create new laws but to codify ancient Lombard law in so far as it needed to be corrected and amended.[18]

Laws could be supplemented and enhanced: in other words, it was possible to 'find' provisions which had not been given legal expression but which had been preserved in the moral consciousness of the people, in an ideal treasure-house of justice, as it were. Thus, the feeling for law and order inherent in the people was accounted as a second source of law, supplementing its divine origins. Above all, law was held to be retained in the memory of the wisest of men, the experts in law. But these experts – the *lǫgsǫgumenn*, the 'law-speakers' in Scandinavia, the *rachinburgen* and *échevins* in France, the *witan* and *liberi et legales homines* in England – did not produce new legislation. They knew the 'old way' of ancient custom. At least, this is how they saw their job as legislators.

Everybody is subject to custom and law, especially the ruler. His most important function is to uphold the law and see that it is observed. The belief that the ruler must concern himself with the protection of the customary law, and must be just and gracious, runs through the many 'King's Mirrors' produced in the Middle Ages, which contain exhortations to monarchs and lay stress on their individual qualities. This was natural at a time when royal power was identified with the personality of the ruler.

At his coronation the king swears to uphold the law.

Nowhere in the Middle Ages can we find any trace of a special state law: the ruler must uphold the existing law and act in accordance with it. Should he transgress the law, his subjects are not required to submit to injustice. 'A man is called upon to oppose his king and the king's judge, as soon as the latter does wrong, and he shall continue to oppose him in all ways and with all means even if he is his relative or his lord. And in so doing he does not break his oath of loyalty', says the 'Saxon Mirror'.[19] Isidore of Seville alters Horace's words to warrant the concept that the king is he who acts justly – otherwise he is not king ('Rex eris si recte facies, si non facias, non eris').[20] Intentional transgression of the law by the ruler deprives him of the legal bases of his power, and liberates the subjects from their oath to him. The subjects are also called upon to uphold the law even against the ruler if he has broken it. The obligation to uphold the law does not derive from any treaty or agreement but from the concept of the universal power of the law to which all men are subject. Accordingly, law unites all men, and is in itself the general bond between people. This principle is basically at variance with the theocratic concept of monarchy, according to which the king is above the law and answerable only to God.

But, granted that the people had in certain circumstances the right to oppose an illegal ruler or a king who failed to discharge his mission as required by the law, this did not give them the right to change the form of government; the place of the overthrown monarch had to be filled by another. To succeed to the throne, the new monarch had to have rights of succession, and he had to be accepted and anointed by the clergy. Membership of the royal family or kindred, while certainly important, was not in itself sufficient to warrant succession to the throne; for this to happen, both in the barbarian kingdoms and in the early medieval monarchies, the agreement of the 'people' was necessary – in actual practice, the support of the nobles.

In the same way, the agreement of the subjects (*consensus fidelium*) was necessary before new laws drawn up by the ruler could be made binding. As representatives of the people and as embodying the people's inborn feeling for law and order, the *meliores et maiores* were called upon to decide in what measure the new laws introduced by the king corresponded to the existent law inherited from ancient times.

The principle of the supremacy of law and justice and their independence of the monarch can be detected in medieval juristic practice. Thus, in England, although the courts were in the service of the government, they displayed a certain independence of the sovereign and never degenerated into mere instruments of his will. If the statutes and customary law contradicted the king's wishes, the king's courts took up their stance on the side of the law.[21] This principle lies at the root of feudal action against kings who broke the law and offended against the customs of the country. It is well known that Magna Carta was the result of such action taken by the English barons and knights, who saw their initiative as a completely legal one, deriving naturally from the essence of English law. Magna Carta provided for a commission of twenty-five barons, whose task it was, not only to limit the power of the king, but also to restrain him by force of arms should he break his word. Dangerous as this might seem for national unity, it did not contradict the spirit of the law or the understanding of the relationship between the king and his immediate vassals. From the medieval point of view, there was nothing paradoxical in the notion of the *bellum iustum*, the legal rebellion.

In normal circumstances the subjects were subordinated to their legal sovereign. Their obedience was expressed, however, not so much in passive submission as in fidelity (loyalty). Fidelity (*fidelitas*) is distinguished from mere obedience in that it specifies definite conditions in which 'the loyal/faithful' serve their lord, and also in that it implies a certain reciprocity; the vassal is bound by fidelity to his master who, in his turn, assumes certain duties towards his vassal. It is often asserted that relations between lord and vassal were built up on agreement or treaty. But this is to see medieval social relations partially at least through modern eyes, in that feudal relations are thus construed in terms of the bourgeois contract. In fact, the relationships of fidelity and patronage were built up on joint submission to the rule of law, custom, by both the ruler and the ruled; the fidelity binding on both parties is their fidelity to the law.[22] When they swore fidelity it was not simply to each other, but rather to that higher principle to which ruler and ruled alike felt themselves subject.

Law was held to be ancient and its authority rested on this. Innovation as such was not considered, and legislative practice consisted mainly in the restoration of ancient law, the identification and clarification of the customs of the forefathers. Law was backward-looking, focused on the past. This high regard for ancient times and practices is characteristic of all walks of life in the Middle Ages. There was more to medieval traditionalism than mere conservatism and force of custom: a positive gain was seen in appeal to ancient authority ('nihil innovetur, nisi quod traditum est')[23] which alone possessed moral dignity. What was new awakened feelings of mistrust; innovation was regarded as sacrilege and immorality. 'Move not from their places the stones which your father placed there,' preached the fifth-century monk Vincent of Lérins, 'for if it is better to avoid novelties, ancient things must be preserved; if the new is impure, the old learning is holy.'[24] The medieval consciousness is static; the idea of development is, as we saw above, still foreign to it. The world neither changes nor develops: it is God's primordial and perfect creation and remains in this unchanging state. It is characterised by a graduated hierarchy, not by a dynamic process of development. Hence, law too, as a component part of the world order, was thought to be static. Obsessed with fixation of principles, it ignores their origins and refuses to contemplate their change. It is outside time.[25]

In a certain sense, it is true to say that the existence of something in the Middle Ages depended on its having legal status. The first priority of a town seeking recognition as such was to be granted specific legal rights; a guild, a university or any other corporate body existed officially from the moment it was awarded its charter. Rural communes provided themselves with special deeds guaranteeing their legal status; feudal lords exercising judicial or military authority took care to ensure their legal immunity by having this power legalised in the shape of plenary powers conferred by the sovereign and special legal codes were worked out for every medieval institution. No social relationship was effectively existent unless it had the sanction of law.

The major social and political conflicts of the Middle Ages were fought not only over religious issues but over legal issues as well, and this was clear to the people of the time. We have space only to mention some stock examples: the conflict for political supremacy between the German emperors and the papacy centred in the first place on the question of investiture – the right to appoint bishops; the dramatic clash between King Henry II of England and Archbishop Thomas à Becket began in a disagreement over the question of the king's judicial competence; it was John Lackland's disregard for feudal custom and feudal law that led to Magna Carta. Experts in Roman law had to be called in to provide a legal foundation for the French monarchy, and their help was also found necessary in the struggle between Philip IV and Pope Boniface VIII. Law and theology were the oldest and most influential faculties in the medieval university. The adoption of Roman law in Europe, thanks to a whole series of social, economic and political factors, was of enormous import for every aspect and area of public life.

Law was understood as the essential framework of society as a whole; but more than that, each member of society was characterised first and foremost by his legal status. In feudalism, as in barbarian society, status and person were inseparable.

In general, status was inherited, passed on from father to son. It was, however, susceptible of change. The ruler could confer new status and enhanced rights upon one person or another. The peasant who forsook his feudal lord for the town received personal freedom; and when he became a burgher, a member, that is, of the urban community or of a guild, his status was changed. The rank-and-file freeman, and in some cases even the non-free man, could be knighted by doing homage – i.e. taking the oath of loyalty to a feudal lord – and thereupon be entitled to the legal rights proper to his new status. The layman who entered the priesthood became a member of the clergy, legally a special group enjoying special privileges. From this we can see that the medieval estates and other categories of the population as distinguished in law, were not closed and petrified castes with no possibility of transfer from one to another. There was, in fact, a rather high degree of socio-legal mobility in feudal society. The essential point is that status – whether inherited or acquired – remained directly linked with an individual's inner nature, and influenced, as the medieval view had it, his moral self and the basic traits of his character; indeed, it determined him as a human being. In legal documents, social status is not infrequently defined in terms of moral categories. Those of noble birth are described as 'best', 'most worthy'; while common people are categorised as 'low', 'base', 'vile'. Society is divided according to the medieval legislators into the 'nobility' on the one hand and the 'plebs' on the other. Nor is there any equality between rulers and ruled in moral matters either – a very comforting state of affairs for the ruling classes!

All social categories were first and foremost legal categories. The medieval mind did not recognise the de facto status of an individual or of a group of individuals if this had not been juridically identified and defined. It is not so much a question of class differences as such, as of estate indices which determine the individual's social position. A man's value depends primarily not on his belongings but on the rights to which he is entitled. The poorest knight is higher on the social scale than the richest burgher. Neither money nor even possession of landed property attracts *per se* official recognition or special rights. To be of noble estate, to enjoy full rights, one must either be born noble or be the recipient of royal favour. High birth and full legal competence – these are the criteria of membership of the ruling stratum of society. Wealth is normally associated with these criteria but does not in and of itself mark its possessor as a nobleman. Feudal society is a society of legal orders.

It is easy to see that the role of law in such a society was enormous. It was a role that grew even larger as a result of the high degree of ritualisation of social practice. In a traditional society 'normal' behaviour was that of the man who followed accepted example and never deviated from the established norm. Such exemplars acquired the force of moral standards, and departure from them was accounted not only reprehensible but on occasion even as infringement of the law. All the big moments in people's lives – marriage, acceptance into a family, becoming a knight, joining a guild, inheritance and its apportionment, lawsuits, commercial transactions, sale of land, taking monastic vows, excommunication, receptions, diplomatic missions, etc. – all of these were subject to ritualisation and had to be accompanied by the proper procedures, failure to observe which rendered the act null and void. Accordingly, a man's actions took place within strictly defined and immutable juridical forms: action outside their radius was both unthinkable and ineffective.

But, unlike later bureaucratic periods of history, this age of total and all-embracing formalism and ritual was in no sense a 'paper' (or, more accurately, a 'parchment') culture. Many transactions were not fixed in deed form at all; it was held to be enough if the proper ceremony was duly observed. In the early days of the feudal system in Europe, grants of land played a big part and had to be recorded in documentary form. The Germanic peoples, however, having borrowed the *carta*, the official deed, from Roman juridical practice, did not really grasp its essential meaning. The function of the written deed would surely have seemed to be to fix the deal and secure proprietary rights over the land in future. But in the early Middle Ages most people put little trust in a written document – which very few could even read – and failed to understand its juridical nature. Accordingly, the preparation and delivery of the land deed was accompanied by the traditional custom of throwing or handing over a handful of earth, turf, twigs, etc. The deed (*carta*) was seen simply as an object, a piece of parchment, and before inscribing the text it was customary to take the parchment and the writing materials to the piece of land involved in the transaction, so that the 'power of the earth' would penetrate the material and make the inscription effective and inviolable.[26] To make a juridical act effective, magic ritual was necessary.

The deed itself was accepted as a symbol. As such, it did not even have to have anything written on it, and *cartae sine litteris* were not infrequently accepted. A ruler wishing to ensure the obedience of his subjects or to communicate a decree to them could send them a piece of parchment or a seal without writing: the symbol of his authority was enough.[27]

The ritual made the transaction substantive, irrespective of whether a document was provided or not. Hence, a crucial role was played by the witnesses present at the conclusion of the deal. The role of witness was restricted to a comparatively small, localised and stable group of people who were personally acquainted with each other. When a man moved to another locality it was not obligatory for him to furnish documentary proof of his status; his new neighbours would take his word for it that he was what he claimed to be. Since a man's status was not some sort of exterior and inessential marker, but the factor determining his nature and his essential qualities, an individual's behaviour was the best evidence of the truth or the falsehood of his claim to belong to this or that order or social stratum.

In such circumstances, law was seen as the generally accepted form in which essential human business took place, both between individuals and between groups, and was understood by both individuals and groups as the essential factor in their behaviour. In the spiritual life of the Middle Ages law could not but appear as one of the basic categories in human awareness.

But medieval law was no logically articulated and rounded-off system, all of whose parts fitted nicely together. On the contrary, no manifestation of medieval social life was more contradictory and complicated than its law. The law not only united, it also divided people by giving rise to mutually conflicting claims and complicated quarrels. It was to be a long time before law could be looked upon as an abstraction. There was no 'law in general'. In the early Middle Ages, indeed, there was not even one identical law for all the inhabitants of a country. In the Germanic kingdoms occupying territory which had formerly belonged to the Roman Empire, the Germans and the 'Romans' retained their own forms of law; each tribe or people lived 'according to its law', whose customs and precepts every member of the tribe observed irrespective of where he happened to dwell. It was only very gradually that the monarchy succeeded in establishing alongside the body of tribal precepts a system of law generally binding on all subjects. In the same way, the monarch himself was originally the king of a tribe not of a state: *rex Francorum*, not *rex Franciae*, king of the Angles, or the Saxons, not the king of England. The practice of recognising the particular laws and special customs of individual peoples, certain parts of the country, local districts, was carried on into much later times. It was judicially laid down in Nuremberg in 1455 that when a Franconian was being declared an outlaw, the judge must stand near the bridge on the Neuenstadt road on Franconian soil; he must stand on Swabian soil beyond the stone bridge on the Onolzbach road if a Swabian was being outlawed; in the case of a Bavarian, the judge must stand in front of the Frauentor on Bavarian soil; and if the criminal was a Saxon the judge had to stand before the Tiergartentor on the Erlangen road.[28]

Lacking internal coordination as it did, medieval law was readily susceptible of many different interpretations and gave rise to many conflicting claims. The word *law* was synonymous with *justice*; but in point of fact medieval law was not directed towards establishing the 'truth' in our sense of the word. What was 'true' was what was 'proved' in court by means of oaths and sworn statements and the rigorous observance of all the ceremonial steps prescribed by custom. Credence was placed on oaths, rituals, trial by ordeal or single combat rather than in material proof or evidence, on the grounds that truth inheres in the oath, and a solemn act of this nature cannot be carried out against the will of God. The slightest deviation from the accepted formula, the failure of one party to adhere to every detail of the procedure, identified that party as the guilty one, for God does not allow the guilty to triumph over the innocent. The truth cannot be made manifest except via the precise and inviolate formalism of the judicial process.

All of this can be traced back to the barbarian age. But it would be wrong to see in the ritualised nature of medieval law no more than a survival of the preceding age. Throughout the Middle Ages, the retention of customs and procedures genuinely inherited from pre-feudal law is accompanied by the growth and spread of many new forms of ritual and ceremony and by the emergence of new formulas and oaths. This is not simply because the archaic stage lingered on, but rather is implicit in the very nature of medieval society, which was built up on the premise of regulated behaviour on the part of all its members. Informal, unrestrained, unconventional behaviour is not typical of the Middle Ages. One took up one's allotted position in society and tried to behave in keeping with it. A man's role in society set the scene for his behaviour, leaving little room for innovation or unconventionality. Hence the semantic density of the social behaviour of medieval people: every action has symbolical meaning, every action must be performed in the approved way and follow the generally accepted model. All sorts of things – sword, spear, hammer, club, chair, gauntlet, head-dress, key, etc. – have, over and above their pragmatic use, a symbolical meaning which is called upon in court and other juridical proceedings.

The earliest legal texts of medieval Europe are the *leges barbarorum*, the law codes of the barbarian tribes which settled in the territory of the former Roman Empire. Ancient custom is the rule here, though it is only partially fixed in the codes themselves. The few innovations introduced into these codes are also treated therein as 'custom'. Certain customs enshrined in the codes had effectively lost their currency – but veneration for the past, and belief in the sanctity of custom nevertheless dictated their retention, even though they were sometimes in clear contradiction with later norms. Henceforth laws issued by medieval rulers often took the form either of 'amendments of the law' – that is to say, the registration of norms which, it was held, had existed earlier but which had not been entered in the legal codes – or of 'purification of the law', that is to say, the removal of distortions and 'human invention'. Thus, even innovation in the legal sphere had a conservative function. As a result, traditional law became multi-tiered and overgrown with additions; the old coalesced with the new.

In their effort to restore law to its pristine purity the people of the Middle Ages were guided by the concept of ideal law – of law, that is, as it ought to be, in keeping with their ideas of justice. In pursuit of this ideal they sometimes had recourse to forgery. But forgery in the Middle Ages was not always deliberate falsification undertaken for nothing more than selfish gain. Things were much more complicated than that. In 'pious fraud' (*pia fraus*), there was an element of self-deception. The monk who 'corrected' the text of a book of donation while copying it, did so out of his conviction that it was simply not possible for the land mentioned in the deed not to be donated to a holy place (a monastery); for it would be unjust, and *ipso facto* impossible, for it to be possessed by an impious layman. In the monk's eyes this was not forgery but a triumph of justice over wrong. A forged deed crediting some ancient monarch with donation of land to a holy place was seen as doing no more than paying this ruler his due – for he 'ought' to have acted in this way! At the same time, this was seen as a verification of the generally accepted principle that in so far as there was a right to possess land, it could only be inherited from ancient times: entitlement must have a pedigree. In the same way, false evidence was not infrequently given out of a conviction that 'justice' was best served by a nudge in the right direction.

The function of documents was to express the highest truth – justice in the ideal meaning of the term – and not simply record chance facts. For truth was enshrined not in the coarse facts of everyday existence but in that right view of things which was above all the province of the church. The Pseudo-Isidorian *Decretals*, substantiating the supreme authority of the Roman church over Western Europe and ascribing to the Emperor Constantine a corresponding grant in benefit of the Bishop of Rome, were forgeries – but forgeries which expressed an 'ideal reality': papal hegemony in the medieval world.[29]

Speaking about the falsification of documents in the Middle Ages, Marc Bloch points to the paradox that veneration of the past should impel the medieval mind to show the past not as it was but as it ought to have been.[30] Individually both clerical and lay institutions had recourse to forgery in their efforts to establish, at whatever cost, their great age and, hence their legal integrity and respectability. The University of Paris was able to date its beginnings from the reign of Charlemagne; Oxford claimed King Alfred, Cambridge the legendary King Arthur as its founder. Inability to think historically led to these documents being drawn up in contemporary style, not in the style of the age to which they allegedly belonged.[31]

The medieval chroniclers never tire of proclaiming that truth is their main aim and the invariable guideline of their exposition. Yet their accounts are packed with the products of the imagination – to say nothing of the fact that much is simply passed over in silence. 'Truth' meant something very different from the scientific 'truth' on which so much reliance is placed today: to the medieval mind, truth had to correspond to the ideal norms, it had to be in conformity, not with the actual course of earthly events, but with the higher reality of God's predestined plan.[32]

Then again, in a society based on the principle of fidelity to family, kindred, lord, etc., truth could not have a value independent of the concrete interests of the group. Fidelity to the 'truth' took second place to fidelity to the ruler, or to faith in the Lord. Truth was, so to speak, 'anthropomorphous'.

The history of the Middle Ages is full of pretenders and usurpers claiming to be lawful rulers or their descendants. If these impostors were, by and large, accepted by the people at their face value, this was due in the first place to the hopes nourished by the downtrodden and enslaved masses that a just and righteous monarch would appear, who would improve their condition and liberate them from their exploiters and oppressors. Their hopes made them gullible. But it is perhaps unfair to dismiss all these pretenders as tricksters pure and simple, moved by nothing more than self-interest. Often they themselves seem to have been deluded into believing either that they had some sort of case, however shaky, for making the claims they did, or that inspiration 'from on high' was impelling them to take up a mission they could not refuse. The religious mood of a period has perhaps never been more favourable to the emergence of all sorts of prophets, popular leaders and divine messengers.

People lived in a climate of marvels and wonders, which were accepted as everyday reality. The ability to think for oneself was as yet comparatively weakly developed; the collective mind dominated the individual one. The belief in images, words, symbols, was limitless and taken uncritically for granted – circumstances in which forgery and falsification found a natural habitat.[33] The figment was hardly distinguished from the reality, and what seemed 'due' or 'fitting' was readily preferred to what merely 'was'.

Medieval people were very credulous. Tales about animals that spoke, possession by evil spirits, visions and miraculous cures; reverence for relics and other holy objects, the tendency to explain earthly happenings by the configurations of the heavenly bodies and supernatural phenomena – none of this is surprising if we remember the extent to which the medieval mind was ruled by religion, the ignorance and illiteracy in which the great mass of the population was plunged, the total absence of objective scientific thinking and of orderly sources of information. The hard lot of the downtrodden peasantry inevitably fostered hopes of miraculous help from above. Medieval people believed not only in the Day of Judgment, which would come 'at the end of time' and at which everyone would be rewarded or punished according to his or her deeds, but also in more immediate divine wrath or recompense in this world.[34] It was not marvels and wonders that had to be explained, but their absence.[35]

But we must not assume that there were no limits to credulity. Not every miracle was given credence, and a boundary between the true and the false, between the natural and the supernatural, was certainly recognised.[36] The medieval assumption was that while normally the law of causation operated, in certain circumstances it could be 'suspended' and a miracle could then take place. The theologians repeatedly emphasised that the ability to perform miracles was not what made a saint a saint, and was not even the sole proof of his saintliness, but this was not something likely to appeal to the medieval mind. A saint who did not perform miracles might well be venerated; but from the point of view of the man who was little versed in the niceties of theology and merely wanted a quick return on his pious outlay, it was a pure waste of time to do obeisance to his relics or make a donation to his church or monastery.

[179]

Neither the concept nor the practice of law in the Middle Ages can be understood in isolation from the real social and political conditions in which it took shape and in which it operated. The feudal state cannot really be compared with the modern state; the analogy is false. The ruling class in the Middle Ages shows as a rule no tendency towards cohesion. The feudal lords forming it were, along with their groups and factions, in a permanent state of rivalry among themselves and of 'permanent revolt' against the royal power. The sovereign was not synonymous with the power nor was he its only bearer, since every feudal lord of the slightest importance tried his best – not always without success – to concentrate power over his people in his own hands and to rule them himself. Hence the state was not centralised or unified; there was no organised administration. The unity of the state, in so far as it existed, was embodied in the person of the sovereign. If he was to possess real power, the monarch had to have at his disposal the same means as his feudal lords had – private forces.

The distinction between 'public' and 'private' was not consistently adhered to in the Middle Ages. The state property was not distinguished from the patrimony of the monarch; the king was sovereign over all his subjects, while at the same time some of them could become his private dependants, to be under his protection. Kings and princes regarded their accession to power as an act of personal succession, inherited from their ancestors. The inheritance procedure regarding landed property or allods, as set out in the Salic Law, was subsequently to become the procedure for succession to the throne in France: the Salic decision that the paternal portion should pass only to the male issue was interpreted in such a way that the female issue of French kings were excluded from the line of succession to the throne. The power of a medieval ruler was real in so far as it was coextensive with his seigneurial rights. Relations of vassalage and of private dependence were intertwined with one's status as a subject. Magna Carta is the most important document in the history of English government, but essentially it is no more than a regulation of relations between the king – the supreme seigneur – and his direct vassals, the barons.

At the same time, seigneurs discharged public functions in their own name, for property and power were indissolubly linked; great landed property was *ipso facto* power (the landowner ruled the land and the vassals who lived on it), while power conferred property rights (the possession of political, juridical and military prerogatives implied the transformation of the area over which these prerogatives extended, into the personal possession of the person exercising these prerogatives).

No clear distinction was made between ideal and positive, i.e. law as ideal, complete and perfect justice, and law as it was actually applied in practice or set out in ordinances and codes. Hence, people's actions had to be guided not only by actual laws and prescriptions but also by norms of conduct which were nowhere codified but which nevertheless corresponded to the medieval feeling for justice and for law and order. Medieval law as written was fragmentary and full of gaps; it was completely unsystematic, many areas of life being juridical no-man's-land. The most important relations in feudal society were regulated by local custom, which had either never been written down at all or was only partially committed to writing at a much later stage. If we compare Carolingian legislation with the legislative activity of Western European rulers in the period of mature feudalism, the extreme poverty of the latter becomes at once evident. Hardly any area of human affairs remained unaffected by the legislative enterprise of the Carolingians, who saw themselves as the heirs of the Roman emperors, continuing the great tradition of the ancient law-givers; whereas the feudal system remained virtually without a written legal code. Whether it was the election or the succession to power of a prince, the exact order to be observed in the inheritance of fiefs, the extent and nature of vassalage services, the delimitation of the juridical rights of ruler and subject, relations between church and state – these and many other equally crucial questions affecting the working of the feudal system were never unambiguously defined in law. All these questions were settled in *ad hoc* fashion as and when a dispute had to be settled or an uncertainty cleared up. In place of unambiguous settlement by law, binding on all interested parties and setting a precedent for the future, it was increasingly to custom, which varied according to place, time, person and many other decisive factors, that appeal was made in the day-to-day handling of feudal juridical problems.

In circumstances such as these, the 'law of the strong' came into its own. What could not be satisfactorily settled in court on the basis of juridical proceedings was settled by the sword and civil strife. Powerful lords were not over-inclined to take their affairs to law, and either had recourse to violence when they could not be certain of a favourable decision, or simply set up their own courts. Single combat, war, blood feud were the invariable concomitants of feudal law. But the current view of the Middle Ages as the age of the 'law of the fist', the age when things were settled by arbitrary force in place of law and custom, is unfounded. It is a view which arose at a time when emergent bourgeois law was taking over from an increasingly discredited medieval law which could no longer meet all the demands made on it.

There was certainly plenty of violence in medieval society, but it was not a society built on violence, nor did the extra-economic constraints which played such a major role in feudal production relations reduce simply to violence. The ruling classes in any society resort to violence when they are faced with the necessity of bringing the masses to heel, just as the oppressed meet violence with violence when they are no longer able to put up with being exploited. Naturally, the ruling class in a feudal society – the armed and pugnacious nobility – was particularly prone to resort to violence. But it is equally true that any society feels the need for law, for the juridical formulation of realistic and practicable laws, and this need was felt as keenly in the Middle Ages as in any other historical period.

Obsessed as it was with tradition, feudal society was a peculiarly fertile field for *de facto* social relations to assume the halo of antiquity and take on the force of law. We have already seen how its antiquity was held to be the most important characteristic of medieval law, so much so that even innovations were regarded as really restorations of ancient if unrecorded ordinances. Renovation was understood as restoration, progress as a return to the past; for only that which had existed from time immemorial carried moral force and incontrovertible authority. This attitude was typical not only of the sphere of law but of literally all other social spheres, in production relations as in theology, in philosophy and in family matters. Development and change were inevitably construed in such terms as *reformatio*, *regeneratio*, *restauratio*, *revocatio*. The ideal state was seen as having existed in the past, and what mattered was either to restore it or to return to it. Unconventional behaviour, a taste for novelty, for innovation, are not typical of this society. One distinguished oneself not by departing from example but by sticking to it as closely as possible. For this, a rigid framework of convention was necessary, within which one always knew exactly how to behave in a given situation; and in the construction of this framework, in the ritualisation of all sides of social behaviour, custom and law played an enormous part. They did not simply shape relationships – they very largely constituted these relationships, providing not only a ready-made schema for general use but also detailed scenarios for use in particular situations.

If medieval government is not noted for its legislative activity, this is due in part to the prevalence of customary law. All aspects of life were governed by custom; custom was all-embracing, and precisely because of this it was impossible to set it down in any sort of integrated and codified form. Each locality lived by its own customs, which were different from those of its neighbours. By its very nature, customary law is local law, and this renders it all the more intractable to unambiguous fixation in written form. The many codes of custom, 'mirrors', tracts, fall far short of an exhaustive account of customary law. The most that could be achieved was to establish precedents – concrete instances which would have to be taken into subsequent account when an identical or closely similar situation arose. But it was not simply a question of the impossibility of getting the whole intractable mass of customary law reduced to codified form. Medieval society was very largely an illiterate society. The peasantry and most of the feudal gentry could not read or write. For them, written law had little meaning. Hence, even when many legal ordinances had been codified in writing, practical

[183]

conduct was guided less by the letter of the law than by custom, by recollection of how people used to act in similar circumstances and by what one's moral conscience suggested as the proper course of action.

Here we touch on the main difference between custom and law. Once laid down as law, a norm became immutable: henceforth, the letter of the law would have to be rigorously obeyed. The law freed itself from the circumstances which had given rise to it and took on its own independent existence. This is the essential point: by acquiring written form, law became 'alienated' from its begetters, who thereafter could no longer influence it or amend it; its interpretation would now be the exclusive monopoly of the judiciary and of the ruling power – in no case of the community, which nevertheless would be obligatorily subjected to it. Custom, on the other hand, being unwritten, had not cut the umbilical cord linking it to the community, to groups and strata of real people; and while it appeared to those affected by it not to change, imperceptibly it did change in answer to new needs as they arose. Custom is not stored up in people's memories in unchanging form; it is created by people who may not be aware of this, and remain convinced that this is how it was 'long ago'. There was no 'alienation' of customary law from the community; it remained a creative source. Medieval law was *ratio vivens*, not *ratio scripta*. Whenever customary law had to be invoked, its interpretation was guided, almost unconsciously, less by what one remembered than by the real needs of the case, the *de facto* interests of the parties.

Thus, while inferior to written law as an articulated, systematic, unambiguous and perfected instrument, custom was a creative factor in medieval law, a means whereby a wide cross-section of medieval society could share in the interpretation and implementation of law. The legislator had to reckon with customary law which was obligatory on all, and which even the ruler could not change. The prestige of the monarch was safeguarded by the doctrine that all law was protected and preserved in his person. In practice, however, of the two systems of medieval law – written legislation and unwritten custom – customary law was the more important and the more directly applicable to the problems of real life. Misgivings *vis-à-vis* 'unheard-of novelties' had their effect on official legislation as well, and this left room for customary law to continue to develop under cover of traditional and unchanging social order.

If it is one-sided to dismiss the Middle Ages as an age with no law but that of the 'mailed fist', it is equally superficial to see therein unrelieved lawlessness and arbitrariness. Feudal society was built up on dominion and subordination. No one in medieval society was completely free in all respects, for everyone was subject to a lord. If we are to understand the exact meaning of the relationship of dominion and subordination in feudal society, we have to be clear about the real content of such concepts as freedom and dependence.

The social relations of the Middle Ages are above all interpersonal relations. Relations between people are not yet screened by relations involving things, commodities and other material values, as is the case in bourgeois society. Precapitalistic societies are marked by direct, immediate relations between people; the social body has not yet been affected by the mechanism of 'alienation', which becomes all-powerful in a society geared to the production of goods. In this latter stage, relations between people are concealed behind relations between the goods which represent people in the marketplace; as Marx puts it, relations are then 'fetishised'. As they became reified, human relations lose their immediacy, the individual is replaced by his goods, and his personal qualities play no role whatever in these relations. 'Commodity fetishism' was unknown to the Middle Ages. In particular, the value of this or that article was not determined by the market, or by the labour input; everything bore its maker's imprint, its properties were linked to the personality of its creator. In medieval society goods and money had not combined to dictate the shape of social relations. The role of such a regulator was played by law.

When we speak of the interpersonal nature of social relations in the Middle Ages – particularly in the earlier period – we have to remember that the human personality was not yet individualised: it was still very closely connected to the collective, the group, of which it was indeed an inseparable part.[37] It was the victory won by a market economy, the consolidation of the rule of money, that was later to destroy the system of interpersonal relations, free the individual from the corporate integument and confer freedom of personality. The personality gains foothold and takes over in a society which denies the personal character of social relations.

Medieval social relations are shot through and through with the principle of mutuality, of reciprocity, which played no small role in the forging of these relations. The vassal finds himself a lord. The links thus set up between the two are not natural, as they were in barbarian society, but purely social (although the organic groupings either retain their previous identity, e.g. the family, or are retained for a long time, e.g. kinship relations under feudalism). In addition, in contradistinction to the collective ties of barbarian society, feudal ties are built up on an individual basis. The ties between lord and vassal, between protector and ward, are constructed on the assumption that, in some form or other, both sides have accepted certain obligations. The vassal undertook to serve his master, to help him in every way, and to be personally faithful to him at all times. On his side, the lord undertook to protect the vassal, defend him, and to treat him justly. Entering upon this relationship, the two exchanged solemn oaths and performed the ritual act of homage which rendered their bond indissoluble. Any infringement of the feudal treaty by one party liberated the other from his obligation to it. A poor helpless man who found a patron for himself asked him for protection and support, promising in return to be obedient in all things; the patron undertook to feed and protect his client. A peasant giving up his rights to a property in favour of an ecclesiastical or lay magnate and seeking dependence on the latter, was entitled by law to expect to be protected by his new patron, and to expect that the landowner would release him from having to undertake public service on behalf of the state. The real content of the relationship between lord and dependant consisted as a rule in the exploitation of the latter by the former, and the relationship was regulated by the principle of reciprocity of obligations and services agreed by the two sides.

In contradistinction to the doctrine of the unconditional obedience of subjects to the divinely appointed authorities, with its emphasis on the role played by one's duty or *service* instead of on the *person* performing that role, feudal law is based on the relationship between two *persons* who admittedly stand on different rungs of the hierarchic ladder, but who are in identical fashion included in the scope of the law, and who are individually responsible for the fulfilment of their obligations as undertaken. In the same way, the rule of the king is no longer founded on the unilateral 'descent' of power from him to his subjects, but on cooperation between him and his vassals, whose relationship to him is a personal one.

It is hardly necessary to point out that the principle of reciprocity is far more readily identifiable in the relationship between knight and baron than in the relations between land-owner and peasant; but in all cases the relationship is based on a definite personal bond. It is in this sense that the feudal dependence of the peasant is radically different from the dependence of the slave, who was treated by his owner as a thing, something to order about and make use of, but never as a person.

The man of the Middle Ages could not be turned into a disposable object like the slave in antiquity, principally because he was not an isolated unit, like a cow, which could be easily 'alienated'. Medieval man is invariably a member of a group to which he is very closely bound. From top to bottom medieval society is corporate. Associations of vassals, knightly orders, monastic brotherhoods and Catholic clergy; town communes, merchant and trade guilds; defensive unions, religious brotherhoods; village communities, kind-reds, patriarchal and individual family groupings – these and similar collectives spliced individuals together in closely knit microcosms which gave protection and help, and which were built up on a basis of mutual exchange of services and support. Some of these groupings were organic in nature – a man was born into one, lived and worked within it, satisfying all his social needs within the radius defined by it. Other groups were less closely knit and did not completely absorb the personality of the members. But in one way or another, medieval man was always related to a corporate body. The ties binding people within a group were much stronger than the ties between groups or between individuals belonging to different groups; social ties in medieval society were above all ties within groups. Each group had its own regulations – constitution, statutes, and code of behaviour either written or traditional, which was strictly binding on all the members of the collective. These regulations were not imposed on the collective by any higher power or authority; they were worked out by the group itself on the principle of general agreement and self-rule (or were borrowed from a similar corporate body as, for example, urban law). In the sphere of corporate relations there took shape the principle of representation, something completely alien to the concept of the unlimited power of the ruler.

Each type of social group had its moral attitudes, its socio-political ideals. The group to which an individual belonged gave him his occupation and guaranteed him a certain life-style; in many cases it also ensured his material existence. But over and above all this, the group recommended or rather prescribed the way he behaved, the way he thought and the way he reacted to things. The corporate social structure of the Middle Ages was at the same time a mental conformism.

The corporate body repudiates non-traditional behaviour on the part of its members, anything that runs counter to its accepted standards. Those who break the rules are subject to moral censure, are punished and even expelled from the group. In this context, the exact manner of the deviation from the norm is not too important. The craftsman who produces an article better in quality than is normative in his guild, or who works more efficiently or quicker than his fellows, is punished, just as is the negligent craftsman. It is not the threat of competition that occasions these punitive measures but simply the fact of deviation from the accepted standard.

The conclusion suggests itself – the corporate nature of social life in medieval Europe prevented the development of human individuality; it arrested initiative, robbing people of the chance of opening up new ways of life, and subjecting the individual mind to the collective mind of the group. The guilds and other corporate bodies generated by the whole structure of material existence in the Middle Ages and the division of labour inherent in the feudal system used their influence to strengthen the prevailing relations within society. These bodies represented a form or mould in which society was much more likely to reproduce itself in its own image than to change or develop. They conserved those production levels that had been attained, and discouraged innovatory ideas among their members.

All this is true; yet we have to see the other side of corporate life in the Middle Ages. The guilds and other corporate bodies did not all enjoy equal rights; but they were constituted on the principle of the equality of their members. The corporate group united people who not only belonged to one profession or were engaged in the same sort of work but who were also equal in socio-legal status. Within the confines of such a group there were no master–subject relations as there were in the vertical scale uniting feudal lord and vassals, who belonged to different socio-legal orders and to different groupings – some belonging to knightly orders, others to the barons who held estates immediately from the Crown, etc. Social ties within the corporate group are not 'vertical' but 'horizontal'. By requiring its members to observe its discipline, to live and even think according to its sole example, the corporation nourished them at the same time, in a spirit of equality, of mutual respect for the rights of all members of the group. It united them in defence of these rights and of the group's general interests against any possible interference or encroachment from outside. The principle of the equality of the members of the corporation remained its crucial index even when it was not observed in practice. Guild unity could be ruptured by the emergence of differentiation among the craftsmen, just as the unity of citizens in the town communes could; but the idea of equality stuck in their minds and served as a rallying point for its restoration. Equality was never quite reached in the Middle Ages, but the gap between the ideal and the reality was never allowed to weaken the ideal.

Thus we see that the social structure of feudal society in Western Europe was characterised by two contradictory but functionally associated organisational principles: on the one hand, the relations between lord and vassal (dominion and subordination) and on the other the corporate relationships. Masters and subordinates formed part of corporate groups which defended their rights and guaranteed their specific social and juridical status. By leaving no room for the free development of the human personality, the corporation created the conditions for its existence within certain prescribed limits: allowing it, that is, an area of action, a radius which did not run counter to the interests and aims of the collective. Medieval law reflects this duality: rejecting novelty as reprehensible and even criminal, it defended the status which a man enjoyed by virtue of his adherence to a given social group. The corporation was a sort of nursery where the self-respect and dignity of its individual members were inculcated. The man who relied on the support of his fellows, and who felt himself equal to them, learnt to respect himself and those like him. People were bound together in their group not by fear or by deference to higher authority but emotionally by feelings of fellowship and of mutual respect.

If we are to gain more than a superficial understanding of the social structure of medieval Europe we have to take into account both the 'vertical' link of lord and subject, and the 'horizontal' link provided by the corporate body. Individually, the vassal was subordinate to his lord; but he received his status from the group, from the socio-legal instance, the corporation, and his lord and master had to bear this status in mind.

The role of the corporate society in the development of the personality becomes clearer if we compare the corporative structure of Western Europe with the comparatively individualised social and ideological relations obtaining in the Byzantine Empire. In Byzantium, the ruling class was not united as it was in the West in groups of lords and vassals, and it was easier for upstarts to move upwards from lower to higher social strata. In theory, the individual in the Eastern Roman Empire had a better chance of rising in the world and improving his socio-legal status. But closer study of this Byzantine 'individualism' will convince us that it had little to do with the genuine development of human individuality.

Byzantium knew nothing of the feudal treaty, the loyalty of the vassal or the group solidarity of peers. In place of the 'horizontal' ties linking people of the same status, there prevailed the 'vertical' linkage from the sovereign downwards to the subjects.[38] Byzantine society was marked not by mutual assistance and exchange of services but by the unilateral and servile dependence of the lowly on their masters. The most powerful personages, the princes and the very rich, who had attained high state office, were completely devoid of rights and unprotected by law in relation to the emperor, who could deprive them at will of their property, their rank or even of their lives just as he could at will elevate any man of the people and turn a vulgar upstart into the highest official in the land. It is highly significant that the power of the monarch (Basileus) to punish and exploit his subjects to an unlimited degree was never questioned in Byzantium; it was simply accepted as the natural order of things. It is quite impossible to imagine anything like Magna Carta – a legal compromise between the monarch and his vassals – in a Byzantine setting. The 'individualism' of the Byzantine aristocrat was the individualism of the lackey looking for a career and a chance to enrich himself, devoid of personal dignity, cringing before his superiors and ready to demean himself for a gratuity.[39]

At a reception given by the Byzantine emperor one of the knights of Lorraine taking part in the First Crusade was outraged to see that 'one man could sit while so many great warriors had to stand', and proceeded to place himself ostentatiously on the throne.[40] An example of the uncouthness of Western courtiers amid the niceties of Byzantine ceremonial? No doubt; but here we also see the personal dignity of the knight, something which was retained even in the presence of the monarch, the *'primus inter pares'* – not the master among slaves.

It might look as though only one personality really existed in the Byzantine Empire – the sacred person of the Basileus himself. But the fact is that it was the imperial office itself that was considered sacred, the office and everything connected with it, while one Byzantine emperor in two was removed by violence, mutilated or murdered. Even while he was in power – apparently, total power – he was the slave of the most complicated court ceremonial. The subjects who prostrated themselves before the emperor one minute would betray him the next; there was no trace in this relationship of knightly loyalty or personal commitment. From top to bottom they were all slaves. Hence, the Byzantine attitude to law was also totally different from that of the West. Byzantium is distinguished by possession of the most substantial of the medieval law codes – the Code of Justinian, unifying Roman law – and by a total absence of any feeling for law and order, any regard for law as the guarantee of the observance of human rights. The principle of 'whatever pleases the emperor is law' is the principle of autocratic lawlessness. Autocratic rule and human individuality are incompatibles. Servility became established as the behavioural norm: the result was arbitrariness and despotism, hypocrisy and 'Byzantinism'.

The West had its share of lawlessness and perfidy, but throughout the Middle Ages in Europe it was never forgotten that the monarch must obey the law set over and above him. The royal power was not in a position to rule if it ignored the interests of the corporate estates; on the contrary, it convoked these orders and sought their support in all complicated political situations. The corporate nature of the feudal state is explicable first and foremost by the existence of powerful and influential corporate groups, whose members were united by sharing status and equality of rights.

It can be seen that the relation between the individual and the corporation was contradictory in the extreme. While rigorously delimiting the area in which human personality might develop, and channelling it into a code of regulations, the corporate group at the same time helped its members to value their human dignity as individuals, their solidarity as members of a group, and the equality they shared. True, it was a relative degree of equality, valid only within the confines of the group, but it was a necessary step on the road

[192]

to the recognition, at a much later date, of the equality before the law of all citizens.

No less contradictory and idiosyncratic in content is the medieval concept of freedom. 'Freedom' in its medieval meaning is something quite different both from the ancient and the modern concept. It was not simply the antithesis of servitude and dependence. No one was completely independent in medieval society. The peasant was subject to his master, but even the feudal lord was the vassal of a greater lord. A proprietor was master on his land, but it was a fief given him for service and obedience. The coalescence of seigneurial rights and the obligations of vassalage is characteristic for every member of the feudal hierarchy right up to the monarch who heads it: for in a sense he too is a vassal, having taken the oath of fealty to emperor and pope, or he regards himself as a vassal of God. Possession of complete and final sovereignty is unknown in this society. Every member of feudal society is dependent on someone, even if the dependence is no more than nominal. At the same time, significant strata of this society regarded themselves as juridically free. Hence, freedom was not construed as the antithesis of dependence; freedom and dependence were not mutually exclusive. On the contrary, such concepts as 'free dependence', 'free service', 'free obedience', etc., had real meaning.[41] And just as freedom did not exclude dependence, so too dependence did not imply the absence of all rights.

A wide spectrum of degrees of freedom and dependence is in fact characteristic of medieval society. No one limited definition of freedom is universally valid. Freedom and dependence are relative states, not absolutes. One's freedom increases or decreases depending on the nature of one's rights. One and the same man can be at one and the same time free and unfree: dependent on his feudal lord and free with regard to all other men. It was difficult and often impossible to define the status of one or another man or of a social order unambiguously and definitively; the juridical categories were fluid and variable, and the medieval courts were always having to take up cases involving personal rights. Definitions of dependence changed in the course of time; for example over a long period, it was impossible to establish who belonged to the class of serfs, as the dependent peasants were called in France. The fact that in Western Europe the peasant was not free in relation to his landlord did not mean that he had no rights at all. The dependent peasant who carried out heavy labour service and paid his taxes in money or kind, who had no right to leave his lord and was juridically subject to the lord, was nevertheless not in a state of total servitude, nor was his dependence regarded as arbitrary. The lord of the manor was obliged to safeguard certain rights enjoyed by such a peasant; he had to take into account those customs which limited the extent to which he could exploit the peasant, and which defined the other claims which the lord could make on the peasant's labour and person. The lords had to do, not with individual peasants but with collectives, whole villages or districts, which enabled the peasants to offer resistance in cases where the lords tried to depart from custom and step up the exploitation of the peasant. It is significant that one of the most usual and widespread forms of peasant resistance against their lords was the appeal to law; going to court to have a disputed custom investigated and restored, to have documents verified, was the form of resistance which stressed the highest social value of the Middle Ages – law.[42] It would be historically inaccurate to draw any sort of parallel between the dependent peasants in the Western European feudal system and the Eastern European serfs of the sixteenth to eighteenth century. The total absence of rights which was a characteristic of the Russian serf, and by virtue of which he was hardly distinguishable from a slave, was something very different from the specific juridical situation enjoyed by the dependent peasant in Western feudalism.

The legal treatment of the status of human personality had a strong religious component. The doctrine that all men were equal before God and that Christ died to save all men spiritually, was combined with the church's teaching that inequality on earth was the result of the Fall. Since true freedom, as the church taught, could only be found in heaven, it was up to everyone to bear earthly adversity and injustice in a spirit of meekness and humility. 'Is not every man born to labour as a bird to flight? Does not almost every man serve either under the name of lord or serf? And is not

he who is called a serf in the Lord, the Lord's freeman; and
he who is called free, is he not Christ's serf? So if all men
labour and serve, and the serf is a freeman of the Lord, and
the freeman is a serf of Christ, what does it matter apart
from pride – either to the world or to God – who is called
a serf and who is called free?' in such terms did St Anselm
of Canterbury seek to justify inequality in society.[43]

Christianity, which had started out in the late Roman
Empire as a denial of and opposition to the establishment,
soon altered its stance to one of conformity with the prevailing forms of social exploitation. In feudal society the church
developed its theory of the organic structure of society, in
which each member is an indispensable part of the whole,
and must, as such, carry out his allotted task. Parallel with
the feudal system there evolved the ecclesiastical doctrine of
the three-fold functional structure of society, consisting of
ordered strata (*ordines*): the clergy (*oratores*) whose task it is
to care for the spiritual health of the kingdom, the knights
(*bellatores*, *pugnatores*) who defend it, and the ploughmen,
the labourers (*aratores*, *laboratores*) who feed it. Any
infringement of this harmonious reciprocity could bring
about the most disastrous consequences for the whole
organism. 'The house of God is three-fold', wrote Adalberon, bishop of Laon (late tenth/early eleventh century),
'but belief is one. Therefore some pray, others fight, and
others again labour; altogether they form three orders, and
their separation is not to be endured.'[44]*

Together with the doctrine of the moral value of suffering
and passive endurance, medieval Christianity developed a
doctrine of freedom. In contradistinction to the pagan gods,
who were subordinated to an implacable destiny, the Christian God was entirely free, with no limits to his freedom;
freedom indeed was the token of his omnipotence. To this
free God corresponds man, endowed by his creator with free
will: he is free to take the path of righteousness, and he is
free to depart from it and take the path of sin and evil. That
freedom which is God's prerogative becomes a virtue of man.
As a result of this freedom every human being is in himself
the arena for the struggle whose outcome is salvation or

---

* Asterisks indicate addenda. See p. 315.

damnation.[45] Christ's act of redemption confronts every individual with the problem of choice and the free fulfilment of his moral duty. By giving priority to the salvation of the individual soul and by taking freedom of will as a cardinal tenet, Christianity put a higher value on the human personality, which it represented as in direct and immediate relationship with God.

As we have already pointed out, this relationship was regarded in the Middle Ages as a service. If man served God faithfully and was obedient to him in all things, he would attain freedom. Those faithful to God, those who believed in him with all their soul, would be free; but those who persisted in their pride and were recalcitrant to God's will, only imagined themselves to be free – in fact they were unfree, the slaves of their passions on earth and condemned to the torments of hell in the life to come. In this sense the 'free bondage in the Lord' (*libera servitus apud Dominum*) was opposed to 'the servile freedom of the world' (*servilis mundi libertas*). Only the faithful servant enjoys true freedom in the highest sense. St Augustine had already distinguished between the *vera libertas* of the devout and the *falsa libertas* of the sinful. Augustine links the concepts of 'justice', 'peace' and 'subordination', since only submission to God and unity with him can serve as a guarantee of peace and justice on earth. Thus on the teleological plane as well we see an approximation and coalescence in sense between the concepts of 'freedom', 'service' and 'fidelity'.

In the Middle Ages, fidelity was the most important Christian virtue. In both the courtly epic and the courtly romances, the main hero is the faithful, valiant vassal who performs countless exploits of derring-do. He even overshadows the king and pushes him into second place. In the *Chanson de Roland* Roland is a far more active and lively figure than Charlemagne. In later works the monarch is allotted an even more passive role: Charlemagne turns into a sick old man, Arthur snoozes at his Round Table, and the heroic principle is completely embodied in the faithful vassal.[46]

Not freedom and dependence but service and fidelity are the central socio-political and moral-religious values in medieval Christianity. These values are treated in very similar fashion by theology and by law, for, after all, law was regarded as part of Christian morality. The dialectical relation between freedom and unfreedom had both a speculative and a practical sense. Law was a global and all-embracing entity to which all things were subjected. It formed the general link binding people together. But this link was not the same in degree for all people. The unfree were bound to a lesser degree by the prescriptions of law, the free to a greater degree; in fact, the more free someone was, the more privileges he enjoyed, the more strictly he had to abide by the law and the greater the weight of moral responsibility he carried for exact observance of the law. The feudal lord enjoyed a far wider range of privileges than did the dependent peasant, but precisely because of this he was bound to observe a code of behaviour which required him to submit to a whole series of restrictions which were invalid for commoners. 'Noblesse oblige'.

In this respect the distinction between the unfree and base-born on the one hand, and the free and noble-born on the other, lies in the fact that the former were not free to choose their situation or their behaviour; their birth, their blood determined that for them. The free-born man, however, could opt to become a knight, the vassal of a noble seigneur, to whom he would swear the oath of fealty; he would voluntarily take upon himself certain specific obligations, including observance of the code of chivalry with all its rules of ritual and ceremonial behaviour. By this act of free will, the nobleman consciously recognises the law, just as a priest deliberately and at the dictate of his own conscience seeks ordination. The free man lives by his own will and sets his own limits, while the unfree man lives by another's will, in submission not to the law but to the will of this other. The hierarchy of privileges, of freedom, of dependence and of servitude was also a hierarchy of services. A vassal's service to his lord found moral sanction and enhancement in the analogy of the Christian's 'free service' to the Creator.

We see then that man's freedom was not denied in feudal practice. But it was a very particular kind of freedom, quite different from 'freedom' as understood in modern times. A man's rights in the Middle Ages, as a matter of fact, were not his individual rights. If he was to make use of his rights, a man had to be a member of a corporate group or corporation from which he acquired these rights; and it was the corporate body which protected these rights from being eroded or ignored. Outside the social group, a man ceased to be a member of society; he became an outcast, defenceless and devoid of rights.

It was not only juridical rights that accrued to the individual in so far as he belonged to this or that social group; his professional skills could only be practised and his mental qualities expressed within the framework of the collective. Essentially a man's social status, his ability to work, his ideology, were not his own personal qualities but a property of the corporate group.

Feudal society was a society of clearly specified social roles assigned and fixed by custom or by law. The individual was bound in the most intimate way with his social role, and it was his performance in this role that enabled him to make use of the rights accruing to the incumbent of such a role. More, his individuality was very largely determined by the role he played in society. Not only his rights were corporate; so were his inner nature, the way he thought and the way he behaved. Medieval man *was* a knight, a priest or a peasant – not someone *behaving as* a knight, a priest or a peasant. The social order of the Middle Ages saw itself and accepted itself as the natural order of things as ordained by God.

The corporation shaped the individual. From a modern individualistic point of view, the medieval group stunted the development of the personality. But in the Middle Ages – up to a certain point, at least – this was not recognised as constraint; rather, it was seen as the natural form in which alone the individual could develop his capabilities. Within the confines of his own social sphere the individual enjoyed a relatively large measure of freedom and could accordingly express himself in his daily activity and in his emotional life. His belonging to a group did not as a rule weigh heavily upon him; on the contrary, it was a source of contentment and made for confidence. Thus, the medieval personality lacked the generalised – and hence abstract – character it has acquired in modern times. It was rather a concretised personality playing its allotted role in a general social order, which was understood as divinely instituted, and identifying itself mainly through and in terms of this social role. Since individuality merged with social role and social status, law acted as the main regulator of the whole of social existence.

Not all corporate bodies and social groups were integrated in identical fashion, however, and there were very wide differences in the degree to which they determined the individuality of their members.

The monotony and the very low differentiation of the social and productive activity of the peasantry made for conservation of traditional forms of thinking and behaviour. The peasant felt himself at one with his natural environment. His horizon was bounded to a very great extent by the village horizon. His life depended in every detail on the rhythms of nature. As we saw above, time for the peasant was cyclic, bound up with the changing year and the agricultural seasons. In the peasant mind, the Christian world-view was an accretion to a massive stratum of magic and mythological beliefs, which had by no means lost their power.[47] The peasant saw himself as a member of the agricultural community rather than as an individual. Inwardly, the medieval collective was not united: low individual productivity subordinated its members to general routine patterns, and served at the same time as a source of conflict, disagreement and inequality among them. To some extent, the antagonism between the peasants and the feudal lords made for peasant unity, but the division of the land-tenants into categories with non-identical rights and obligations, and with holdings which varied markedly in size and yield, acted as a divisive factor. Nevertheless, the peasant mind remained collectivist. Non-conformist behaviour was scarcely imaginable in the village or the countryside; where it occurred, it was mainly in the shape of change of employment from agriculture to a craft or trade or perhaps a move to the town. In choosing to remain a peasant, a member of a community – i.e. a dependent tenant to whom feudal society had denied most rights – was submitting to an all-embracing social conformism. Oppression by the feudal landlord was compounded by spiritual dependence on the priests, and by mental backwardness and ignorance.

For many centuries, folk culture remained oral; like village music it was never written down. All that the historian can find out about the spiritual and emotional life of the peasantry is contained in chance references and solecisms in authors belonging to much more elevated social circles, who treat peasants with scorn, hostility or contemptuous pity. In the lexicon of the medieval writer, the *rusticus* is an uncouth boor. The peasantry formed the silent majority of medieval society, and made its voice heard only at times of exacerbated social conflict and of mass movements such as rebellions, heretical uprisings and outbursts of religious fanaticism. As a rule, the feudal lords were well able to handle such outbursts.*

At the same time, the governing orders exercised a great deal of influence on the mental and spiritual life of the peasantry with the aim of persuading the peasants to accept their lot with due humility. The priest's sermon and the liturgy were highly effective ways of ensuring control over the behaviour of the oppressed classes of society. In the Lives of the Saints, a most popular form of writing during the Middle Ages, composed by monks, it is stressed over and over again that any alleviation of the lot of the poor is exclusively in God's hands and in the hands of the saints, who are unfailingly represented as the defenders and protectors of 'the least of these'. It is, however, significant that over a long period the heroes of this hagiographic literature were exclusively representatives of the upper classes of society, and the 'saints' were primarily bishops and priests. Thus was the belief inculcated in the ordinary people that sacral powers were taking care of them; and it was for their spiritual welfare, for the salvation of their souls, that these powers sent down punishment from on high in the shape of sickness, natural calamities and cruel and unjust rulers. The message for the ordinary man was simple: rely on miracles, not on your own strength.[48]*

Certain possibilities were open to the nobleman to develop his own individuality. Living an isolated life in his castle, at the head of his obedient and servile microcosm, he could himself lay down its rules and routines. In relation to the world outside, he was a relatively autonomous unit. His warlike profession was very largely an individual skill, in that he had to rely on his own strength, courage and experience in battle. Even when campaigning in his lord's army the knight acted very largely on his own initiative and at his own risk. His relations with other feudal lords were also mainly of an individual nature, consisting as they did in mutual visits, feasts, quarrels, parleys and marriage contracts.

More than anyone else in feudal society, it was the members of the aristocratic order who had to abide by very strict rules governing their conduct. Entering upon or quitting a lord's service, declaring war, taking part in a tournament, attending at court, acting as judge – for all their actions rules were laid down which had to be meticulously observed, and a strict ritual was prescribed which had to be carried out to the letter. The code of chivalry set out the complicated procedures of etiquette, the slightest departure from which could tarnish a knight's honour in the eyes of other members of his class. The code did not require the knight to be so meticulous in his conduct towards the unprivileged classes; but in his own milieu he had to be continually on his guard against any infringement of the rules of behaviour. His noble birth and his high social status laid obligations upon him which restricted the extent to which he might develop his own ego. When we say that in the feudal system of social relations it fell to the knight to 'play a leading (and far from easy) role', this is no mere metaphor. It was a role that had to be sustained in constant mindfulness of the audience for whom he was 'playing', whether it was the king or his own immediate superior, a lady or another knight like himself. The key issue is honour: this is not inner awareness of one's own worth, not the self-awareness of a man conscious of his own individual qualities as those traits which distinguish him from others, but rather the prestige which a man enjoys in his own milieu. He sees himself through the eyes of others, and his prowess crystallises not in his difference from others in that milieu, but in his identity, his congruence with them.

So, etiquette is no more than an elaborate scenario for behaviour in society. Even where it might seem that all that is needed is a bit of personal initiative and resourcefulness, the knight must not be guided by common sense but must

[201]

act in conformity with the requirements of the corporate ethic. A knight bearing tidings to the king in the heat of battle, must not approach him directly but wait to be called to audience, even if the delay means disaster on the field.[49] Medieval culture is a good example of an elaborate semiological system which is seen at its best in relations between members of the dominant order. Every action of the knight, every article he uses, his garments and their colour, his words and expressions, the language he speaks – all of this is invested with symbolic significance. Socially, the feudal upper classes expressed themselves in ritual and symbol. In a dominant position and enjoying the maximum degree of juridical freedom possible in an age of general corporate determination, this class was nevertheless not free to select its own ways of behaving. The inevitable result was that the individuality of the knight had to express itself in fixed and conventional forms.

Here, the literature of chivalry is instructive. The earliest of its basic forms is the epic. The epic corresponds to a way of thinking associated with the predominance of collective principles and of stable group attitudes, both social and mental. The personages of the courtly epic embody conventional ideas and qualities – courage, fidelity and strength vis-à-vis villainy, treachery and cowardice. They are abstract types rather than real people. The hero of chivalry has no individuality.

Evidence of the changing relationship between the individual and his milieu is to be found, however, in the courtly lyric. At its best, the love poetry of the Minnesänger and the troubadours reveals an exceptional ability to penetrate into and to analyse the inner world of the individual. The love celebrated by the Provençal poets of the twelfth and early thirteenth centuries (in contradistinction to what might be called its 'family' or 'dynastic' form) has an individual ring to it: one woman only is dear to the poet, and he will exchange her for no other. What inspires the troubadour is not nobility of birth or riches (though the poets are by no means indifferent to these assets!), but the beauty and the courtoisie of his lady. Here we see the concepts of nobility of origins and nobility of soul beginning to take their separate paths.[50]

And yet, whoever the lady is, the portrait we are given of her in the Provençal lyric is stereotyped, and her beauty is hymned in the usual clichés. The catalogue of the lady's charms, from her 'beautiful fair hair' and brow 'whiter than the lily' to her 'white hands with their long, slender, smooth fingers' and her 'charming body, soft and youthful', becomes a literary convention.[51] The lady celebrated in these lyrics has no marks of identification: she is an abstract and ideal figure, apprehended in the main, nevertheless, by the 'eyes of the body'. She is also anonymous; as a rule, the poet gives her an amorous pet-name. Nor are her inner qualities individualised to any greater extent. The beautiful lady is tactful, lovable, worldly-wise; she dresses tastefully, is a coquette in moderation, she is well-born, intelligent, and can carry on a sophisticated conversation. In short, she is a compendium of those qualities which were given the overall name of *courtoisie*. To judge from the troubadour lyrics, relations between lovers varied considerably from the platonic 'service' of an inaccessible lady, a sort of worship which ennobled and elevated the poet, to the most intimate intercourse which the troubadours not infrequently describe in explicit and naively coarse language. Soon, however, a definitive ritual for courtship and amorous relations was worked out, which became obligatory for refined people who set some store on their reputations. A lady was bound to have a lover and to treat him as such, while her knight was expected to keep the 'secret love' secret, and to serve the lady of his heart in exactly the same way as a vassal served his lord. The terminology of feudal institutions was easily transferred to more intimate relations.[52] The passion for classification which is characteristic of the whole epoch gave rise to a 'scholasticism of love', a *sui generis* codification of canons of amorous behaviour and the expression of feelings. Poets gained added lustre from their affairs with noble ladies and sought to build up reputations as fearless and daring lovers. It was not just the material value of tribute and plunder that made knights go on military expeditions, but the chance thus offered to acquire fame through an ostentatious (and therefore symbolical) squandering of wealth; and in the same way, in courtly love the socially most valuable dividend was the renown accruing to the poet through his praise for his conquest – his lady – and his feelings for her. The poet's individuality was constrained by a set of stereotypes; directness of expression was replaced by mannerisms, artificiality, conventionality and play on words.[53]

These traits of the courtly lyric may be taken as an index of the growth of a corporate awareness in chivalry. By elaborating an ideal type of love and turning it into a ritual, the troubadours created a special sublimated world which existed for only one social group of the feudal hierarchy, screened off from the ordinary people on the one hand and the higher aristocracy on the other.

But over and above the traditional features which are characteristic of medieval society in general, the courtly lyric has something quite new to offer. The position of woman in this context is totally different from her position in official, feudal marriage, which was understood as the union of two houses. Courtly love cannot arise between husband and wife. One of the troubadour lyrics expresses this in unmistakable terms: 'A husband offends against honour if he loves his wife as a knight loves his lady; for in this the worth of neither increases, nor can the relationship yield anything that is not already there by law.' The verdict reached by the 'Courts of Love' said to be held by Eleanor of Aquitaine (if these courts existed at all and were not invented by the poets) was that there could be no courtly love between husband and wife.[54] Courtly love is illegal, officially beyond the pale; but the more deeply it touches the inner world of the individual, the more clearly it illuminates his spiritual resources. The courtly lyric provides a new basis for human self-expression.[55] For the first time in European literature, the analysis of intimate experience takes a central place in the writing of poetry. Individual passion becomes virtually the main aim in life. The poet acknowledges that love enriches him inwardly. Feeling is one of the moral and aesthetic categories of chivalry; and if the lady hymned by the troubadour remains a non-individualised embodiment of the ideal of womanly beauty fashionable in the courts of Southern France, immersion in his own inner self, ardent recapitulation of his own adventures, the cultivation of love's joys and sorrows, all of this amounts to a reappraisal of moral values and constitutes a step forward in the development of the knight's self-awareness.

More strictly bound by etiquette in his social setting than peasant or burgher in theirs, the knight had nevertheless a better chance of discovering and developing his personality in the cultural sphere, though even here his emergence as an individual in his own right was subject to certain limitations.

The situation of the town dweller was quite different. The most heterogeneous elements went into the formation of this stratum of society. The social structure of the medieval town was far more complex than the relatively homogeneous structure of the countryside and the villages. In itself, the burgher's activity as a producer of goods generated a completely different attitude to life. His dependence on nature and her cyclical changes was already far less than that of the peasant. In place of a direct metabolism with nature, a qualitatively new medium was created for the circulation of the products of human labour. This is the key importance of urban production and the exchange of manufactured products. In the towns, relations with nature are second-hand. *Homo artifex* has to rethink his role in the world. Man face to face with a nature he has transformed can ask himself a question that could never occur to the peasant: are these products, and the tools he has used to make them, works of God or works of man, i.e. his own creations?[56] A more complex understanding of the relationship between art (in the wide sense of the word, as used in the Middle Ages to mean all sorts of skills) and nature arises. Town-dwellers rationalise their ideas of time and space. In this process, the personality of the burgher was bound to be affected with consequent changes in his self-awareness.

Nevertheless, the life of the medieval town-dweller continued to be hedged about by all sorts of regulations. Naturally, these regulations were first and foremost due to the conditions involved in production, the effort to save small handicrafts from competition and secure better conditions for the expanding production of commodities, the organisation of markets, and the subordination of apprentices to the control of master craftsmen.

But the roots of *Zunftzwang* (compulsory membership of a guild) which prevailed in the towns went deeper than this and can only be understood in connection with the essential peculiarities of social life in the Middle Ages. Guild rules did not so much restrict a man (for a long time, he was subjectively not aware of any restriction) as stamp his behaviour with a generally significant form, which identified him in the clearest possible way as a burgher.

The behaviour of burghers was laid down and regulated by guild and town codes of rules. Together with the regulations governing the production process and other sides of economic life, these codes contain provisions for the care of the poor, they specify the baptism service, the authorised dress for apprentices, even lists of swear-words and the fines payable for using them, and much more. In the 'Wedding Regulations' of Augsburg, description of the marriage rites and procedures is not less detailed than the full and factual account of the *'leges Barbarorum'*. Here we learn the maximum number of guests that the burgher may invite to the wedding, the number of times it is permissible to change one's clothes during the first two days of the wedding, and how much the musicians should be paid; the order of the wedding procession is set out, and we learn how many women may accompany the bride to the bath, and how many men should perform the same service for the bridegroom; everything, even what would seem to be the most ordinary of everyday practices, is ritualised and made subject to the rules of the municipal magistrate.[57] The rules for laying on a feast, with their petty details – how the participants should behave and what to do if the guests get out of hand – remind us of the casuistic German law-codes.[58]

In guilds we can find strong evidence of the efforts made by medieval citizens to unite in a corporation – efforts in which we can see not only specific urban conditions but also the typical traits of the human personality of the epoch. The guild – the association of craftsmen – was the organisational form in which they and their families spent their lives. It was not only production and marketing interests or the social struggle that united them in the guild, but also corporate membership, justice, the need for protection, religious functions, the organisation of leisure, entertainment, mutual assistance. It is worth while remembering that the word *Zeche* meant 'drinking-bout', 'blow-out', the word *guild* was derived from the Old English *gild* meaning 'sacrifice', and the Old Scandinavian word *gildi* meant 'feast', 'festivity' and also 'payment' or 'cost'. The guilds of the early Middle Ages had a sacral character and were connected with pagan cults. Members of the guilds called each other 'brother'; democratic forms and traditions played a rather large part in the medieval town in spite of the high degree of differentiation in the commune and the guilds.

The relation between the craftsman and his product was highly specific; he saw it as part of himself. The concept of the *chef d'oeuvre*, the 'exemplary product', had a moral tinge, for only a conscientious worker who worked honestly and produced nothing but high-quality goods could be a guild member. The attention paid to the quality of every article produced by a guild's craftsmen bears witness to the absence of mass production and the limited nature of the market for which they worked. In the Icelandic sagas we find a curious example of the envy felt by a master craftsman of his own product. The Norwegian king Olaf Trygvason ordered the most powerful warship in the land to be built. The vessel was almost ready for launch when it was discovered that it had been damaged – during the night someone had bored holes all along the sides. The king offered a reward for the discovery of the culprit, who would be put to death. The chief boat builder Thorberg then admitted that he himself had damaged the vessel. The king ordered him to make good the damage. After Thorberg's repairs the boat was even more beautiful than before.[59]

Belonging to a guild was connected with a complex of emotions which a man shared with other members: pride in his guild, whose reputation and authority he would jealously defend, participation in meetings and general decisions, assertion of his dignity as a fully-fledged burgher *vis-à-vis* the town patricians and the nobles, and a feeling of superiority *vis-à-vis* the unorganised craftsmen, the apprentices, pupils, servants – the common people of the town. A master craftsman sought and found in his work not simply a source of material prosperity: his work gave him satisfaction in itself. Hence his work and its product could be a means of achieving aesthetic pleasure. Perfection in a craft was handed down from generation to generation, forming a tradition of excellence and pushing the productive and the artistic possibilities of the craft to their utmost limits. A craft was a skill, and skill was artistry. The free work of a master craftsman within a guild was a means of asserting his human personality and heightening his social awareness.

The union of productive, ethical and aesthetic principles in the work of the master craftsman gave this work a very high social significance. It provided a basis for the development of the human personality to the maximum possible in the corporate society of the Middle Ages. The burgher was a citizen of his community, an owner, a working individual. The multilateral nature of his social relations raised him above the representatives of the other orders in feudal society.

The built-in limitations of production based on handicrafts were, of course, at the same time the limits to which this society could develop. The horizon of the medieval burgher remained limited, and the narrow, closed social groupings at one and the same time united the citizens (in communes, guilds, corporations) and divided them (disunity among guilds, hostility to manufactures that began to appear towards the end of the Middle Ages, the narrow provinciality of the towns, which prevented them from realising the need for national unity). Urban society was incapable of rapid development; though it was dynamic in comparison with the agrarian society, it shared with the latter the tendency to reproduce itself on too narrow a base and in over-close adherence to traditional forms and standards.

Over a certain period, however, it was precisely in the towns that the human personality was able to achieve a certain growth, a specific medieval individuality. The distinction made by F. Tönnies between *Gemeinschaft* and *Gesellschaft* is relevant here.[60] Tönnies applied the term *Gemeinschaft* ('community') to the Middle Ages to indicate what he saw as the integrated quality of this medieval individuality, and its close organic unity with its social environment. *Gesellschaft* ('society') on the other hand is constructed, not on immediate personal relations between individuals, but on relations between the depersonalised owners of commodities – i.e. the bourgeois society.

CHAPTER VI

Medieval attitudes to wealth and labour

The world-view of any society will include that society's concepts of property, wealth and labour. These are not only politico-economic categories but also moral and ideological ones; labour and wealth may be highly valued or despised, their role in human affairs can be variously assessed. Economic activity is a component part of social practice, of the interaction between man and his environment, and of man's creative action on this environment. It reflects the vital preoccupations of a society, and if we are to penetrate the mental climate of this society it is particularly important for us to try to understand its attitudes to labour and property.

Labour can be seen as a curse which the human race has to bear, or as a blessing, enabling man to separate himself off from the rest of the world and make himself the lord of nature. Wealth can be seen as an end in itself or as a means of achieving other ends. Hence, the attitudes to labour and wealth which prevail in a given society are indissoluble components of that society's world-view, determining the behaviour of its members and setting the ideals towards which they strive. Of course, the ideas of property and labour prevalent in any given society are generated by the production relations characteristic of that society; but the ideas themselves enter into these relations and are an essential factor in their operation.

From the outset, the medieval attitude to labour and wealth was quite different from that of the ancient world. Far from regarding labour as a virtue the ancient world did not even consider it as something befitting free men. The classical ideal centred on the individual – member of a polis, of a state, the citizen absorbed in his social, political and cultural life, and having nothing to do with physical labour. Labour was something better left to slaves or to freedmen. The citizen was a warrior – he attended the national assembly, took part in athletic competitions, performed religious sacrifices, went to the theatre, feasted with his friends; his personality developed entirely outside the sphere of material production. Wealth was something which enabled the citizen to lead this sort of life. Thus the economic theories of the ancient world can be reduced to the one question: what form of ownership provides the best citizens? Ancient civilisation of the Classical period did not recognise the dignity, the religious-moral value, of physical labour. Plato rejected the visible, tangible world as a pale copy of the world of ideas, and Aristotle emphasised man's political nature; both regarded productive labour with aristocratic contempt. Noble idleness is desirable. For the ancients, labour was the negation of leisure, a sort of deviation from the normal tenor of life. It must be pointed out, however, that their notion of leisure was not simply inactivity. The Classical Greek σχολή (Latin *schola*) means free time, leisure, relaxation, idleness; but it also signified the time allotted to learning and learned discussion, schooling, in particular philosophical schooling (whence the medieval *scholastica*).

As regards labour, the term πόνος had a second meaning, closely allied in the ancient Greek mind with the first: burden, suffering, misfortune, calamity. Physical labour – toil and pain – was the lot of the unfree and the lowly, a heavy, dirty business which degraded man to the level of the animals. The free man used the services of slaves and attendants, who were the tools and the instruments assuring his welfare. Initially, one exception was made – for farming. But towards the end of antiquity even farming ceased to count as the civil virtue it had been in the patriarchal period of, say, Cincinnatus. In the Empire period, the view that those who engaged in physical labour, especially slaves, were innately base was generally accepted by the ruling class. Certain thinkers disagreed with this negative attitude to labour (the Cynics, Seneca, Epictetus), and we may see in their views preparatory steps towards that break with the old slave-owning morality which finally found expression in Christianity. The only people who put any value on labour were the labouring masses themselves. A total lack of interest in mechanical inventions which might have alleviated physical labour was combined with dreams of robots and other wonderful contraptions which would ensure permanent leisure for mankind – which is perhaps indicative of the general attitude to physical labour in the ancient world. Labour, it was held, could not dignify a man; it was senseless and brutalising; it did not have, indeed could not have, inner beauty. The image of Sisyphus ceaselessly pushing a stone up to the top of a mountain only to see it roll down again could only have occurred to a society which regarded labour as a punishment. Idleness, freedom from having to give oneself any trouble, was the ideal not only of well-to-do people but also of the poor; the slogan of the proletariat was 'bread and circuses', and existence at someone else's expense always seemed to be the best way out of their difficulties.

Preaching 'if any would not work, neither should he eat' (II Thess. 3:10), Christianity broke radically with this attitude to labour. A society of small-scale producers could hardly regard labour as something disgraceful. People began to look upon work as the normal state of human beings. True, if it was a *necessary* state, this was not because man was thus created but because of the Fall; that is to say, labour was still seen as a punishment. The essential point, however, is that idleness was now accounted one of the most grievous sins. Every man had to carry out his allotted function, occupy himself with his work, though not all varieties of work – necessary for the community though they might be – were equally acceptable to God. Like labour, wealth was no longer viewed as an end in itself or as a means to securing an idle existence. Attitudes to wealth were defined by hopes of salvation in the world to come; for the possession of wealth, while it might help, could also actually hinder the soul's chances of entering into eternal bliss. In the possession of wealth, the followers of Christ – who had preached poverty and asceticism – saw something very questionable and morally hardly justifiable. The words of Matthew's Gospel (19:24), 'It is easier for a camel to go through the eye of a needle, than for a rich man to enter into the kingdom of God', served as the source of much spiritual and social conflict throughout the Middle Ages.

The economic postulates of the medieval church corresponded to the social reality of feudalism by treating wealth not as an end in itself but as a means guaranteeing the existence of every member of society '*secundum suam conditionem*'. Production in the early Middle Ages was not geared to accumulation and profit. Its aim was to ensure a 'commensurate' existence for each part of the whole: *corpus Christianum* corporately divided according to the will of God. Here, wealth serves as a means towards achieving and consolidating social power, while in bourgeois society wealth in and by itself constitutes decisive social power. In medieval society the actual form in which wealth is embodied – in lands or goods and chattels or money – was not a matter of indifference. Property was viewed in various lights depending on how it was embodied and to what order the owner belonged, in contradistinction to bourgeois wealth, which is not connected with any social or ethical criteria.

Naturally, in feudal society people belonging to different social classes did not always see labour in the same light; and differing attitudes to labour and property underlie many of the social antagonisms of the Middle Ages.

'A gift demands a gift'

Several factors went into shaping the medieval attitude to property and wealth. Christianity certainly played an enormous part, as in so many other aspects of medieval civilisation; but it did not act alone, and no less a part was played in this context by the values prevalent among the barbarian tribes who settled on European territory in the days of the declining Roman Empire. In many ways, the structure of barbarian society, whether Germanic or Slav, recalls the system of social relations prevalent among other peoples in a pre-class or early class stage of social development. That is to say, the social attitudes, the beliefs and ideals of the European barbarians were often very similar to those found among the so-called primitive peoples. Pre-class society has certain specific social institutions, variants of which are encountered all over the globe. These institutions and attitudes are partially at least eliminated during the process of development from barbarism to civilisation; for a class society acquires a new set of morals and ideals, a new religious system is established and radical changes take place in all branches of social life. Nevertheless, even in the class society, alongside the new systems of relations, ideas and beliefs, certain archaic relations are retained and often continue to play a very important role in the new setting.

Medieval Europe is a case in point. However deeply Christianity affected the general world-view, it was not able to eradicate all the mental attitudes that had dominated the age of barbarism. The result was a complex synthesis of barbarian, Christian and classical values.

The civilised neighbours of the barbarians were unanimous about one thing – the barbarians were not slow to help themselves to other people's goods. The thought of the treasures stored up in the rich countries drew the barbarians like a magnet; and plunder was the main motive for their military expeditions. As they saw it, violence paid off far better than toil. Young men flocked to noble leaders, hoping that a quick and successful campaign would yield plentiful booty which the leader would then divide up among his warriors.

But what was to be done with wealth thus acquired? As Tacitus already tells us, when they were not away on military raids, the German body-guards spent most of their time feasting. A lot of the plunder went into feasts at which the warriors publicly and ostentatiously ate too much and drank themselves silly. Loot from a successful raid was not merely a way of feeding the warriors, but also the best way of holding them together and of affirming the leader's authority. The barbarians tended to despise military deeds which were not widely publicised. They had to be celebrated in the songs of the bards and thus fixed in the memory of the warriors and of all the members of the tribe. The plunder – treasure, garments, arms – bore eloquent witness to the virtues of the heroic way of life and to the prowess of the leader and his men, and was boastfully paraded. Gold and silver were not yet used by the barbarians as money; exchange of goods was on the most direct and natural level. Coins plundered from more advanced peoples were turned into ingots, cut into pieces, or made into rings, bracelets, brooches and so on.

Valuable vessels and jewellery often came in for the same treatment.

So wealth accruing from warlike expeditions conferred social distinction. In barbarian society wealth was neither a means of commercial exchange nor something to hoard up, it was not even put into circulation: rather, it had a valuable semiological function.

This conclusion would seem to run counter to the well-known fact that the barbarians were very fond of burying and hiding the treasure they plundered. All over the territory settled by the Germanic tribes buried hoards of Roman coins are found. The Viking hoards in Scandinavia are especially rich, and some scholars even speak of a 'silver age' in Northern Europe of that period, so frequent and rich are the finds of Sassanid, Byzantine, German, Anglo-Saxon coinage, most of it silver. Several hundred thousand hoards have already been discovered and the number is rising continually. Are we entitled to deduce from this that a monetary system had been developed in tenth- and eleventh-century Scandinavia, and that coins were used as currency? This view has had its supporters, while some scholars have even written about the 'commercial boom' in the northern countries brought about by the activities of the Vikings. The adherents of such a view think it likely that at times of danger – e.g. during attack by raiders – the local inhabitants hurried to hide their valuables and failed to dig them up again after the danger had passed.[1]

But this point of view seems questionable. In the first place, the Icelandic sagas, dating from much later, often refer to people who buried hoards of coins, making it quite clear that not only were these hoards not subsequently dug up but that there was never any intention of doing so: the money was buried for ever so that no one could make use of it. Rulers often buried their money before death, making sure there were no witnesses; the slaves who did the digging were put to death. Archaeological finds yield evidence of the widespread practice of burying treasure in swamps and marshes; this 'marsh silver' could not be retrieved for use. In the second place, it is well known that trade in Scandinavia at the time when these hoards were being buried *en masse*, was

[217]

primarily carried on by means of exchange in kind; certain commodities, e.g. home-spun cloth, were used as currency, or wealth was expressed in terms of head of horned cattle. Coins acquired as loot during predatory excursions or as tribute were not used as currency in Scandinavia. The Vikings must have known very well how highly gold and silver were valued in other countries, and they themselves were very far from despising them – witness the trouble they took to hide coins and other objects made from the precious metals – but as a rule they did not use them in trade or as a currency.

Thus, on the one hand the Norsemen prized precious metals and went to any lengths to lay their hands on them; on the other hand, they never used them for trading purposes, but buried coins in the earth, in swamps and even sank them in the sea. And while they wore articles such as pendants, brooches and necklaces, made of gold and silver, which they liked to flaunt in public (the men no less than the women), they treated coins in a way that was completely incomprehensible to peoples who knew the commercial uses of money and equally incomprehensible to many scholars today.

If we are to understand the way the ancient Germans and Scandinavians treated precious metals, we cannot approach this problem from a narrowly economic standpoint; we have to see it in the wider context of the spiritual life of peoples making the transition from barbarism to civilisation. According to concepts still current among them, the treasures a man owned incorporated in some way his own personal qualities and were intimately bound up with his fortune and happiness. To be deprived of them was equivalent to perishing, to losing one's most important qualities and one's prowess as a warrior. Let us recall the struggle that arose over the Rheingold – the inherited treasure sunk by the legendary Niflungs (in German, *Nibelungen*) in the Rhine which was in the long run to be their ruin. Gold, as the ancient Germans and Scandinavians saw it, was a materialisation of its owner's good fortune. Guided by this idea, the Norsemen tried to conceal the coins they plundered, with no real intention of ever digging them up again; as long as it lay undisturbed in the ground or at the bottom of a marsh, the hoard preserved within itself its owner's success, which was therefore inalienable. In the eyes of the barbarians gold and silver possessed magic and sacramental power.

This power did not pass from the metal when it was used to make bracelets and other ornaments. These were not buried; on the contrary, they were flaunted, as unmistakable indices of social position and prowess. The bracelets and rings which the warriors solicited from their leaders were not merely material gifts: in them a portion of the leader's 'success' passed to the recipient, who thus partook, as it were, of the leader's essence. 'Dispenser of the rings', 'liberal with bracelets' – these are the epithets we find given by grateful skalds to the leaders and kings who had bestowed such gifts on them. A leader who was sparing of gifts, who did not hand out rings and jewellery, was simply not worth serving, for he was stingily withholding the magical powers and the good fortune in which his men should have a share. Generosity, no less than military prowess and valour, was what characterised a true leader. The true leader was generous; his generosity was a token of his nobility. In one of the poems of the *Elder Edda* about the Scandinavian hero Helgi, we read that 'to his faithful company he generously gave red gold won by blood'.[2]

The rich booty taken by the barbarians in times of war and in the course of predatory expeditions was not turned into a currency for the acquisition of wealth in our sense of the word; it was not used to buy cattle or lands or any other sort of property. It was distributed, consumed, or it became a hoard invested with sacral properties and exercising magical influence on its owner.

This was a way of looking at treasure that could not survive the coming of Christianity and the spread of monetary commercial relations among the erstwhile barbarian peoples. People began to grasp the earthly role of money, the material value of gold and silver. But under the feudal system wealth continued to be regarded above all as an instrument in social relations, as a means of establishing and reinforcing social authority.

The specifically barbarian attitude to money can also be identified in a very important feature of their social structure

– the *wergild*. Normally this replaced the blood-feud and was paid for the murder or mutilation of a man or for certain other serious crimes. The law-books – the 'barbarian codes' – contain detailed assessments of the due recompense to be paid to the victim or to his relatives. Recompense was fixed after due consideration of the social status, the age and sex of the victim (sometimes also of the culprit), the circumstances of the crime and a series of other factors. In the Germanic 'law-codes', the wergild is usually expressed in terms of a certain sum of money: this sum to be paid (if we can take the 'codes' at their face value) whenever a certain crime was committed against someone belonging to a given social order (noble, free, semi-free). There are, however, grounds for believing that in practice the scale of values set out in the codes was not the only criterion used in fixing the amount of wergild. Every concrete case seems to have produced *ad hoc* criteria affecting the sum awarded. The principles underlying assessment by the adjudicators are not clear. We may assume that compensation depended in no small measure on the power and social prestige of the injured party or his family. Naturally, the aim was to get as much compensation as possible under the law. But in many cases we find people who have to pay wergild actually insisting on increasing the sum. At first sight this seems very strange, but it becomes understandable if we bear in mind the special nature of wergild and its meaning for the people of that time. The amount of the wergild reflected the social position not only of the recipient party but also of those paying it; the higher the wergild, the more this redounded to the social prestige of the individuals concerned and their kin. Thus, wergild was something more than the (not inconsiderable) monetary sums that were paid by way of material compensation for loss or injury.

Although the 'barbarian codes' specify the amount of wergild and of all other dues in terms of money, these payments were in fact usually made in goods – after all, there was not so very much money about. Not all commodities were acceptable in payment of wergild, however. Cattle were always acceptable. Many codes specify the number of animals – usually cows – held to be equivalent to the monetary value of a given wergild. Other goods that were acceptable included slaves, weapons, armour, land, woven cloth. Anything put up and accepted as compensation in lieu of monetary settlement had to be of good quality and without defect. There were other, limiting factors: thus, among the Norwegians, only *óðal* land was supposed to be acceptable as wergild: inherited land, that is, in the possession of the family for several generations and virtually inalienable. 'Bought land', recently acquired and involving none of the difficulties attending the disposal of odal, was not acceptable in lieu of wergild.[3] Here there seems to be a special relationship between family and wergild. The compensation paid for a slain relative could not become an alienable object, and the lands and other property forming it would remain in the possession of the family for ever.

The wergild symbolised reconciliation between two feuding families. It also served as a graphic demonstration of the social status of the victim and his kin. As the sum of money or other valuables paid on the reconciliation between a murderer and his victim's kin had such an important semantic function, it could hardly be freely disposed of and freely spent. Sometimes people on their deathbeds left their wergild to the church, along with their other possessions. In these circumstances, nothing is known of a murder or any other crime punishable by payment of wergild. In the bequest, the amount under this heading is specifically isolated; which suggests that some particular significance was accorded to the wergild: in some special way it was connected with the man and expressed his social dignity and status.[4] Great landowners who had made land donations to a monastery sometimes redeemed these after a certain interval by paying the proper wergild. This is a clear example of the link between a payment protecting the life of an individual, and his hereditary property.[5]

As in any pre-class society, exchange of gifts played an enormous part in barbarian society. The establishment of friendly relations with others, marriage, visits by guests, the successful conclusion of a trade deal or of a peace treaty, funeral feasts, award of patronage – these and many other social occasions were invariably accompanied by an exchange of gifts. Any gift implied reciprocity. A gift from a leader was an award for faithful service and a pledge of the recipient's devotion in the future. A gift from equal to equal required a gift in return. 'A gift demands a gift' says one of the aphorisms in the Old Icelandic lay *The Words of the High One (Hávamál)*.[6] The same principle is recorded in Old Germanic law as well: a gift had no virtue unless the recipient made an equivalent return. Among the Lombards, a gift had to be acknowledged by means of a special compensatory payment – *launegild*, although by this time it was nothing more than a symbolical gesture.[7]

Thus the very idea of a unilateral gift was alien to the barbarians: they recognised only exchange of gifts. It is interesting to note that the Indo-European languages had originally the same word to express the concepts of 'give' and 'take'. One or the other meaning of the verb *dō* had to be supplied according to its grammatical context.[8] This is true of Old Scandinavian: the verb *fá* has both meanings, and only the context and the syntax will tell us which of these is to be used in any given case. 'Giving' and 'receiving' are apparently closely associated in the minds of many peoples on the archaic stage; exchange – of property, of feasts and services – expressing and reinforcing feelings of friendliness and confidence as it did, was a universal form of social intercourse.[9]

At the root of the exchange of gifts lay the conviction that the given object carried with it some part of the essence of the giver, and that in this way the recipient entered into closer contact with him. If no gift was made in return, the recipient was in some degree dependent on the giver. The warrior who received a gift from his leader was not troubled by this dependence – on the contrary, he was always striving to strengthen his ties with his leader, hoping to acquire along with the gift something of the 'success' which made the leader what he was. A gift from a powerful man could be answered with faithful service or songs of praise; but a gift from an equal could be fraught with great danger for the recipient unless the latter could send something in return. Magic dependence on another man could involve loss of one's own personal integrity and freedom, even the ruin of the recipient who failed to make a return gift.[10] Hence either one hastened to repay a gift, or one tried to avoid accepting it.

It is very difficult if not impossible for us to comprehend the nature of the dangers that lay in wait for the man who accepted a gift and failed to repay it. It is clear that what I call 'magic dependence' (in view of its non-material character) was perceived by the ancient Scandinavians in quite a different way. The sharp distinction between the ideal and the material which dominates our present-day ways of thought, was completely alien to the barbarian mentality. We saw above how time was apprehended by them in material terms. Similarly, the 'fortune', the 'luck', which the warrior might obtain from a leader rich in it, was just as materially real as the ring or bracelet handed to him by the leader. Recipient and giver were closely interrelated, as it were; and the person who received the gift remained under the influence of the giver. The dependence was magical in nature.

Gifts were continually being exchanged in barbarian society; often quite modest gifts without much material value. In *Hávamál* we read:

> A kind word need not cost much,
> The price of praise can be cheap:
> With half a loaf and an empty cup
> I found myself a friend.[11]

What matters is not the value of the gift but the friendly relations which result from the exchange of gifts. Thus the author of *Hávamál* says:

> No man is so generous he will jib at accepting
> A gift in return for a gift,
> No man so rich that it really gives him
> Pain to be repaid.

> Once he has won wealth enough,
> A man should not crave for more:
> What he saves for friends, foes may take;
> Hopes are often liars.

With presents friends should please each other,
 With a shield or a costly coat:
Mutual giving makes for friendship
 So long as life goes well.

A man should be loyal through life to friends,
 To them and to friends of theirs,
....

A man should be loyal through life to friends,
 And return gift for gift,
Laugh when they laugh, but with lies repay
 A false foe who lies.

If you find a friend you fully trust
 And wish for his good will,
Exchange thoughts, exchange gifts,
 Go often to his house.[12]

There is no mistaking the close connection between friendship and the exchange of gifts. Gifts are the most important, indeed the crucial factor in the establishing and maintenance of social relations. Generosity shows that a man has made a success of his life and is socially respected, while meanness is a man's undoing; a miser is literally beyond the pale:

The generous and bold have the best lives,
 Are seldom beset by cares,
But the base man sees bogies everywhere,
 And the miser pines for presents.[13]

Generosity, boldness and good fortune go naturally together, just as cowardice and miserliness do. The moral evaluation of the qualitative antithesis is evident. The miser is afraid of receiving a gift and shies away from it because he knows that he will have to give something in return. The man who gives nothing to others risks his social well-being:

 . . . give a ring,
 so that you are not
 the recipient of bad wishes.[14]

[224]

'Bad wishes' or curses could be very dangerous, since words are invested with magical power; the barbarians believed that malediction could bring evil powers to bear on a man and ruin him. Was not the word just as real and 'materially' effective as the act? Again we are brought face to face with the absence in barbarian thinking of any sharp dividing line between the material and the spiritual spheres. Reality is not divided into mind and body, into natural and supernatural; everything is active, everything is capable of taking part in and affecting human affairs, and so the action the barbarian performs, the word he utters, can have far-reaching consequences, even to the extent of upsetting the world order. Hence, one has to be permanently on guard. We have to bear this in mind when we are reading *Hávamál*. It contains many exhortations to be prudent and avoid precipitate action. We find not infrequent hints in histories of Old Norse poetry that this prudence reflects 'peasant cunning', the small-mindedness of the 'little man' with his fears and his limitations, in sharp contrast to the 'grand style' of the nobles and the Vikings, the heroes who do things in a big way.

It hardly needs to be stressed that the norms governing the lives of the ordinary *bönder* – farmers and peasants – were radically different from the warlike code of chiefs and Vikings. Circumspection in deed and word – especially when not on one's home ground – was called for: circumspection at meetings, during visits, at feasts, with unknown or rich people, brevity in speech, wariness, resourcefulness, shrewdness, determination to keep one's independence while at the same time avoiding disputes and making enemies, sobriety, self-control in eating and drinking, moderation in all things including knowledge, diligence and thrift – these are the qualities recommended in *Hávamál*. In my opinion, however, it would be quite unfair to see in such homilies no more than the worldly wisdom of the crafty smallholder. The aphorisms of *Hávamál* are the product not of a class society but of a weakly differentiated society; and any attempt to classify these maxims into 'aristocratic' and 'peasant' compartments is artificial and hardly in keeping with historical reality. The matter-of-fact and utilitarian nature of what has been called the 'egoistic' morals of *Hávamál* really reflects the very special position of man in a world full of dangers, a world in which anything and everything can affect him directly. It is a world all of whose elements and manifestations are linked to each other by mysterious and incomprehensible bonds; a world which can only be approached with caution and guile. This is why the desirable qualities of nobility, boldness and honour are accompanied in this Eddic lay by egoistic and cynical advice; there is no need to contrast them as expressions of two different world-views.

One of the main requirements for a happy existence is the maintenance of friendly relations with people. One must be continually exchanging visits with friends, and, on each such occasion, exchanging gifts with them. The original connection between hospitality and the exchange of gifts is linguistically attested in several Indo-European settings.[15] Taking part in feasts and exchanging gifts – these were the main channels of social intercourse among the barbarians. With many peoples, exchange of gifts had reached such a pitch that it developed into a whole system of elaborate ceremonial. Certain articles or fruits of the earth were ceremonially passed from hand to hand in exchange for others; these objects were not consumed or used but were passed on or amassed, so that they could be publicly exhibited. Their importance lay not in their use value but in the fact that in them were palpably embodied the social ties between the people making the exchange. Ceremonial exchange united people belonging to different family and tribal groups.

Among primitive peoples the reciprocal hosting of feasts sometimes led to extraordinary competitions in generosity, with the hosts trying to stupefy the guests with their largesse. It was then up to the guests to act as host in their turn, and not fail to match or surpass the same lavish standards. There is an element of belligerence here which sometimes becomes explicit: the aim being not so much to do the guests a good turn as to leave them in no doubt of the host's superiority. On occasion, in their determination to outstrip all comers in conspicuous waste, the hosts would destroy their entire stock of food and chop their boats into pieces, without so much as a thought for what was going to happen after the feast was over. The aim of such feasts was to confirm the moral superiority of the spenders, something much more important to them than mere material well-being.[16]

In this extreme form, ceremonial exchange and competitive feasting are not found among the European peoples in the early Middle Ages. But the idea that feasts and the exchange of gifts had a very big part to play in social relations was inbuilt in the Germanic mind.[17] In *Hávamál*, one of the most important leitmotivs is provided by the feast and the need to conduct oneself thereat in proper fashion.

The feast was one of the most important social institutions among the Scandinavians. On their ceremonial journeys through the territory subject to them, the leaders – king and jarl – were entertained at feasts laid on by the local population. All matters of interest were discussed at these feasts, and sacrifices and libations to the pagan gods were performed. The union of the country under one king brought no change whatever in the role of the feast.[18] This ancient and venerable custom remained the keystone of the Scandinavian political system. The ruler travelled systematically throughout the country at the head of a bodyguard, which tended to increase – so that the need for provender increased in the same measure. In certain parts of the country the king had estates, where he would put up for periods during these peregrinations. It was then up to the local inhabitants to supply the produce necessary for the proper entertainment of the king and his retinue.

As the royal power increased and was consolidated the character of the feast changed in that it lost its original voluntary character; now all *bönder* were obliged to provide for the king's festive requirements. But, as before, the feast remained the main channel for direct contact between the peasants and their leader.

The Icelandic sagas describe these feasts in great detail. The company that assembled in the great banqueting hall of a Norwegian king included his retainers and the most influential bönder. The host sat at the head of the table on a raised dais; the seat for him was supported on wooden posts decorated with carved images of the pagan gods under whose protection the house was supposed to be. Round the walls were benches for the guests and retainers. In the centre of

the hall was the hearth with a blazing fire. The feast lasted
many hours if not several days. It was the occasion for the
king to learn all the local news, to decide various matters and
issue orders. In conversation with the nobleman and bönder
it would become clear whom he – the king – could rely on
and who was hostile to him. Not infrequently the feast ended
in violence, even bloodshed – after all, weapons were either
lying beside the feasters or were hanging on the wall. Any
disturbance of the peace at a time and place where people
were drinking together was severely punished. Seated in the
seat of honour, the ruler dispensed his favours to his retainers
and his allies, presented them with rings and arms, settled
disputes and fixed wergild. An indispensable or at least highly
desirable participant in the festivities was the skald who
would deliver a song (sometimes improvised on the spot) in
praise of the king and either craving a reward or thanking him
for one received. *Egils saga* tells of the behaviour of a well-
known Icelandic skald at a feast given by the English king
Athelstan (or Adalstein as he is called in the Icelandic sources).

While he [Egil] sat . . . , he was twitching one eyebrow
down on to his cheek and the other up into his hair
roots. Egil was black-eyed and with brows of dark
brown. He would drink nothing, though drink was
fetched him, but twitched his eyebrows up and down,
now this way, now that.
King Athelstan was sitting in the high-seat. He too had
laid his sword across his knees, and when they had been
seated so for a while, the king drew his sword out of the
scabbard and, taking a fine big gold ring off his arm,
drew it over his sword's point, stood up and walked on
to the floor and reached it across the fire to Egil. Egil
stood up, plucked out his sword, and walked on to the
floor. He stuck his sword in the round of the ring, drew
it towards him, then went back to his place. The king sat
down in the high-seat. When Egil sat down he drew the
ring on to his arm, and with that his eyebrows fell into
line. He then put down sword and helm, took hold of
the horn which was brought him and drank it off. Then
he chanted:

> 'King, corslet's god, has given me
> A ringing springe for clawtongs,[19]
> To swing from hawktrod hangtree,[20]
> Handgallows goldenhaltered.
> Aloft on sword I lift it,
> My gallows-spar of spearstorm;
> This swordhand's snare wins favor
> And fame for ravens' feeder.'

From then on Egil drank his full share and conversed with other men.

In addition, Athelstan sent Skallagrim, Egil's father, two chests full of silver as wergild for his slain son; he also promised Egil wergild for his brother in the shape of land or money as he wished:

Egil took the money and thanked the king for his gifts and friendly words. From then on Egil began to grow cheerful, and chanted:

> 'My browcrags griefbraised
> O'erhilled my eyehollows;
> Yet forehead's rough furrows
> Were smithred to smoothness.
> The prince has now prised up
> (Gold armrings' despoiler)
> High edge of my eyecliffs
> From maskland of face.'[21]

Here we have a particularly clear example of an exchange of valuables: the king gives Egil money and valuables, and the skald thanks him in song. This would have been seen as a completely fair exchange as the Scandinavians and the Anglo-Saxons valued poetry very highly indeed. It was not only that the skald's song appealed to the leader's vanity: since words – and particularly poetical words ('bound speech') – possessed magical power, lampoon was a way of causing genuine harm, while eulogy reinforced the well-being and the success of the monarch to whom it was addressed.

Other participants at a feast also received gifts – indeed it was the custom for no one to leave the scene without a gift of some sort. Great attention was paid to the quality and the value of the gifts, and a man would react bitterly and angrily if someone else of the same status was more lavishly rewarded than he. The sagas of the Norwegian kings tell the story of Áki the rich *bóndi*, who once invited two kings – of Norway and of Sweden – to a feast. He received the king of Sweden in the old banqueting hall, but for the Norwegian king a new hall was built and decorated with new tapestries. The Swedish king and his retinue had to drink out of old vessels and horns, while new vessels, polished and smooth as glass and adorned with gold, were prepared in honour of the Norwegian king. When parting with his guests Áki asked the Norwegian king, to whom he had given 'splendid gifts', to take his son into his service; to the Swedish king he offered 'noble gifts', also. The Swede did not conceal his resentment and asked Áki why he, being 'his man', had seen fit to offer such very superior hospitality to the king of Norway, by giving him 'the best of everything'. Áki answered that he had provided the Swede with old things because the Swede was the older, while the Norwegian king, being a young man, had been given the new things that befitted him. Áki went on to deny his subordination to the king of Sweden: 'As to your reminding me that I am your man, why, I consider it no less true that you are my man.' This was a direct insult, and the Swedish king slew Áki. In revenge, the Norwegian king and his men slew several members of the Swedish king's retinue.[22] Not too much reliance can be put on the details of this story, but it is not without interest as it provides a graphic illustration of the value the medieval Scandinavians placed on the rules and symbolism of hospitality.

Just as a gift had to be repaid, an invitation to a feast had to be rewarded. Bönder and nobles who entertained kings were rewarded with gifts. In Norway, the custom was for the king to show his gratitude for being entertained at a feast by granting the host a piece of landed property, which was called *drekkulaun* – from *drekka*, 'to drink', 'to feast', and *launa*, 'to reward', 'repay', 'thank'.[23] There was, however, more to a feast than a simple exchange of gifts; the gifts and hospitality laid on by the bönder in honour of the king had a deeper significance. The feast and the libations which accompanied it were a means of ensuring the people's welfare which depended on the king. At the festive board goblets were raised to the pagan gods and the king. On the king and his relationship with the gods depended whether there would be a good harvest, whether the cattle would be fertile and whether the herring shoals would come close inshore. As we saw above, the barbarians believed that they could influence time and its real content. The feast was the chief means employed of influencing time; but for this to be effective a personal relationship had to be set up between the farmers and the king, who embodied the 'fortune' and the 'success' of the country and its people.

Social relations in the world of the barbarians had a direct person-to-person character. The same goes for relations between the farmers and the king, and never was this more strikingly demonstrated than at times of ceremonial feast.

As the royal power became stabilised and as Christianity rendered the king's role as the director of religious affairs superfluous, not to say impossible, the character of the feasts changed. From being the main channel for contact between the bönder and the leader, they turned into an instrument for exploitation of the people by the king and his retinue, who could force the farmers to pay their tribute in the form of produce. Kings began to grant their retainers the right to appropriate such tribute for themselves; the practice began to resemble the award of fiefs.[24]

Not that feasts ceased to be an important medium of social relations. According to Norwegian law, the mark of a free man enjoying full rights was that he managed his own household, rode a horse and took part in feasts; there was no impediment in the way of such a farmer or *bóndi* owning and controlling property.[25] Long after the victory of Christianity over paganism, the custom of holding obligatory feasts every year persisted; and all householders, apart from the poverty-stricken, were required on pain of punishment to supply a given quantity of beer for the feast.[26] The feast was an occasion for the conclusion of property and marriage deals; the formal taking over by an heir was accompanied by

[231]

a feast, and at feasts feuding parties made peace; 'acceptance into the family' of an illegitimate son, that is, his investiture with personal and inheritance rights as a free kinsman and member of the family, was also the occasion for a specially arranged feast.

Among the other Germanic peoples we find the ceremonial feast playing no less important a part than among the Scandinavians. Like the Scandinavian kings, the Anglo-Saxon kings too travelled about the country, stopping to feast with their retainers and nobles. According to the *Laws of Aethelbert*, the first written example of English law (beginning of the seventh century), the king was mainly concerned with fixing due punishment for any action undertaken against him at a time when he was feasting at some country estate.[27] It seems that fighting and bloodshed were by no means rare at feasts, and 'ancient law' prescribed that the guilty party had to pay compensation not only to the victim but to the master of the house where the feast was taking place and also to the king.[28] Later, in the tenth century, those responsible for the maintenance of law and order in the provinces were required to assemble regularly at feasts, where they discussed affairs of the day and decided whether the law had been infringed in any way.[29]

The guilds – associations of people having common political or economic interests – also organised feasts; indeed, the very word *guild* is derived from *gildi*, a feast, offering, festival.

For these people, the communal consumption of food and drink had a profound social, religious and moral significance; the table-companions made new friends and old quarrels were patched up. In an appeasement formula which has been preserved in an Icelandic saga, we are told of the enemies who reached agreement and paid their wergild: 'You are to make peace and come to agreement over food and drink, at the þing and in the national assembly, in the church and in the king's house, and wherever people are gathered together, and you are to be as peaceable as though there had never been any disagreement between you. You will exchange knives and morsels of meat and all things like kinsmen and not like enemies.'[30]

[232]

Hospitality to guests was a cardinal and inviolable obligation on the part of any householder. Of the legendary king Geirröðr it was said that he was 'so sparing of food that he starved his guests if he thought that too many of them had come'. In the original of this passage the word *matníðingr* is used. But *níðingr* meant 'villain', 'scoundrel', 'base criminal'; the term was one of very strong legal and moral condemnation, being used of traitors, treaty-breakers, disturbers of the peace, those guilty of murder or other serious crimes, cowards – indeed, of anyone who was held to be useless to the community. So the term *matníðingr* does not mean 'miser' in our present-day sense of the word, which carries no very strong moral condemnation; rather it signifies a villainous reprobate who actually refused people hospitality. It was the worst accusation that could be levelled at anyone, and the story goes on: 'It was a great slander that Geirröðr was not hospitable.'[31]

The need to pay continual attention to one's guests is stressed over and over again in *Hávamál*; generosity, solicitude and, above all, gifts – we are told – safeguard friendship:

> Greetings to the host. The guest has arrived.
> In which seat shall he sit?
>
> ....
>
> Fire is needed by the newcomer
> Whose knees are frozen numb;
> Meat and clean linen a man needs
> Who has fared across the fells.
>
> Water, too, that he may wash before eating,
> Handcloths and hearty welcome,
> Courteous words, then courteous silence
> That he may tell his tale.[32]

We find ourselves in the presence of a society in which all aspects of social life have been regulated and ritualised, even the consumption of food and drink.[33]

In the barbarian view, peace was equivalent to feasting: the two things were virtually synonymous. The *Einherjar*, the heroes fallen in battle and taken by Óđinn to the hall of the gods – Valhalla – divide their time between the battles they engage in every day, and the peaceful feasts that follow the bloodshed. It was the warrior's ideal, at any rate.

For the farmer, however, military expeditions and plunder could hardly be his source of livelihood; nor could he count on gifts from the king. Such welfare as he has comes from his own labour:

> Early shall he rise who rules few servants,
>   And set to work at once:
> Much is lost by the late sleeper,
>   Wealth is worn by the swift.[34]

Naturally, it was not easy to earn very much in this way. However:

> A small hut of one's own is better,
>   A man is his master at home:
> A couple of goats and a corded roof
>   Still are better than begging
>
> A small hut of one's own is better,
>   A man is his master at home:
> His heart bleeds in the beggar who must
>   Ask at each meal for meat.[35]

The ethical norms in barbarian society are diffuse; they are not formulated with the clarity and finality characteristic of biblical commandments. Hence, it is not easy to reconstruct the barbarian attitude to work. As is well known, no small part was played in their economy by slaves, who were of course given the heaviest and dirtiest jobs – looking after the cattle, dunging the fields and so on. Female slaves worked in the house and reared the master's children. The main agricultural tasks, however, especially tilling, were performed by the masters themselves, the free men. In the Icelandic *Rígsþula* – a sort of mythological sociology of barbarian society – the work of slaves is described thus:

[234]

> They manured the fields,
> And built folds,
> They gathered peat,
> And fed the pigs,
> Guarded the goats.[36]

As if that were not enough, Thrall – the founder of the 'race of slaves' – 'stripped bast, made hurdles and carried brushwood for days on end'.

The free man, Karl,

> domesticated oxen
> and handled the plough
> built houses,
> erected barns
> made carts
> and tilled the soil.[37]

His wife span and looked after the house.

Clearly, the authors do not consider these agricultural tasks as beneath the dignity of a free man. The nobleman, however, will not concern himself with tilling or putting up farmyard buildings – he is completely taken up with entertainments, and military expeditions, the sort of thing that will ensure him fame and plunder. In the *Rígspula*, Earl is a dashing warrior, always ready to go on the warpath, who owns a large number of country estates; he is a keen hunter, fond of horse-racing and of throwing the javelin. He lives in a richly furnished house, eats fine foods and drinks wine. Together with his wife, who is also of noble birth, Earl lives 'in comfort, prosperity and good fortune', increasing his family. He distributes generously of his treasure and makes presents of swift horses, costly raiment; he throws rings and golden bracelets to his companions. For the ordinary man, however, work is the only way he can get the means to keep himself alive.

The connection between labour and property – the realis-ation that the former can generate the latter – can be traced in the records of barbarian custom. The right of possession was seen as deriving from the actual tilling of the land in question. Hence, the peasant could take squatter's rights on communal land in so far as he was able to cultivate his holding. According to Norwegian law, a farmer was entitled to clear for ploughing an additional piece of common land (*almenning*) stretching as far from the boundary of his own piece as he could throw his sickle or knife.[38] In the same way, meadowland was deemed to be taken by the first man to put a scythe to it;[39] and in the forest, as much wood could be taken as a man could cut down and transport before sunset. A husbandman who cultivated a piece of land over a lengthy period without any other claim being made on it from any quarter, was entitled to regard it as his own. On the other hand, anyone who failed to make proper use of his land in the long run lost his rights to it. In other words, the right of ownership was not understood in any abstract sense: a piece of land being tilled was held to belong to the tiller.

But for the ownership of a piece of land to be established beyond question, something more was needed than hard work on it; ownership had to be consecrated by certain prescribed ritual procedures, which alone ensured that the rights of an individual would be recognised by the community. The juridical terminology of the Scandinavian is particularly interesting, as it very clearly reflects their ideas in this context (unlike the Latin used in the historical documents of continental Europe). The Scandinavians used the word *helga*, 'to sanctify', 'to consecrate', 'to make inviolable', to indicate titular rights to a piece of land. The rituals by means of which the act of possession was consecrated placed the land and the right to it under the patronage and protection of higher powers, and at the same time linked the possession in the closest possible manner with the person performing the ritual. The most important means of taking and consecrating possession was fire. An Icelander, wishing to appropriate a piece of no-man's-land, wasteland, had to spend a day, from sunrise to sunset, circumambulating it and lighting bonfires at certain prescribed distances. It was permissible to fire an arrow with burning tow and the fire sanctified the spot where the arrow fell.[40] The appropriated land was often dedicated to the god Thor; this was enough to make it impossible for anyone else to lay claim to the

[236]

land. In Icelandic, the expression *helga sér* still means 'to declare one's ownership'. Land and other goods which underwent the sanctification and dedication ceremony were protected by law, and any infringement of their inviolability was punishable by fine.

Thus, the mediating role played by the gods conferred a sacral character upon the acquisition of landed property. Labour and religion, the norms of law and the trappings of magic, were brought together and interwoven. The *de facto* situation had to receive not only juridical recognition but also religious sanction; hence inevitably it also acquired a symbolic meaning. By cultivating his ground a man entered into a sacral-magical relationship with nature and with the gods. A productive activity was given a symbolic setting, which enhanced its significance and lent it a new dignity.

To judge by the aphorisms contained in *Hávamál* and by the Icelandic family sagas the farmer's ideal could be summed up simply as the hope of a comfortable existence. The desire for luxury which was characteristic of the nobleman was alien to the ordinary free man. For neither of them, however, did wealth – whether earned through hard work or taken as plunder in battle – represent an end in itself. Wealth is not very highly valued in the world-view prevalent in this society. In *Hávamál*, which seems to sum up the mental attitudes of the pre-feudal period, it is the ephemeral nature of wealth that is stressed, its inessentiality, its insignificance in comparison with the higher values inherent in observance of social morals. Wealth is transient:

> It is always better to be alive,
> The living can keep a cow;
> Fire, I saw, warming a wealthy man,
> With a cold corpse at his door.

....

> Fields and flocks had Fitjung's[41] sons,
> Who now carry begging bowls:
> Wealth may vanish in the wink of an eye,
> Gold is the falsest of friends.[42]

[237]

Wealth does nothing for a man's dignity and can even be detrimental to his personal qualities:

> The nitwit does not know that gold
>   Makes apes of many men:
> One is rich, one is poor –
>   There is no blame in that.
>
> ....
>
> In the fool who acquires cattle and lands,
>   Or wins a woman's love,
> His wisdom wanes with his waxing pride,
>   He sinks from sense to conceit.[43]

The main thing is that it is not wealth that elevates a man but his good name: that is what remains in people's memories even after his death:

> Cattle die, kindred die,
>   Every man is mortal:
> But the good name never dies
>   Of one who has done well.
>
> Cattle die, kindred die,
>   . Every man is mortal:
> But I know one thing that never dies,
>   The glory of the great dead.[44]

The last line in this translation does not give all the shades of meaning that are present in the original. *Dómr um dauðan hvern* means literally: 'The judgment [verdict] on each of those who have died'. S. Piekarczyk is right to stress that these words reflect the weight of public opinion which was brought to bear on the individual.[45]

The contrastive pair formed by wealth and good name is highly characteristic of the world-view prevalent in barbarian society. Wealth is valued only in so far as it contributes to the attainment of fame and public esteem. But as we have seen, this does not depend on the accumulation of wealth but on showing oneself to be lavish, a giver of gifts, a liberal host at feasts – in short, on turning wealth into a sign of personal prowess. The feast and the gift are key concepts linking their economy and their culture.

The sin of cupidity

Medieval feudal society differed fundamentally from the barbarian society which preceded it. It was built up on class antagonism, on the political and social dominance of the feudal landowners over the dependent peasantry. So attitudes to labour and property in feudal society differed radically from those in the pre-class society. Nevertheless there is a close link between the two. Our present task is not to analyse property relations under feudalism; rather, we wish to show how property and wealth were understood in this society, how they were valued from an ethical viewpoint, what was the purpose of wealth. It is hardly necessary to point out that different classes looked on labour and property in very different fashion. At the same time, feudal society was dominated by Christian morality, whose norms were obligatory upon all of its members, and shared to greater or less degree by all classes and social groupings.

Feudal society was founded on property – on the immense holdings of the nobility and the church on the one hand and the small holdings of the peasant or the artisan on the other. And yet throughout the Middle Ages the possession of property was never expressly approved or justified: it was permitted, but only under certain conditions and with pretty extensive provisos. For while Christianity gave its blessing to the feudal structure in general, its attitude to property was somewhat contradictory.

The Church Fathers were at pains to point out that Adam and Eve, being without sin and in direct contact with God, knew nothing of labour or of property. The Lord had created the earth, its fruits and all living creatures for man's use and enjoyment; but these things were to be held in common. It was people's cupidity after the Fall that led to the institution of private property.

Thus, property and individual possession are not of God

but are the result of human cupidity and the shortcomings of human nature after expulsion from paradise. This viewpoint, which links private property with primeval sin, was also accepted by the medieval church. According to the law of God, all things are held in common. 'Mine' and 'thine' are the outcome of man's greed. Christ had no property and lived in poverty, an example which was followed by his disciples. As it is said in the Gospel of St Matthew (6:19–21, 24): 'Lay not up for yourselves treasures upon earth, where moth and rust doth corrupt, and where thieves break through and steal: But lay up for yourselves treasures in heaven, where neither moth nor rust doth corrupt, and where thieves do not break through nor steal; For where your treasure is there will your heart be also. . . . Ye cannot serve God and mammon.' And again in verse 26: 'Behold the fowls of the air: for they sow not, neither do they reap, nor gather into barns; yet your heavenly Father feedeth them . . .'

The medieval Christian could not but take these commands seriously. Ideally the righteous man was a poor man; for poverty was a virtue which wealth could never be. Property was the embodiment of earthly interests which distracted man's attention from the life to come and the salvation of his soul. Faith demanded the renunciation of earthly things and earthly interests. So a true follower of Christ could only look upon wealth with suspicion. 'Scorn earthly riches', said St Bernard of Clairvaux, 'so that you may gain heavenly riches.' Property was seen as a hindrance in the way of the love of God and of mankind, for it generates selfishness and the struggle to acquire things; and in the process altruism is overcome by avarice and enmity. 'And so the first and basic condition for the attainment of perfect love', taught St Thomas Aquinas, 'is voluntary poverty.'[46]

The sermons preached by the medieval theologians on the need to renounce property contain more than a trace of rhetoric. If few people were prepared to take such teachings seriously, they were not just paying lip-service to their inability to follow the Christian doctrine of poverty literally. If the great mass of believers were to succeed in reconciling the prescription of evangelical poverty with the possession of property, there had to be people in society who would take it upon themselves to practise voluntary poverty, thus setting others an example, which, even if it could not be followed by the backsliders, at least gave them some comfort. By behaving righteously and renouncing earthly delights, these godly men were saving the whole of the human race. In the monastic orders the vow of poverty was a basic condition. The Benedictines not only eschewed all forms of property but were even forbidden to use the words 'my', 'mine' and 'thy', 'thine'; in their place the founder of the order, St Benedict, prescribed the word 'our'. 'The concept of common property was even extended to the physical bodies of the monks. There was discussion as to whether a monk was entitled to look upon the limbs of his body as his personal property; was he entitled to speak of 'my head', 'my tongue', 'my hands' or was he to say 'our head', 'our tongue', 'our hands' in the same way as one said 'our head-dress', 'our cassock'. In monasticism medieval renunciation of the world and of the self led to the annihilation of the individual personality.'[47] In the post-Benedictine orders of the Franciscans and the Dominicans not only personal but communal property as well was forbidden. The monks were supposed to live entirely on charity.

For most members of feudal society it was practically impossible to live in a state of evangelical poverty. The clergy were well aware of this. If society was to exist and function as a whole, some property had to be tolerated. 'It would be wrong to say that men must have no property', admitted St Thomas Aquinas,[48] who reasoned that the Fall not only caused private property to appear but also rendered its retention inevitable: for, in a state of worldly sinfulness, a man naturally cared and worked for himself and his own affairs more than for others. However, it was not so much private property itself that the theologians condemned as its abuse. According to them, a man should not own more property than was absolutely necessary for the satisfaction of his needs. As Augustine said: 'he who has more than he needs has what does not belong to him'. The early Christian ideal of a community of believers, who have renounced all possessions and take no thought for their sustenance, is replaced in the Middle Ages by the ideal of the smallholding, the possession

[241]

of which allows basic needs to be satisfied. Accumulation over and above this minimum was considered a sin; for it was dictated by cupidity. As defined by St Thomas Aquinas, 'cupidity is the sin which leads man to try to acquire or to retain more wealth than he has need of'.[49] On the basis of this concession, the church recognised a real social requirement. And its teaching that a limited amount of property, though an evil, was permissible because it prevented a greater evil, incorporated and satisfied the main aims of the small landowners and small craftsmen and artisans who formed the backbone of medieval society. Christian condemnation of property reduced in practice to the condemnation of profiteering and money-grubbing; and the question of what was permissible and what impermissible property was assessed, not so much by its dimensions, as by the aims pursued by its owners and the means they used to get their hands on it. A cardinal criterion, too, was the mental attitude, the spiritual state of the owner. Wealth, as St Thomas Aquinas said, could not be accounted an end in itself; it was no more than a means for the attainment of other ends that lay beyond the purely economic sphere.

The biggest proprietor in feudal society, and one bound by many ties of common interest with the great lay landowners, was the church. As one might expect, it did nothing to encourage any change in the institution of private property, or to bring about any redistribution of property that might approximate more to the ideal of small holdings and the satisfaction of limited needs. In a class society, the commandment 'Thou shalt not steal' protected property in a way that was very much in the interests of the 'haves'. At most, the church countenanced a partial redistribution of wealth by urging the faithful to give alms to the poor. The 'have-nots' of the world were regarded as being closer to Christ than the well-to-do; in the poor man was seen the image of Christ. Hence charity was encouraged in every way possible. Rulers and noblemen normally supported a fairly large contingent of beggars and poor people at their courts, to whom they gave food and money. It was not unusual for these hand-outs to assume very large proportions indeed, and rich people were in the habit of providing substantial sums for the destitute. Noble ladies were particularly zealous in this field, and some persons of royal origin did not shrink from sacrificing part of the state income to the needs of the poor. Paupers and beggars were widely supported by the monasteries; in some years, for example, up to seventeen thousand poor people were fed at Cluny.

Medieval charity was, however, inspired less by love for one's neighbour as preached by Christianity than by the donor's concern for his own spiritual salvation. If a rich man could save his soul by giving alms to the poor, that was what mattered; the beggars to whom he gave a portion of his wealth did not concern him overmuch. This is shown by the fact that throughout the Middle Ages there was not one single attempt to get to grips with the root causes of poverty; the poor continued to be fed, the donors gained virtue, and the situation remained as it was. For the coexistence of poverty and riches the church provided a logical explanation: 'The rich are created to be the salvation of the poor, and the poor are created to be the salvation of the rich.' Giving charity to the poor was seen as a sort of insurance for the rich. Alcuin wrote that by giving alms to the poor one might go straight to heaven. Hrabanus Maurus echoed him: material riches given to the destitute are turned into heavenly riches.[50] Thus it was actually necessary for the have-nots and the ne'er-do-wells to exist, and it never entered anyone's head to try to get rid of poverty; just as the beggars themselves came to see themselves as God's chosen and made no attempt to better their earthly lot. On the contrary, poverty was seen as an ideal to be aimed at, and the church allowed the taking of the oath of poverty by those who were drawn to it by reasons of 'humility and concern for the common good, not out of self-interest or sloth'. The papacy, it is true, apprehensive lest anti-property convictions should become too popular, announced that poverty was not a general obligation but rather a vocation for a chosen few. It would be a long time before poverty was recognised in medieval society as a social evil, as an index of social malfunction.[51] Poverty was not seen as a contingency to be got rid of, but rather as a state of self-abnegation and renunciation of the world; with the result that the business of poverty was very much part of the medieval scene. Not riches but poverty – above all, poverty of spirit, humility – was the ideal of medieval society.

Every society has its heroes, every society produces its ideal type of man, who serves as an example to be followed. This ideal type plays a very important part in moral education, and can therefore be itself construed as a reflection of the moral condition of society. This is especially true in the case of an authoritarian society like the medieval one, all of whose culture bears the didactic imprint. In such a society the ideal type of man is a not unimportant ingredient of its moral climate. What was this paragon like?

The ideal human type of the antique polis was the all-rounder, the citizen who had fully developed his talents. Among the qualities that went to make a harmonious personality, an important part was played by physical development; the athlete, the Olympic champion, embodied this ideal to perfection. The ideal human type of the Middle Ages was infinitely removed from the antique one. The cult of the body, of visible beauty, has nothing in common with worship of the sufferings of a God who has chosen to embody himself in mortal flesh. In so far as we can speak of a 'physical ideal' in the Christian Middle Ages, this is represented by the tortured body of Christ, crucified to save the human race. The Middle Ages did obeisance not to the bodily strength and the harmonious proportions of the athlete but to the wasted frame and suppurating sores of the sick. Nursing the sick, washing their wounds and seeing therein the suffering Saviour was a service as pleasing to God as the giving of alms.

The ideal of medieval society was the monk, the saint, the ascetic, the man who had most completely renounced earthly interests, cares and temptations and who was therefore of all men nearest to God. The Greek word ἄσκησις means 'exercise' – in particular, 'gymnastic exercise'; the ἀσκητής is the athlete, the wrestler. The same word was used in the Christian Middle Ages for the man who neglects his body and mortifies the flesh for the sake of exercising his soul. Perhaps nothing is more expressive of the contrast between the antique and the medieval mind than the shift in the meaning of this word. The medieval ideal is not this-worldly,

earthly and practical; it is transcendental, having outgrown
its earthly ties. The ideal of the saint was a general one, with
a hold on all strata of society. Of course, the various strata
and estates of medieval society also had their own individual
ideals. For example, there was the knightly ideal. But even
this ideal was long subordinated to the universal ascetic ideal,
for what was held to be admirable and worthy of imitation
about the knight was not only his physical prowess and
warlike spirit – not even the conscious effort he made to live
up to his order and his adherence to a strict code of behaviour, but his subordination of all these qualities to a higher
ideal; the knightly class was called upon to place its arms at
the service of God and the church. The Crusader – the loftiest
type of the man-at-arms, *miles Christi*, exemplifies this ideal
type of knight.[52]

The whole of society cannot be judged by its ideal type.
But the type serves as an index of the prevalent mental
climate, of the moral norms accepted in this society, and it
reflects the system of values by which its members are in one
way or another guided. The social ideal of the Middle Ages
did not favour the accumulation of material goods, nor was
it compatible with vanity or ostentation. Medieval literature
is unsparing in its condemnation of showy attire. Women's
fashions, which are perhaps the best guide to social taste and
social trends, did not change over centuries, and we are on
the threshold of the Renaissance before we find a desire for
quick changes, for innovation and extravagance, creeping in.
The successful and wealthy could not be taken as objects of
admiration and examples to be followed.

The religious-ethical glorification of poverty and recognition of its sacral character found their supreme expression in
the preaching of St Francis of Assisi, who called upon people
to 'follow naked the naked Christ' and who solemnised a
mystic marriage with Our Lady Poverty. It was no part of
St Francis's plan to release the poor from their miserable lot;
on the contrary, he accepted material inequality on earth,
seeing poverty as a virtue and as an example most worthy to
be followed.

Christian moral attitudes did not prevent the steady development of trade and industry, but created a specific mental

and spiritual climate in which this development took place. The accumulation of wealth and the undue adulation of earthly goods were targets for attack by all those who were dissatisfied with the social order as it stood. Ideologically, dissatisfaction of this sort drew for its sustenance on the evangelical ideals of poverty and asceticism, and this continued to be the case right up to the Reformation. Opposition to feudalism, which took in these days the form of religious heresy, used these ideals as its ammunition, and strove to realise them in practice. Predictably, all efforts in this direction came to naught – yet in themselves they are very characteristic of a society which was based on property and exploitation and which nevertheless preached the virtues of poverty and humility. Medieval man laboured, prospered and led a sinful life, doing obeisance to the saints and repenting of his own imperfection. Hypocrisy was not unknown in the Middle Ages, far from it – but to reduce the gap between the way people lived and the ideals they professed to nothing more than sanctimoniousness would be an oversimplification. Medieval man was conscious of the dichotomy between the kingdom of heaven, the abode of the blessed where justice ruled, and the earthly world sunk in sin and riddled with temptation. As a rule, man was not able to tear himself away from the embrace of this earthly world, and he paid for his weakness by being in a state of mental ambiguity and inferiority. The mass sectarian movements, the social convulsions accompanied by self-flagellation, mass repentance and pilgrimages to the Holy Places, the dispersal of one's goods and taking the vow of abstinence – all this reflects both the social and the spiritual conflicts of feudal society.

'Serving' and 'distributing'

As we examine the attitude to wealth and property which underlies the values held by the ruling class in feudal society, we come across something that may strike us at first sight as paradoxical: the ethical attitudes of this ruling class – the knights and nobles – quite closely resemble the attitude to wealth which was characteristic of barbarian society. Furthermore, it is a resemblance which extends beyond this to a wider area of feudal ideology and social psychology. Such concepts as 'honour', 'fame' and 'high birth', as used in feudalism, seem to be directly borrowed from the ideology of the period preceding the emergence of the class society.

Of all the virtues that could grace the feudal seigneur, generosity took first place. The seigneur was surrounded by his family, his retainers, his vassals, all of whom served him, supported him and did his bidding. The power of a noble seigneur is determined by the number of persons serving him and owing allegiance to him. Otherwise, he is not 'senior'; he is not lord and head. The seigneur is, of course, a landed proprietor, drawing revenue from the peasants who work his land. Were it not for such revenue from his dependent tenants, he would not be in a position to maintain his retinue and feed his many hangers-on. The income he derives from his estates enables him to give feasts and receptions, to receive guests and hand out gifts – in a word, to live in the grand manner. A seigneur is behaving 'normally' when he is generous, careless of cost, open-handed and spendthrift, and indifferent as to whether he is spending more than he receives. Any gap between income and expenditure can be filled by squeezing the peasants a little harder and fining them; robbery and war booty bring in additional sums. Economy and thrift are qualities running counter to the ethics of his estate. His income is looked after by the bailiff, the steward and the reeve, and all he has to do is eat and drink and give away his property – and the more lavishly, the more spectacularly he can do this, the more vociferously will he be praised and the higher will be his social standing and prestige.

Wealth as seen by the lords was not an end in itself, nor was it something that should be accumulated or used for economic improvement or development. The landowner who sought to increase his income did not do so with a view to stepping up production; it was simply a way of widening his circle of friends and retainers, allies and vassals, among whom he would then distribute his largesse of money and goods. Pushkin's stingy knight, secretly gloating over the sight and sound of the money he keeps in armoured chests in the cellars, may be a figure characteristic of the Renaissance – but he has nothing at all to do with the knights of the Middle Ages. Feudal extravagance was one of the ways in which the proceeds of the exploitation of the servile classes were distributed among the members of the ruling class. But this form of feudal distribution was very specific in its effects. The seigneur could get little satisfaction from the knowledge that he owned treasure if he was not in a position to squander it and exhibit it – or, to put it more accurately, to squander it in spectacular fashion. It was not simply a matter of eating and drinking one's way through a fortune; it had to be done in the full glare of publicity at a crowded table with lots of free gifts.

The way wealth was handled in feudal society often reminds us very strongly of the 'potlatch' of the North American Indians, who would invite other members of the tribe to feasts and try to impress them by squandering their entire food stocks and chopping their fishing boats into pieces. In these and other ways they demonstrated their generosity and extravagance. Marc Bloch has described some very similar practices from feudal times. There was the knight who ordered a ploughed field to be sown with pieces of silver; another required his food to be cooked not with wood but with very expensive wax candles; a third sought to catch the public eye by burning thirty of his horses alive.[53] These wanton acts of wastefulness always took place before an audience of other noblemen and their vassals with the aim of startling them – otherwise an act of such conspicuous waste would have no point.

Competitions in wastefulness of the potlatch type found in archaic societies and the gargantuan feasts put on by the medieval nobility have something in common: in both there is an aggressive generosity, an effort to overwhelm the guests with one's extravagance, and to score points in an extraordinary sort of social game, in which the stakes are prestige and influence. Of course, behaviour of this sort on the part of feudal nobles was dictated by obedience to tradition rather than by a dominant frame of mind; and it is true that in the more outrageous acts of extravagance, contemporaries saw something unusual, a departure from the norm. But an essential trait of courtly psychology is here laid bare, albeit in somewhat hypertrophied form.

For the feudal lord, wealth was a means of retaining his social influence, of affirming his 'honour'. In itself, being rich did not command respect; on the contrary, the merchant with plenty of assets, who used money to make more in commercial or money-lending operations, awoke all sorts of emotions in the medieval breast: hate, envy, scorn, fear – but not respect. The seigneur, on the other hand, carelessly flinging his revenues to the winds and living beyond his means, had only to invite guests to a feast and hand out gifts he could not afford to be universally renowned and looked up to. The feudal lord saw wealth as a means for attaining ends lying far outside the purely economic sphere. Wealth was an index of the lord's success, of his generous and magnanimous nature. He had to show off. For the rich lord, the supreme moment of pleasure in his wealth came when he could squander it in the company of as many people as possible.

Like all semantic systems with a social significance, this one too had to be translated into practice via an obligatory ritual and a series of established canons. Feasts, entertainments, courtly gatherings, tournaments, took place at regular intervals duly accompanied by the proper ceremonial and protocol. The public life of the knight was spent either on the battlefield or in diversions organised at his lord's court. The lyrics of the Provençal troubadours provide perhaps the best evidence of the extent to which every detail of knightly behaviour was ritualised. Courtly love which is their theme is understood as service of a lady, exactly similar to a vassal's service of his lord. The lady bestowed her favour on the knight just as the lord gave him a fief or a gift. The troubadours liked to use legal language and feudal terminology to describe their amorous langour. Sometimes the poet actually calls his lady-love 'seigneur'.[54] Recent research has shown that courtly love, which the troubadours had ritualised down to the last detail, was an important factor in the consolidation of the lesser nobility attached to the courts of great feudal lords, since it was an indissoluble component not only of their amorous life but of their social behaviour as a whole.

In their idealised picture of relations at court, the poets give pride of place to the idea of generosity. The court of the great feudal lord is above all a place where people 'give and receive'. The theme of giving and the distribution of gifts is linked in troubadour poetry with the theme of the decadence of the world – a very popular theme in the Middle Ages. The world is seen as a battlefield where virtues confront vices. Among the worst and most heinous defects must be reckoned arrogance, stinginess and cupidity. 'No more do barons bestow gifts on youths as they used to do long ago', laments one poet, who sees in this a symptom of the intrusion of evil into the world. Meanness must be opposed by a noble generosity, which the poets see as the crucial criterion of the state of society. 'To give' and 'to make a gift'; to a troubadour, this is the prime virtue. The split between wealth and the joy of dispensing it is tantamount to the collapse of universal harmony, for avarice is the mother of all vices, while generosity is the core of all virtues. A man is weighed in respect of his generosity, round which the whole ethical system of chivalry revolves, and which even takes precedence over prowess on the field of battle. 'By means of gifts and largesse a man becomes noble, acquires honour and fame', says one poet; 'I say nothing ill of arms or reason, but gifts govern all.'[55] He who gives will gain divine favour. 'Valour teaches us to be lavish with our income', said the poet Peire Cardenal. Generosity, hospitality and a readiness to hand out gifts were the distractions of the nobleman, the only way for him to reach the supreme pinnacles of love. In the eyes of a troubadour, the rich miser is a monster who fails to grasp the significance of his privileged position and who acts contrary to God's will.

The troubadours' appeals to the generosity of the feudal lords come in all keys – from the bluntest of extortionate demands to the subtlest of hints. According to the morality they preached, which was doubtless shared at court, the sole justification for wealth and power is that by being passed on from the owner they can contribute to the happiness and welfare of others:

As soon as you gather goods together,
Divided they can do good,
Without selfishness and falsity.
(Giraut de Bornelh)[56]

The question of the incomes of the lesser knights, the cadets – i.e. unmarried men without fiefs – was a burning social problem in feudal society.[57] The lyrics of the court poets reflect the conflict between rich and poor knights and the tensions that existed between different levels of the feudal hierarchy.

Relations between seigneur and vassal are presented by the poets as relations of mutual service, help and friendship. 'To serve', in their lexicon, often meant not 'to take', but 'to give' 'to offer', 'to spend'. In the lyrics of the Old Provençal poets, we are constantly coming across such compounds as 'serving and giving' or even 'serving and giving something from one's own property'. The Provençal poets never tire of stressing that the power of the feudal lords resides in their generosity. 'Ignoble is he who serves not nor gives, and does not behave as reason bids us' (Bertrand Carbonel). 'The owner of a castle who, serving and giving, attains to happiness' – only he deserves the poet's praises (Richart). Rich and renowned is the castle of the seigneur who 'serves' and 'gives' in lordly and magnificent fashion. We even find the expression 'to serve by means of one's property'. The concepts of 'giving' and 'taking' along with 'serving' and 'accepting service' are here intimately correlated within the ideological nexus of the reciprocal lord–vassal relationship. Thus, the feudal concept of service is indissolubly linked with the concept of the bestowing and squandering of property. Where it not so, how could there be friendship and loyalty between two knights? Only the generous squandering of wealth can make a man famed and respected.

'If a man scorns fame and generosity, he is acting without dignity. God exhorts men to dwell on their fame and good name . . .' (Montanhagol). Lords who transgress these rules of courtly morality do not deserve the love of fair ladies:

[251]

The baron who in secret feasts
Behaves unacceptably vilely,
But a hundred times worse than he is the lady
Who then accepts him. (Magret)[58]

Like relations with one's vassals, love for one's lady entailed a lot of outlay. The chief merit of the gift, however, did not lie in its material value; indeed, the troubadours censured those who solicited more opulent gifts, and tended to regard such behaviour as immoral. The real meaning of the gift lay in the actual act of giving, in the tie between individuals which the gift established or consolidated. Custom required not a single gift unilaterally given, but an exchange of gifts. Quite often it was not the knight who made an offering to the lady but she to him, and there was nothing humiliating in this. Service was understood both as giving and as receiving gifts. The better to understand the close connection between the concepts of 'serving' and 'gift' we must rid our minds of the idea that 'service' was always undertaken for the sake of material reward; service, like the proffering of gifts, was a form of social intercourse which united people in cohesive sets. Wealth was a means whereby such links could be socially sustained. At one point in the poetic competition between Raimbaut de Vaqueiras and the Marquis Albert de Malaspina, the former accused the marquis of extorting money from merchants travelling through his domain. The marquis replied that if he did so it was not out of greed but merely so that he could then distribute the plunder to others.[59] For medieval seigneurs exchange of gifts was no less important than the question of donations to the church for the purpose of saving souls. Giving, donating, was an inexhaustible theme for pointed discussion. John of Garland wrote *In Praise of Noble Donors and On the Reasons for Giftgiving* (*Commendatio nobilium datorum et de causis dandi*), while other authors expatiated on the dangers inherent in accepting gifts. How and to whom gifts should be made is one of the themes of twelfth-century literature.[60]

Generosity is an inseparable trait of the monarch, as, in general, of any great lord in the courtly romances. Generosity is the 'lady and queen' without whom all other chivalric qualities are reduced to naught. As we are told in the *Romance of Lancelot*, the ruler must distribute horses and gold, raiment, 'prime' revenues and 'rich lands' – whereby 'he loses nothing but will gain in all'. In the Arthurian cycle, generosity and gifts appear as the sole factors making for cohesion among the knights.

We need not dwell here on the ruthless exploitation of the peasantry by the feudal lords: it is well enough known. Peasants were subject to corvée and to quit-rent, either in money or in kind and to many other kinds of extortion; often the poorest peasants were driven to ruin and desperation. Nor did it take the nobility long to decide to lay its hands on the wealth of the townspeople as well. Medieval knights saw nothing disgraceful in relieving others of their wealth; indeed, they often boasted of their predatory skills and exploits. Respect for other people's property was not uppermost in their minds. The history of the Middle Ages is one of interminable wars and civil strife. Each and every campaign, even if it ostensibly pursued worthy ends 'pleasing to God', was accompanied by pillage and rape. The seizure of wealth was followed by its distribution among one's comrades-in-arms, the bestowal of gifts on vassals and companions, and the ostentatious consumption of whatever was left, at feasts. To recapitulate: only as and when turned into a palpable symbol of high social standing and privileged position could a nobleman's wealth be squared with feudal morality and with the style of life and mode of behaviour required of him by his membership of the noble order.

We see then that the exchange of gifts, the festive distribution and squandering of wealth, and the spendthrift attitude to property, so characteristic of the barbarian age, were equally characteristic of feudalism. But this is not to say that feudalism simply took over these institutions and traditions from its predecessors, and that the medieval scene is no more than a rerun of the past. Many archaic features of medieval life do indeed display remarkable tenacity, but nothing is gained by dismissing them as mere atavisms. The crucial question is: what was the role of these traditional institutions in the new economic and social climate?

The gift, the feast, the ceremonial exchange of objects or

services and their semantic function as the indices of wealth – these are specific manifestations of social relations in the societies we have been considering. Under feudalism, these relations were primarily of a person-to-person nature. Members of the society entered into direct personal contacts with each other, relations which were based on kinship, on marriage, on proximity as neighbours and on common membership of a group, and on patronage or dependence on and subordination to the lord. However these relationships might differ in nature and function, they always found expression in the shape of direct personal relations between individuals – in sharp contrast to the relationships of bourgeois society, which are 'reified' and 'fetishised' as relationships between commodities. 'Wealth', says the hero of a French epic, 'is not fine furs, nor money, nor castle walls, nor horses; wealth is kinsmen and friends . . .'[61]

It is the personal relationship between lord and servant – a relationship with which the whole structure of feudal society is imbued – that gives the feudal concept of property its specific character. This is very far from what is usually called private property. Roman law defined private ownership as the right to the free possession and disposal of property and the right to make unrestricted use thereof, including its abuse (*jus utendi et abutendi*): the feudal law of ownership was different in principle. The main category of feudal property – land – was not something that could be freely alienated. The feudal proprietor could not appropriate for his own use all the revenue from his lands and was deprived of it altogether if he failed to perform the services that went with ownership. At the same time, as long as the peasants working on his land paid their rents and carried out the services required of them, their allotments were safeguarded and he had no right to expel them. Strictly speaking, the concept of 'private owner' cannot properly be applied either to the medieval landlord or to his vassal. The landowner was regarded not as 'possessor' but as 'holder' (*tenens*) to whom land has been assigned by a higher authority, and for his tenure to be viable certain conditions had to be observed. The rights of the *tenens* were always limited. Even in cases where he exercised *de facto* independent ownership over a piece of land, he was still regarded as having received it from a seigneur above him, and in several areas of feudal Europe the principle of 'no land without a seigneur' was adhered to. Independent properties with no known human seigneurs were called 'fiefs in the air' or 'fiefs held of the sun'.

The concept of 'partial ownership' does little to clarify the specific nature of feudal ownership. It is not so much a question of the 'limitation', the 'incompleteness' of feudal ownership (concepts which creep in when we try to compare feudal ownership with classical or bourgeois ownership) as of the *personal* nature of the relationships connected with it. Property is always a relationship between people. But private property is a reified form of social relations, while feudal ownership is an interpersonal form, containing in essence all the social relations of medieval society. If bourgeois ownership confronts factory workers and agricultural tenants as impersonal wealth, feudal land ownership is always personified for the peasant in the person of the seigneur and in the authority, the judicial prerogatives and the traditional ties inseparable from him. Bourgeois ownership can be entirely anonymous, while feudal ownership always bears a name which it confers upon the feudal lord; for him, the land is not just something to be owned, but also his native soil, with its history, its local customs, its beliefs and its prejudices.

Landed property relations under feudalism are above all relations between those in authority and those subject to authority. The vassal entering the service of a feudal lord and accepting his patronage swore an oath of fealty to him and pledged himself to help him in all things, to defend him from his enemies, to do his bidding and to perform such services as were incumbent upon him. For his part, the lord undertook to protect the vassal, to care for him and not leave him to fend for himself. The exchange of oaths and pledges might be accompanied by grant of a fief, but to qualify for this the vassal had to be in a position to perform knightly or other 'noble' service. Grant of a fief usually meant a land grant, but it might also be no more than the right to the revenues from the land, or the right to customs and other forms of extortion, judicial rights and the income therefrom, and so

[255]

on. The key issue was not the object granted but the fact of the grant itself; the conferring of a fief entailed obligation on the vassal's part to serve and obey his lord. The fief gave the vassal the material security which was needed if he was to serve his master properly. The lord could, however, attain the same ends without conferring any sort of grant: he could simply receive the vassal into his establishment and provide for his upkeep. Thus, in essence, the feudal relationship between seigneur and vassal consists above all in the establishing of a personal link: master and servant, patronage and service. In these relationships the principle of reciprocity, the mutual exchange of services, is as clearly visible as it was in the forms of ceremonial exchange we looked at above.

Like the exchange of gifts and participation in a feast, the establishment of vassalage relations had its due ritual; as oaths were exchanged, certain special rites were performed, which were designed to reinforce the personal ties being forged and lend them juridical force and inviolability. The vassal went down on his knees and put his hands between the hands of the seigneur. This meant literally that he 'came into his hands', made himself his 'man'. When granting a fief the seigneur handed the vassal a twig or some other object symbolising the transfer of the holding. The profound symbolism of these procedures found adequate expression in contemporary art.

The miniatures illustrating the medieval law-codes often show people with several hands and two faces. This is not simply a grotesque fantasy: it is a way of reproducing the actual content of certain juridical procedures – investiture, paying homage, '*commendatio*', the act of becoming a vassal. The artist sacrifices reality to the need to incorporate in one configuration all the implications of the juridical act – hence the additional hands. The feudal lord, seated on a chair, holds between his hands the hands of the vassal who is swearing fealty to him, pointing at the same time with an additional hand to the land which is being granted to the new vassal as his fief. Elsewhere, the lord is shown in the form of a two-faced Janus; on the left, he holds the hands of a vassal, while on the right he offers the symbol of landed property to another man. What is represented here is the transfer by the lord of a fief owned by one vassal to a second, without the knowledge of the first. The duplicity of the lord is shown literally: he has two faces and two pairs of hands. Such illustrations are collocations of acts taking place at different times; they are synchronic and diachronic at one and the same time. The medieval artist chooses to represent successive acts in one single configuration, thus emphasising the close inner ties between them in a symbolic fashion which would have been immediately clear to his contemporaries.

The handing on of an inherited fief was also accompanied by symbolic procedures, as was renewal of oath upon change of seigneur: the vassals of a dead seigneur had to swear to his son, just as the heirs of deceased vassals could only take over the fiefs of their dead fathers if they swore fealty to the seigneur. Even annulment of the treaty of vassalage had its specific ritual. Indeed, all aspects of feudal fealty were thus symbolised and ritualised; divorced from the semiological system of formulas and rituals, these relations were unimaginable and had no juridical force. In particular, the relationships of land grant and vassalage could only acquire social significance in this symbolic form. *Ipso facto*, these social and political institutions also became cultural factors. The cultural symbolism, which is a universal trait of the spiritual life of the Middle Ages, absorbed this sphere of social activity as well, lending it a higher significance and raising social ties to the level of ethical values.

Pointing out the essential difference between the feudal and bourgeois forms of land ownership, Marx wrote that for the former to turn into the latter several things were necessary:

It is inevitable that . . . landed property, which is the root of private property, should be drawn entirely into the orbit of private property and become a commodity; that the rule of the property owner should appear as the naked rule of private property, of capital, divested of all political tincture; that the relationship between property owner and worker should be reduced to the politico-economic relationship of exploiter and exploited; that the personal relationship between the property owner and his property should come to an end, and that the property itself should become purely *material* wealth; that the marriage of interest with the land should take over from the marriage of honour, and that land like man, should sink to the level of a venal object. It is inevitable that the root of landed property – sordid self-interest – should also manifest itself in its cynical form. It is inevitable that immovable monopoly should become mobile and restless monopoly, competition; and that the idle enjoyment of the products of the sweat and blood of other people should become a brisk commerce in the same. Finally it is inevitable under these conditions of competition that landed property, in the form of capital, should manifest its domination over the working class and over the property owners themselves, inasmuch as the laws of the movement of capital are either ruining or raising them. In this way the medieval saying *nulle terre sans seigneur* gives way to the modern saying *l'argent n'a pas de maître*, which is an expression of the complete domination of dead matter over men.[62]

Such was the long and arduous path that feudal ownership of land had to traverse in order to become a commodity subject to the laws of market production which are in flat contradiction of its own essence. In feudal society, land was not 'dead matter' dominating people; people were fused with the land, as it were. The feudal lord participates in a 'marriage of honour' with his hereditary fief. Nothing could be further from his thoughts than to treat this fief as no more than a source of wealth or an object to be traded. The ties that link the feudal lord with the earth and with the dependent tillers of the soil are not those of naked material interest; they form rather an intricate nexus of exploitation, political power, subordination, tradition, habit, emotion, patronage and respect (Marx points to the 'emotional side' of the feudal landowner's attitude to the peasantry and the poeticisation (*Bodenpoesie*) inherent in Romano-German feudalism).[63]

Labour – curse or salvation?

The medieval attitude to labour was no less contradictory than the medieval attitude to property. Of course, the ruling class had nothing to do with productive activities of any kind, and, in so far as such activities were the province of the lower, unprivileged strata of society, tended to despise them. From the knightly point of view, only war, chivalric exploits and entertainment – what Marx trenchantly described as 'heroic laziness' – qualified as occupations worthy of a nobleman; the provision of material comforts, the heavy, dirty jobs associated with growing food, were essentially the province of the common herd. The organisation and direction of the agricultural and productive process were not, as a rule, in the hands of the nobles, who were only too glad to place this burden on the shoulders of the workers and the estate managers. Only some monks and a few categories of lay feudatories, who for one reason or another had forsaken the knightly way of life for commercial and financial interests, took an active part in production and tried to organise it with a view to increasing their returns. In general, however, the feudal lord's interest in husbandry was limited to making sure that he got his revenue from the peasants and other subordinates. Of the two aspects of economic activity – the production of material goods and their distribution – it was only the second that was of any great interest to the ruling class. And here there is another essential difference between the feudal system and the industrial bourgeoisie, which organises and revolutionises production and guides it. His preference for making use of products, for converting his revenue into symbols of social prestige, specified the position and the role of the feudal lord in the production process.

But there is more than this to the attitude of the ruling class towards labour. The clergy did not share the nobility's preference for 'heroic indolence' as an ethically acceptable way of life. The church's position as regards the moral value of labour was dualistic. On the one hand, in man's obligation to labour the church saw both the result of his imperfection and a striking manifestation of it. As long as Adam and Eve were in paradise they were in a state of innocence and took no thought for their sustenance. The Fall entailed divine retribution; now man would have to earn his bread by the sweat of his brow, and Adam was expelled from the Garden of Eden to till the earth from which he had been made (Genesis, 2:23). This biblical verdict on labour as a punishment became an integral part of the Christian ethics of the Middle Ages. Christ, the clergy pointed out, did not labour. Having gathered his disciples around him he encouraged them to give up their earthly occupations and become not labourers but 'fishers of men'. Christ's associates had no need to bother their heads about what they were going to eat; their teacher could provide for them without any difficulty; it is enough to recall the parable of the five loaves with which Christ feeds five thousand people (not counting the women and children) and the seven loaves which satisfied the hunger of four thousand of his followers (St Matthew 14:15–21; 15:32–8).

So labour was not a postulate in man's state of innocence; he did not have to work when he was walking with God. In general, man was called upon to concern himself, not so much with what he could put in his stomach or with his physical welfare, as with his spiritual salvation and with life eternal. 'Not by bread alone . . .' The theologians rated the contemplative life, which brought man into closer contact with holy things, higher than the active life, Mary rather than Martha, and therefore monks occupied a higher degree on the ladder of spiritual ascension to God than any of their fellow humans. St Bernard of Clairvaux identified three degrees of this ascension corresponding to three kinds of people – lay, clergy and monastic orders: 'the first are in the mill, the second in the fields and the third in bed'.[64] The 'mill' stands for the earthly life of the world; the 'field' refers to the souls of lay people, on which, as on a field, the clergy have to labour by preaching God's word; 'on the bed rests the holy love of those betrothed to Christ' – that is, the monks. On the whole, labour was not rated very highly

On the other hand, labour was recognised as something inseparable from man's condition: in ordinary, day-to-day life people have no option but to work. The Christian sociology of the Middle Ages was based on the principle of the organic nature of society, each of whose members had an allotted function in the integrated upkeep of the aggregate. The *laboratores* and *aratores* were just as necessary elements of the social organism as the *oratores* and the *bellatores*. In service to the whole organism, the church saw the justification for productive labour. The decisive factor here was the intention for which the labour was undertaken. The accumulation of earthly riches was not something likely to get the blessing of the theologians. Christ had condemned usury and had chased the traders out of the temple; for the pursuit of wealth deflects man from his main *raison d'être* and serves bodily needs rather than spiritual ones.

For the Christian theologians, labour was above all educational. Origen put it as follows: 'God created man as a being who needs work in order that he may fully exercise his cognitive powers.' Man is the arena for a permanent battle between the forces of good and of evil, and only in the light of this confrontation can his actions be morally evaluated. Idleness – the 'enemy of the soul' – breeds vice and threatens the immortal soul, while work subdues the flesh and makes for self-discipline and application. But only in so far as it serves these aims and is conducive to spiritual progress can labour's educational role be justified. While the first anchorites renounced all contact with the world and gave themselves over to contemplation, monks as they were integrated into corporate form adopted a new attitude towards worldly occupations. Followers of Christ were recommended to divide their time between prayer and work, 'lest the spirit of temptation that lies in wait seize upon the idle mind' (St Bernard of Clairvaux). Thus, it was not so much the practical uses of productive work that counted as the aim served by the work – 'the attainment of spiritual perfection'.

The key notion here was moderation: it was necessary to identify the precise measure in which work was good and pleasing to God, without becoming an end in itself and a means of worldly enrichment. The situation of many monasteries in the wilderness or in dense forest far from human habitation ensured that monks had to do hard physical labour; and they were in no small measure responsible for

[261]

the clearance of land that took place in Europe at this time and for the development of agriculture. But, as the *Speculum Monachorum* stressed in the twelfth century, concern for their work must not be allowed to divert their attention from spiritual matters. 'Spiritual exercises are not done for the sake of bodily exercise, but bodily exercise is done for the sake of the spirit.'[65] By the Rules of St Benedict, monks skilled in a craft were allowed to practise it, but, 'if any one of them should pride himself on his skill, presumptuously imagining that he is thereby benefiting the monastery, let him be forbidden to practise his craft'.[66] For monks, work could not be an end in itself. A water-mill was constructed in one of the French monasteries so that the monks should have more time for their prayers.[67] Not all categories of work were considered permissible. Preference was given to agricultural work, while the brethren were forbidden to engage in trade and many crafts. Not only in the early Middle Ages but in the thirteenth and fourteenth centuries as well we find the clergy forbidden by synodal ordinances to engage in weaving, making cloth or footwear, dyeing, milling, brewing, or work as blacksmiths or bakers.[68] In the early Middle Ages it is rare to find craftsmen being canonised as saints – the exception is St Eligius, who was court jeweller to the Frankish King Dagobert. The work most pleasing to God was agriculture. The sons of farmers were allowed to take holy orders and to enter monastic orders, and some prelates of the church were of peasant extraction.

In his *Colloquy* the English bishop Aelfric (early eleventh century), discussing the importance of various trades and crafts for human existence, declares that the best and most useful activity is that of the tiller of the soil. All crafts are useful, but 'we all of us prefer to live with you Ploughman rather than with you Blacksmith, for the Ploughman gives us food and drink, but what have you to offer us Blacksmith in your smithy except sparks, the sound of hammering and the wind from your bellows?' 'Let us all help each other with our crafts and let us all abide in concord with the Ploughman who feeds us.'[69] It is a point of view which is completely natural for an agrarian society.

Thus, from the clergy's point of view, labour, as long as

it was not an end in itself, did not conflict with asceticism; on the contrary, it was a useful adjunct, which helped to keep mankind from sliding into sin.

All this, of course, was on the ideal and theoretical level. Practice was a different matter, and the same monastic orders which started out with strict regimes of poverty and self-discipline were later to turn into powerful landlords owning a vast amount of treasure; and it was precisely on their lands that agriculture and other forms of husbandry reached the highest degree of rationalisation and efficiency ever attained in the Middle Ages. The order of the Knights Templar fell victim to the greed and rapacity of its own members, who amassed so much wealth that the French king, Philip IV, thought it worth while to kill or exile the Templars in order to confiscate their property. His example was followed by other rulers.

Popular disgust with the great monastic orders for abandoning their vows of poverty and asceticism found expression in the appearance of the mendicant orders, whose members were forbidden to own property of any sort whatever and who lived by charity alone. From the twelfth and thirteenth centuries onwards, people in Catholic Europe grew more and more discontented with the Papal Curia, which had become a powerful owner of wealth and which continued to extort money from the faithful in the shape of tithes, 'crusade money', payment for church offices and the indulgences sold by papal agents for the absolution of sins. There was little common ground between the high ideals of the church and its actual practice – in fact, in many respects they were the exact opposite of each other, something which gave rise to much acute social and mental unrest. The clergy attempted to defend itself by asserting that the pope and the church used their wealth not for their own gratification but as a general fund designed to help all those in need.[70] But such claims were not likely to fool anybody, and criticism of the church and of the papal throne itself on the grounds of their greed and avarice became more and more bitter. It is enough to recall the *Gospel according to the Silver Mark*, or Langland's Lady Meed, the incorporation of venality.[71]

The peasant and the craftsman could not view labour in

the same way as the clergy. To them it was not a means of self-discipline and deliverance from the temptations which might beset the indolent, but harsh necessity. The never-ending cycle of the agricultural seasons and the work connected with them, the repetition of the same productive processes from year to year and from generation to generation, subjected the peasant to a labour routine from which there was no escape. The organic connection between the peasant and the soil he tilled was conditioned *inter alia* in no small measure by the fact that he worked with his hands; his work required him to use his own physical strength, since there were virtually no technical means which might have lightened his task, being a transmissive mechanism between him and nature.

It would, however, be misleading to see in the lot of the medieval peasant no more than its dark side. Medieval man was well able to see his mundane task as a producer in a more poetic light. Along with the Old Testament personages clustered round the doorways of the Gothic cathedrals are statues and bas-reliefs representing toilers engaged in various stages of the agricultural cycle. These sculptural calendars follow the workers through the tasks typical for each month and season. Ploughing, sowing, harvesting, threshing, fruit gathering, wine-growing, planting trees, setting a scythe, mowing, hunting, felling trees – all of them pictures that continue an old artistic tradition, enlivened with close observation of the living scene; they are imbued with the artist's interest in ordinary people absorbed in their daily productive activities. By acting on nature, man at work is glorifying the Creator, and the active life takes its due place beside the contemplative life. Each is in equal measure sanctified. At Chartres, the virtues and the industrious maidens are arranged symmetrically, with the latter on the right-hand side – which, as is well known, takes precedence over the left-hand side. Gradually, work receives its moral and religious sanction. No doubt, the representation of agricultural tasks reflects the growing self-awareness of the people and their deepening understanding of the importance of productive work in the general scheme of things.

Under the pressure of this new attitude of workers to their

work, even the theologians began to reconsider their view of labour. Hitherto, appealing to the Bible, they had declared work to be a punishment from on high for man's fall from grace. In the twelfth and thirteenth centuries, the theologians began to stress other ideas in this same book of Genesis (2:15) – namely, that Adam *tilled* the Garden of Eden, and hence, before becoming a form of penitence, labour had been an activity enjoying God's blessing.

A 'theology of work' is developed. Work is pleasing to God. The first worker was the Creator himself, *summus artifex*, architect of the world. In the cathedral at Laon God is portrayed as a worker, counting off on his fingers the number of days necessary for the Creation, and is then shown sitting resting after completing the work. Representations of various trades and crafts are frequent in medieval cathedrals. The windows donated by the guilds at Chartres collocate the workers with the saints, for labour too has its dignity and its sanctity. At Semur, the windows contain no scenes from the Lives of the Saints; what is shown in the most minute detail is the process of cloth-making.[72] Not infrequently, productive work is glorified in iconography devoted to religious subject-matter: for example, Noah's construction of the Ark, or the building of the tower of Babel. The artists are at pains to show the enthusiasm of the builders as they carry stones and erect their buildings; the faces and figures are not individualised, the masses of workers move in unison, one single rhythm runs through them expressing the joy and high endeavour of labour shared in common. In the decoration of churches architects and artists did not have complete freedom of choice as regards subject, and in the cathedral in its function of 'Bible for the illiterate' only such themes were permissible as were in strict conformity with theological canons. The fact that agricultural occupations and crafts could be portrayed in such sanctified surroundings bears witness to general recognition of the value of labour as a divinely appointed institution, one of the ways leading to salvation – always, of course, assuming that the work served virtuous ends. Productive work was under the patronage of higher powers, and the medieval guilds chose saints as heavenly patrons. The cathedral itself, while glorifying God, immortalised the industry, the talents and the expertise of the men who built it.

This rehabilitation of the active life reflects the growth of self-awareness among those belonging to the various productive professions and guilds. There is general acceptance of the belief that Christian values are inherent in all honourable callings. Each man has his vocation and may save his soul by exercising it honourably.[73]

Along with rehabilitation of physical labour, the Middle Ages also came to look with a new respect at intellectual labour. In the early Middle Ages, the view had been widespread that intellectual activity did not rate material reward; in particular, teachers did not receive salaries, for wisdom was accounted as a gift of God which therefore could not be the object of mercenary trading. At best, a teacher could be offered gifts in gratitude for his dispensation of knowledge.[74] Such a view could of course survive only as long as knowledge and education were the exclusive province of the clergy;[75] with the spread of urban schools and with the growing demand for educated people, it was not long before the learned professions received full recognition and took their place along with other skills. Payment began to be regarded as legal as long as it was *pro labore*. The enormous popularity enjoyed by outstanding professors at the universities is well known; pupils flocked from many countries to sit at their feet, their knowledge was said to be all-embracing and their authority was constantly invoked in learned discussion. In the taxonomy of medieval culture, the contrastive pair *litteratus* ('educated') – *illitteratus* ('non-educated') is basic.

Poets, however, continued for a long time to be looked down on, and it was virtually impossible for them to live on what they made out of their writing; all they could hope for was a gift from a noble patron. There is only one piece of external documentary evidence concerning the life of the great Middle High German poet Walther von der Vogelweide: in the travelling accounts of the bishop of Passau mention is made of five *solidi* given to the poet to help him to get a fur coat.[78] Unless he had a post as schoolteacher, the poet was on about the same footing as a tumbler or jester. Many fashionable poets were also wandering actors, vagrants, or goliards, as they were called. Complaints about the poverty and deprivation associated with the poet's calling are no fewer in the Middle Ages than in other periods. In the early Middle Ages, awareness of oneself as poet was not as yet developed, and most poetry was anonymous. Poets were remembered, if at all, by their contemporaries (sometimes by themselves too) because of their feats of knightly derring-do, their exploits on crusades, or for their piety; any poetic merit in this would be simply ignored. It is only from the twelfth century onwards that we find the situation changing and the poet beginning to be aware of himself as a creative artist.[76]

We have already spoken about the relationship between the medieval craftsmen and their products, a relationship which is entirely different from the indifference in bourgeois society of worker and entrepreneur alike to the manufactured product. The relative restriction of the medieval urban market, the prevalence of work to order, the very high qualitative standards imposed by the guilds – these are some of the factors determining this special relationship between the master craftsman and the product of his hands. We have to remember that crafts were in the literal sense of the word 'handicrafts'. As in agriculture, there was for a very long time no technical or mechanical intermediary between producer and product; the product came directly from the hands of the maker, the craftsman who had worked on it from the beginning to the end of the productive process. Such a *manufactura* obviously engendered a very close relationship between it and the maker. Work in a guild had 'not yet degenerated into a total indifference towards its objective content'.[77] The finished product embodying the skill, the taste and the working time of its maker was inwardly close to him; it carried the imprint of his personality. All this led to a certain poeticisation, or, one might say, an apotheosis of guild activity. Ethical and aesthetic considerations could not be detached from the guild method of production, and guild members were keenly aware of the dignity of their work. The master craftsman parted reluctantly with his work. 'The old craftsman fights for the pipe which the merchant wants to buy from him.'[78] In any case, the craftsman was

[267]

incapable of seeing in the finished product nothing more than an empty exchange item, a means of obtaining money and other goods. Exercising his skill, he was concerned not with profit at any price but with securing for himself a decent and dignified way of life. 'Our ancestors were not fools', we read in the German *Reformation of Sigismund* (c. 1439), 'they devised the crafts so that each one of us may thereby earn his daily bread, and no one may interfere in the craft of another; thus the world provides our basic needs, and each of us can feed himself.'[79] In this way, a craft exists primarily not for the consumer but for the master himself, mindful of his income on the one hand and his good name and dignity as a craftsman on the other. 'Dignity' in this context implies, along with material sufficiency, the capability of taking due part as appropriate in the public affairs of the town. In this society of small-scale producers the manufactured article is assessed primarily according to its use value, and only thereafter according to its exchange value – to which it is never reduced.

Parallel to the economic content of labour was its role as a source of moral satisfaction. By perfecting a fine article the master craftsman was at once confirming his right to guild membership and asserting his own personal dignity, his social position and his estate in life. It was only as a member of a group that he could assert himself as a legal individual, as a human personality. In this society, labour was understood as a common social responsibility; by means of his productive activities a man took part in the vital work of the whole – whether guild, town or society in general. So the craftsman was aware of the importance of his work. The same awareness can also be found among the peasants. Early in the fourteenth century we find a French peasant declaring, after being excommunicated by the church, that this holds no terrors for him as 'his work will save him'.[80] Labour, which had been represented by the clergy as a punishment visited upon men for original sin, is seen by the peasants as a way of opening the gates of heaven and of leading the soul to salvation.

What is more, labour could be seen as a social advantage enjoyed by the peasantry over the nobility. It is well known

how popular the sermons of the Lollards were in fourteenth-
century England on the theme 'When Adam delved and Eve
span, who was then a gentleman?' Here, the labour of the
forefathers is not a curse but a genuine in-built human activity, while the noble is a superfluous member of society,
since he performs no useful function therein, and cannot have
been thus created in his knightly capacity by God. Behind
Milton's assertion that Adam's work in the Garden of Eden
is proof of his merit[81] stands a tradition spanning many
centuries. Work is just as obligatory for the Christian as
active love, says the fourteenth-century English poet William
Langland in his *Vision of Piers Plowman*. The ploughman's
work is righteous, and it alone opens the way to truth. By
his work, Piers Plowman saves 'alle that halpe hym to erre,
to settle or to sowe,/Or any other myster, that myghte
Pieres anaille'.[82]

We pointed out above that the agricultural year was also
the liturgical year. The natural and the productive cycles
coalesced in the cycle of religious rituals, ceremonies and
festivals. The onset of the main productive processes was
accompanied by prayers and religious-magical rites; the end
of the agricultural cycle was marked by festivals. The established order of things seemed to be divinely ordained and by
that very token acquired moral significance.

Inevitably, in a society full of contradictions negative reactions to work were also bound to make their appearance.
From the point of view of the peasants, labour was frequently
excessive and forced; they had to do far more than seemed
to them necessary if they were to settle their accounts with
their lords. Adalberon, bishop of Laon, developing his
doctrine of the organic structure of society, all of whose
estates – clergy, nobility and peasantry – served the whole,
admitted that 'to supply gold, food and clothes – this is the
duty of the estate of serfs. . . . This miserable estate owns
nothing except what it gets from hard work. . . . Who could
count . . . all the hardships, the curses and torments that the
unhappy serfs have to endure?'[83] The peasant uprisings of the
Middle Ages were due above all to the peasants' resistance
to having to do excess work. The social Utopia of the Middle
Ages was linked with the dream of a blissful state in which

no one had to work hard: the fabled land of Cockaigne, or Schlaraffenland, as it is known in German, where no one worked, where there was plenty of everything and where fruit fell into your mouth. In the kingdom of 'the fifth monarchy' of the revolutionary sects at the end of the Middle Ages there was to be no hard work and all land was to be public property.

When talking about excess working time in a medieval context we must be careful not to overlook its very specific character. In a society built up on what might be called natural husbandry and which was traditional through and through, work could not take up as much time as it did in early capitalist society. It is well known, for example, how many days there were in the year when no one did any work – Sundays, holy days and other church festivals. In fact, work was forbidden on at least a third of the days in the year, possibly more. This meant that on working days work had to go on for a long time. Guild rules laid down that their members worked from sunrise to sunset. Working quickly did not come naturally to a society which was slowly developing and which had a very special attitude to time. More germane to such a society was thoroughness of work, high quality; the craftsman's aim was to reach a master's standards, to make his craft into an art. The product was evaluated from a qualitative, not a quantitative standpoint. The artefact must bear the imprint of the individuality of its creator and must be worthy of him. The product does not overshadow the maker; it is organically bound up with him.

Thus did the Middle Ages re-interpret the meaning of labour in human life. From being a curse laid upon mankind work turned into a calling. This clarification of the dignity and the worth of work played a major part in the general growth of human self-awareness. But complete rehabilitation of work in feudal conditions was an impossibility; and it remained a goal desired rather than realised right up to the close of the Middle Ages.

God and Mammon

P. Wolff has called medieval European civilisation 'a civilisation of labour'.[84] A fair definition, as far as it goes, but
perhaps it should be extended to read 'a civilisation of the
work of small farmers and craftsmen'. Virtually all the principles underlying the ethics of medieval economics were
borrowed from early Christianity, but their enormous
influence on the whole of the feudal age can hardly be
explained by appealing to the force of tradition and to faith
in the ecclesiastical authorities. The fact is that these principles in large measure answered the needs of small-scale
producers. The positive evaluation of labour as a means
towards salvation and as the only justifiable source of property, the recognition that it was lawful to possess property
in sufficient bulk for the satisfaction of personal needs, the
extolling of poverty over wealth – all this found a fertile soil
in the minds of small-scale producers and conferred a high
spiritual value upon their work. The way of life of the ruling
class, of those who idled away their time at the expense of
the peasants and the artisans, fitted in with none of these
principles. It suited the feudal lords and the rich to pay at
least moral tribute to the subjugated masses. Good works,
generosity, prayers and penitence, going on pilgrimages,
letting younger sons enter the priesthood and putting daugh-
ters in convents, bequests to the church, even (as happened
in the case of a few nobles) entering monasteries – these were
some of the ways chosen as a means of compensating for the
injustice which, from the viewpoint of medieval Christianity,
necessarily accompanied wealth and high social position. The
need for acts of contrition and purification, the need for
inner reconciliation with the demands of their religion, was
keenly felt among the nobility also whose public behaviour
was in such glaring contrast with these demands.[85] Less
exalted strata of society, drew some moral satisfaction, no
doubt, from the spectacle of their social betters doing penitence because they felt less certain of salvation than the poor.

It hardly needs to be said that the church did not insist on
literal adherence to the ideal of evangelical poverty and the
total rejection of property. This ideal was understood in a

spiritual sense. As far back as the second century, Clement of Alexandria debating the question 'What kind of a rich man can be saved?' in relation to Christ's words to the rich young man (Matthew 19:21) 'If thou wilt be perfect, go and sell that thou hast, and give to the poor', had given the following opinion: it is not a question of getting rid of one's property and liberating oneself from riches; what matters is 'expelling from the soul wrong ideas about riches, the desire for riches, the effort to acquire riches, preoccupation with riches, these are the thorns of life which choke the seed of the word'.[86] The essential thing was to obtain inner freedom from riches, to resist wealth's power to enslave. It is pointless to throw away one's wealth: it can be useful to one's neighbour, and it can be put to good use in doing good works. Riches should 'serve man, not rule over him'. The art of acquiring money, taught St Thomas Aquinas, is less valuable than the art of using money properly. To transform money from a means into an end in itself is to ensure the destruction of the human soul.[87]

We see then that the whole question reduced to this: how is money to be used? What ends may it properly serve?

Our assessment of medieval civilisation as a civilisation of small-scale owner-producers is reinforced by an analysis of its relationship with money and its ways of using it. If all kinds of wealth were subject in the Middle Ages to some degree of moral obloquy, this was particularly so in the case of monetary wealth. Trade played a great and growing part in medieval society, and as time went on the merchant class made itself a powerful social force in the towns and even extended its influence to the political arena. Nevertheless, throughout the Middle Ages a violent prejudice persisted against people who were engaged not in productive work but in commercial dealings, especially if usury was involved. There is something disgraceful about trade, something sordid and shameful, wrote St Thomas Aquinas.[88] According to the Bible, Cain was the builder of the first city. An English sermon of the fourteenth century contrasts the priests, the knights and the workers, created by God, with the towns-people and the money-lenders, the spawn of the devil.[89] Such an attitude towards dealers in money is very characteristic of small owner-producers, who understand wealth as the yield of their own efforts; in an agrarian society money inevitably appears as a low and ignoble form of possession in comparison with landed property. As they gained ground, trade and profit-bearing capital became more and more of a threat to the economic independence of small owner-producers, whose hostility to both grew in equal measure.

The relentless suspicion with which monetary wealth was viewed in the Middle Ages becomes understandable in the light of the ethico-philosophical principles of the age – above all, the basic principle that what is general takes precedence over what is individual. The part does not exist in its own right but only in its modality as part of some whole. Both nature and society are integral complexes upon which their component elements depend for their existence. Every grain of sand reflects the cosmos and embodies the wisdom of the creator of the world with its harmonious synchronisation and concordance of all its parts. What is individual derives its meaning and its significance from what is general. In human affairs, *universitas* has priority over all the individuals that go to form it. In medieval society a man is not reflectively aware of himself as of a fully independent unit. The unlimited individualism of bourgeois society is completely alien to feudal society. The personal interests of an individual are always in one way or another subordinated to the interests of the whole, whether it be group, corporation, society, church or nation. In concern for the common good he finds his own good – for the latter is inconceivable without or in contradiction of the former.[90] Medieval universalism had not only a social-practical but also a conceptual character. The world had to be conceived first as a whole, if its parts were to be comprehended; for the whole was real, while the individuals were products of this reality and had to be deduced from it by a process of ratiocination.[91]

Closely allied with this basic principle was another, about which we have already spoken: the principle of the general rule of rectitude. The world is built on rectitude, and any infringement of this principle threatens us with chaos and destruction. Justice is at one and the same time a moral and a cosmic principle, to which all human activity must be subordinated. Any departure from this principle is equivalent to transgression of the divine order of things and of natural law. Justice is understood in an extremely wide and far-ranging sense. It implied God's goodness and it provided the basis of the political and legislative structure; it was one of the main Christian virtues, the purity and sanctity of life, a personal integrity which found expression in one's behaviour, a state of rectitude and an innate urge towards the good of all God's creatures. Hugh of St Victor defined social justice as 'that by which the harmony of the whole is sustained, and which denies none their due deserts'.[92] Rectitude is understood as a supra-individual category, to which all the actions and thoughts of separate individuals are subordinated. That is to say, in the principle of rectitude the relationship between part and whole is realised; in consequence of the demands of a higher justice, the individual has to subordinate his demands to the socium. This did not mean that the main end of human existence – the salvation of the individual soul – was to be forgotten; what it meant was that no one had the right to dispose freely, i.e. arbitrarily, of his property. But the idea of justice in its medieval interpretation had nothing to do with the idea of equality. The theologians drew a sharp distinction between the state of innocence of the primordial parents before the Fall and the state of lapsed mankind. In this latter state, certain consequences follow inevitably – private property and inequality between men due to origins, good luck and possessions. The inequality of people on earth is axiomatic for the Catholic thinkers of the Middle Ages.

These principles provide the matrix for such medieval theological concepts as the 'just price' and the inadmissibility of profit through usury. The Gospels, that unfailing source of all medieval wisdom, provided the starting-point: 'therefore all things whatsoever ye would that men should do to you, do ye even so to them' (Matthew 7:12).

It was typical of the Catholic theologians, however, that they should be at pains to provide a basis for moral norms, not only by appeal to divine revelation and the Creator's will, but also by means of rational argument and analogue. Hence, great importance was attached to the analysis of human nature and the nature of things, based on postulates

[274]

of reason and the principles of natural law. Following Aristotle, St Thomas Aquinas construed justice as the expression of proportionality and equivalence in relations among men, each giving others their due. In this sense the concept of *justitia* can also be applied to matters of trade and commerce. Material relations must be built upon a basis of mutual help and equivalence of services, but not on unilateral profit and exploitation. The conceptual matrix is once again provided by rectitude – 'the firm and continual desire to give to each man that to which he is entitled'.[93]

Strictly speaking, medieval theology neither formulated nor ever applied a theory of economics in the exact meaning of the words. Economic activity was of no interest to medieval scholastics as an independent subject for intellectual analysis. Like the problems of labour and property, questions of usury and price were taken up by the theologians in so far as such matters had a bearing on loftier and ultimate problems of existence. So it is inaccurate to speak of politico-economics or of economic doctrine of the Middle Ages. The theologians were concerned not so much to provide a theoretical interpretation of economic practice as to influence it, to subordinate it to religious and ethical ideals, and to decide questions of price in the light of the metaphysical doctrine of value. In their eyes, society was a spiritual organism, not an economic mechanism; and as a result, economic activity had to be controlled and directed towards those moral ends for whose realisation it provided the material means. Seen thus, economics is not an independent entity; it becomes significant only in the framework of a wider ideal whole.[94] Economic problems were seen as expressing themselves in categories of human behaviour.

At the root of the whole matter lay the interpretation of the concept of rectitude. As we have seen, the theologians' attitude to private ownership was determined by the category of higher justice: property was an evil from the point of view of the common good which must necessarily coincide with the divine ordering of things ('By injustice one man calls one thing his property, another man calls something else his property', wrote Clement of Alexandria, 'and thus has division come about among mortals'[95]); yet since man's nature, being in a state of sinfulness, is imperfect, private property must be allowed.

In itself, money is neither good nor bad; the moral pros and cons only emerge in the light of its application. If money is used in a spirit of greed and runs counter to justice – then money is evil. The medieval theologians recognised the necessity of trade if society was to survive. But trade without some profit margin will attract no one. In what circumstances, then, is profit permissible? The answer to this given by St Thomas Aquinas and other theologians reduces to the statement that the final and definitive criterion is that of the common good. Trade is introduced for the public benefit. Commercial profit is justified if it serves the common good, if it is moderate and if it can be accounted a fair reward for the risk, the work and the outlay involved (*stipendium laboris*), a reward which assures the trader's existence. In addition commercial profit may be justified by such philanthropic works as it may be spent on. Avarice and money-grubbing are sins, and any commercial activity undertaken as a means of satisfying these base motives is to be condemned out of hand. But how are we to identify the trader's motives, his state of mind? Where does 'serving the common good for moderate reward' end and 'self-enrichment' begin?

This was a dilemma with which the Church Fathers had already struggled: 'If cupidity is removed, there is no basis for the desire for profit; but if nobody is interested in making a profit, there is no incentive to engage in trade', said Tertullian. The merchant adds nothing to the value of the goods, so, if he takes in payment more than the goods cost him, he does harm to a fellow human being; trade is inextricably bound up with fraud and therefore 'dangerous for the soul' (St Jerome).[96] A merchant can scarcely be pleasing in the sight of God, we read in the treatise ascribed to St John Chrysostom.[97] These difficulties were unknown to Roman law, which took its stance on the principle of the individual ego seeking its own ends. The Roman jurists saw nothing illegal in partners in a commercial deal trying to outwit each other or enrich themselves at the expense of others – the question whether such behaviour was moral or immoral simply never arose. It was, however, precisely this question that was uppermost in the minds of the Christian theologians, for law is inconceivable without inner moral rectitude. Above all, it is up to the trader himself to judge in his heart of hearts whether the motives that guide him are just or unjust.

The church and the lay authorities did not hesitate to intervene in commercial activities if they felt called upon to do so. The church often condemned profiteering, and throughout the Middle Ages the lay authorities tried to regulate prices, especially those relating to basic products. It was a policy dictated by practical necessity, by the constant threat of famine and its associated ills. Freedom of commercial enterprise and practice is about as remote from medieval society as unlimited right to private property. If intervention in business dealings had to be justified, the authorities had only to appeal to the maxims of justice and the common good discussed above. If further authority was needed, they had recourse to the teaching of the church, the words of the Gospels and the pronouncements of the Church Fathers.

The concept of the 'just price' was widely accepted in the Middle Ages and understood on the moral, the juridical and the economic plane at one and the same time. Yet what it implied was never laid down with any precision. It remained an indefinite and confused notion, just as vague as the distinction between the value of an article and its market price in the minds of the medieval philosophers and political theorists. Analysis of the concept of *justum pretium* shows that what was meant seems to have been the current price established in stable market conditions, that is when there was no sharp rise in prices due to profiteering.[98] An 'unjust price', on the other hand, resulted when men of ill-will tried to make as much profit as possible. The key point is that determination of the 'just price' was in the hands of responsible and respected people, who were mindful that the norms of truth and general justice were here involved. The price or the value of something is determined – so taught the medieval philosophers, following Aristotle – by human need. Value then derives from man and only partially from the objective qualities of goods. The measure of this value, however, is common not individual need.

All this was relatively straightforward at a time when

exchange of goods took place directly between producer and consumer, and when the craftsman worked mainly for a customer known personally to him, or gave his product to a second craftsman to be rounded off. In these conditions it was not so difficult to arrive at a value for a given article, taking the maker's earnings into due account; and it was in fact possible to speak of a fitting return for work done. Prices were only marginally affected by the action of free and uncontrolled market forces. Thus the impression was created that prices did not change and could be fixed once and for all. In common law records of the early Middle Ages we often find prices fixed for a great variety of merchandise, ranging from cattle to arms and slaves. The prices thus specified are probably maximum prices. Two factors – public need of the article, and due return for its manufacture and its transportation – were sufficient criteria for determination of the just price.

St Thomas Aquinas[99] and other theologians of the thirteenth century taught that compensation for labour outlay was just; and in such circumstances the concept of 'just price' acquired meaning. It was of course to be expected that Catholic thinkers should see a self-ensuring economy as the ideal to be aimed at. It was St Thomas's view that it would be best if each nation produced enough to obviate the necessity of having to import goods from abroad. Commercial dealing was to be based on simple promise, on the given word. Small-scale trade as it existed in a period dominated by natural husbandry was seen as the ideal. As commercial activity grew, however, and the relations between producers and consumers became more complicated, the role of the commercial middleman increased, and the concept of 'just price' became more and more inconvenient. The application of abstract principles to an area of human affairs as intensely pragmatic as trade was bound to give rise to a whole series of problems and difficulties, the theoretical solution of which fell to the lot of the same theologians and jurists. It was no easy task to reconcile the maxims of ethics and religion with the requirements of everyday life. But it is curious to see that the efforts to rehabilitate in theory the ideal of economic 'innocence' already lost in practice, become increasingly

[278]

strenuous from the thirteenth century onwards – precisely at the time, that is to say, when the purely financial attitude to trade was making more and more headway.

Ecclesiastical condemnation of usury was based on the words of Christ (Gospel according to St Luke 6:35): 'lend, hoping for nothing again'. A financial deal could therefore be no more than a gratuitous service, a friendly grant or loan. Any increment added to the sum granted (apart from a good-will gift in token of gratitude) was to be condemned as illicit gain. The merchant who sold something at a higher price than he paid for it could plead justification by citing his expenses in storing and transporting the merchandise and his need to secure some return on his services; but the usurer could not hope to find any such justification in the eyes of the medieval theologians. Profit made by usurers was immoral and sinful, for they made it while themselves doing nothing; they 'earn money even while they are sleeping', and not only on market-days but on feast-days as well. Usury was understood as the sale of money; accordingly, the right of ownership over that money was also sold. Hence the curious etymology of the term *mutuum*, meaning 'loan': '*mutuum* is so called because what is mine (*meum*) becomes yours (*tuum*); *quasi de meo tuum*'.[100] But it is unjust to ask not only for remuneration for the thing sold but also for payment for its use – it is like asking someone not only to pay for wine but also to pay for drinking it. Money in the Middle Ages was conceived as something to be consumed; following Aristotle, it was seen by medieval thinkers as non-fruitful, sterile (*nummus non parit nummos*), its only use being as a means of exchange. We have already mentioned another argument against usury – that the usurer uses time to make profit, in that he lends money for a prescribed period, upon the expiry of which he gets his money back with an increment. No one, however, may trade in time which was created by God for use by all. Trade in time is 'a distortion of the natural order of things' (St Bonaventura).[101]

The prohibition of usury, originally binding on the clergy only, was soon extended to all Christians. Under the Carolingians, it was condemned not only by the church but by the lay power as well. Throughout the Middle Ages, we find the sins of extortion and usury being condemned by ecclesiastical synods, papal decrees, theologians and preachers. Dante compares Cahors, a town whose financiers were notorious for their usury, with Sodom, and condemns the usurers along with the Simoniacs, forgers, and pimps (procurers) to suffer in the sixth circle of Hell: 'usury is a crime against God's bounty' . . . 'the usurer scorns even Nature'.[102]

It was, however, the theologians alone who stuck to a rigid and uncompromising condemnation of usury. The medieval jurists – legists who had studied Roman law – and the canonists were far less uncompromising on a number of points. Roman law allowed freedom of trade and money-lending and did not forbid interest, basing this dispensation on the principle of the sovereign will of those who take part in commercial dealings. The jurists of Bologna and canonists of the twelfth and thirteenth centuries asserted that 'contractors may naturally seek to outwit each other' and that in designating a price they may 'make mistakes' 'in all good faith' – that is, they may act in this way without the *intention* to deceive. Even among the theologians, there was no clear agreement either on the validity of the arguments against profiteering or on the extent to which it should be condemned. The theoreticians engaged on these problems had to cope with two different approaches to them – that of 'divine law' (*lex divina*) and that of 'human law' (*lex humana*); according to the former, usury was a sin and nothing more, while the second looked more leniently and more realistically on monetary operations, bearing in mind the needs of a developing commercial economy. Human law is not in a position to forbid all that offends against the highest virtue; while divine command requires justice to be perfect and leaves nothing unpunished.

Particular weight was laid upon intention. It was not in itself a sin to make a mistake in calculating a price; what mattered was the intention of the contracting parties. Usury originates in a hope of gain, and all the tricks and subterfuges used to disguise the ill-gotten increment will not save the soul of the usurer. The church was completely uncompromising in its treatment of usurers, even forbidding them to use for philanthropic purposes money obtained through usury.

Usurers and their descendants were required to return all such monies to the debtors they had robbed. In the fifteenth century, when usury in Florence had attained unprecedented proportions, Archbishop Antoninus mounted an extremely outspoken attack on it, exceeding anything his predecessors, the thirteenth- and fourteenth-century theologians, had attempted. The growth of money through usury, he wrote, may appear to be something of a miracle, but in fact it is simply the work of the devil. Of one family of usurers he wrote that four of its generations were doomed to suffer in hell for failure to return the riches amassed by their unjust ancestors.[103] Nor did the church rest content with denouncing usurers and excommunicating them; in the thirteenth century, those who were accused of taking bribes were brought to trial by court of law. Many usurers were subject to social ostracism.

It is obvious that ecclesiastical disapproval and prohibition were powerless to halt the growth of usury, let alone put an end to it. The very fact that as time goes on the tone of these prohibitions grows more and more violent, shows that the sin against which they were directed was proving to be ineradicable. Nevertheless, attacks on usury were a retarding factor on the growth of banking.[104] In the opinion of the outstanding authority on financial history, R. De Roover, it is impossible to understand medieval banking unless we bear in mind the ecclesiastical condemnation of usury. Neither bankers not usurers could afford to ignore these censures. Reluctant to give up their business methods, they were forced to resort to all sorts of subterfuges in order to charge interest without drawing upon themselves the wrath of the clergy, the chief custodians of public morals. As a result, the whole structure of medieval banking took on its own very special character.[105]

As any increment charged over and above the sum lent was regarded as illicit gain (*quidquid sorti accedit, usura est*), some way had to be found of concealing the usurious interest. One of the most widespread methods of securing profit without explicit specification of interest was to use cheques payable in a town or country different from the town or country where the loan was incurred, and accordingly in

[281]

another currency. In such a case, the interest was included in the sum of the debt. The point here is that a deal involving exchange was not held to be a loan, and accordingly exchange of monies or the buying and selling of foreign currency did not fall within the scope of ecclesiastical displeasure. In the account books of the Medici and other Italian money-changing banking houses, we find many thousands of currency exchange notes, but no reference at all to the receipt of interest. All that is mentioned is 'revenue and loss in exchange'. It was a highly inconvenient way of doing business; it complicated procedures, increased costs and meant a lot of extra time and effort spent on book-keeping. Perhaps the main drawback was the growth of the risk entailed in a monetary transaction, which required in addition to the creditor and the debtor a third person (correspondent) by whose agency the transfers were effected. The creditor was dependent on the debtor in the sense that if the latter failed to return the money, the former was unlikely to appeal to the law. As a result, the cost of a loan increased, as the usurers tried to protect themselves against possible loss. Banking developed in very unfavourable conditions, and the crash of a big bank, unable to recoup its loans, was a common enough occurrence. It was not unknown for even a crowned debtor to declare himself insolvent.

Officially, the big bankers were not regarded as usurers. The subterfuges to which they resorted when extending loans at interest were accessible only to people in possession of large capital sums and with representation in other towns and countries. Thus, while big operators could evade accusations of usury, small-scale dealers had no such possibilities open to them, and it was on their heads that the main weight of ecclesiastical censure and public disdain fell. But the consciences of many rich financiers were far from easy, and many last wills and testaments are extant containing instructions for some reparation to be made for the harm done to debtors by their activities. From the middle of the fourteenth century onwards, the number of such wills in Italy begins to drop – evidently it was becoming customary for bankers to continue money-lending without feeling obliged to purge their souls for their impious deeds.

In France and Spain, merchants and bankers were more susceptible to ecclesiastical censure and often consulted with the clergy before undertaking this or that financial operation; some, like the sixteenth-century Spanish merchant Simon Ruiz, refused to take part in any sort of dubious deal.[106] In the struggle to reconcile business with piety, the Spanish were rather more scrupulous than the Italians. The Italians were less inclined to discern spiritual danger in the dilemma, and their account books and personal records often begin with such passages as the following: 'In the name of our Lord Jesus Christ and his blessed mother the Virgin Mary and all the saints in heaven, may they grant us, in their mercy and grace, health and success, and may our wealth and our children be increased, and may our bodies be preserved and our souls saved.'[107] No doubt the fact that the authors of preambles such as this did not sense the gap between the practice of making money and hopes of spiritual salvation, was distinctly helpful in business.

We must ask ourselves, however, how far the sang-froid of an Italian merchant of the Renaissance period can help us to appreciate the state of mind of a medieval citizen engaged in financial dealings of some kind. Business ethics must have borne the brunt of the ecclesiastical attacks on usury, and had to take into account a public opinion sharply hostile to it. The spiritual climate of medieval society, with its built-in contempt for riches and its specific attitude to consumption, was not exactly favourable to the smooth development of a financial system.[108]

It would be a mistake to imagine that the church's attitude to usury closely reflected the interests of the small owner-producers, or indeed of any other class of medieval society. The theologians were guided primarily by general principles of justice and by the gospel doctrine of the evil inherent in material wealth. It was not mere chance, however, that the theologians began to pay particular attention to these questions from the thirteenth century onwards. For it was then that discontent with the spread of usury began to make itself more and more widely felt among the population. It was principally the small owner-producers, the craftsmen, the peasants and the minor nobility who suffered from financial sharp practice, and in so far as this is so, it is reasonable to suppose that ecclesiastical censure of such practices reflected the attitude of these groups. As we have seen, however, such sanctions as were imposed affected only petty usurers, leaving the big bankers with plenty of loopholes. After all, they enjoyed the protection of the princes of this world, who relied on them for loans, and even of the popes, whose financial dealings often reached enormous proportions. It is important to remember, however, that public disapproval of the practice of charging interest on money loans increased the overall risk inherent in such dealings, and made the business of banking both odious and disreputable. It took the transition to modern times to break with this medieval impediment in the way of free accumulation of wealth, and open the door to any and every form of economic activity. 'Money doesn't stink' – but not in every society.

There is a striking contrast between the crass 'materialisation' of social practice in latter-day Rome, a wallowing in sensual pleasures and material values, combined with total contempt for the labour which provided these luxuries, and the specific attitude to man's earthly possessions which arose in the Middle Ages. In terms of economic ethics, the main stages of the transition process from antiquity to feudalism can be set out as follows: from the unbridled hedonism and the acquisitive spirit of Classical society, which turned man himself into a thing to be manipulated, the first transition is to the principial 'dematerialisation' of all social relationships in early Christianity and the symbolic assessment of wealth by the barbarian societies; thence to the triumph – not only economic but moral as well – of small self-contained production and the rehabilitation of labour; the recognition, even if only in the abstract, of the human dignity of all men; then the transformation of property – the source of wealth – into a means of gaining power, into an intermediary relationship between lord and subject, entirely ritualised, and into commercial-monetary activity, disciplined and moderated by the moral censure of 'mammon' which threatens the salvation of the soul.

The social and economic ideas of the Middle Ages inherited

to a great extent from early Christianity, though modified by factors indigenous to feudal society, were inextricably bound up with a wider and more far-reaching system of religious and ethical concepts. This *Weltanschauung* was one that answered the social and psychological conditions of the time and was in keeping with the way people thought. For example, the special relationship with nature which people of a principally agrarian society did not construe as an object, as a datum to be used; an emotional and axiological approach to things rather than a purely cognitive and abstract approach; patriarchalism and traditionalism in social life allied to a regulatory system of behaving and thinking built into a society of small owner-producers; a preoccupation with the past and a negative attitude towards whatever is novel and unheard-of – all these traits of the medieval world-view helped the social and ethical concepts of Christianity to take firm root. [109]

Down-to-earth reality never corresponds to the ideal, the moral postulate. Life is untidy and full of contradictions where moral imperatives and religious precepts are uncompromising and direct. Of course, an ideal must not simply reflect reality – if it is to be an ideal it must be above reality, it must lift reality up to itself, it must present reality in an abstract normative form and set an example which is impossible of attainment. Because of this ideals do not cease to play an essential role in social development, as one of the factors affecting human behaviour. Medieval concepts of wealth, labour and property are an integral part of the life of the period, an element in the culture of feudalism.

CHAPTER VII

Conclusion: In search of human personality

In what has gone before we have examined some aspects of the medieval world picture.* The aspects may at first sight hardly seem to be related to each other. But our study of medieval concepts of time and space, of law as the all-embracing principle of world order, of labour, wealth and property, seems to show the mutual interconnectedness of all these categories. Their connection is determined first of all by the fact that medieval people perceived and construed the world as a unity; that is to say, its component parts were conceived not as independent entities but as copies of the whole, each carrying the imprint of the whole. All that exists is derived from the central regulating principle; all things are arranged in the structural hierarchy and are in harmonic relationship with other elements of the cosmos. Since the regulating principle of the medieval world is God, conceived as the highest good and as that which is perfect, the world and everything in it is seen from a moral standpoint. In the medieval world model there are no ethically neutral forces or things; all things and all agencies are active elements in the cosmic conflict between good and evil and in the universal process of salvation. Hence, time and space have a sacral character; the ineluctable characteristic of law is its moral goodness; labour is conceived of either as a punishment for original sin or as a means of saving the soul; no less clearly bound up with morality is the possession of riches, which may spell spiritual ruin or which may be used for the performance of good works. The moral essence of all the categories of medieval perception which we have studied is at the same time a manifestation of their inner unity and kinship. What medieval man perceived as a unity finding its completion in the Godhead, did indeed possess unity – for it represented the moral universe of medieval mankind.

This is why the significance of the separate mental

categories of the medieval world-view can only be grasped if we treat them as a unity. They must not be viewed in isolation but as components of a whole which we call medieval culture. It is from their prehension in this whole that each component of medieval culture acquires its higher meaning.

The Middle Ages saw the efflorescence of the Encyclopaedias, the Summae, the Specula. All of these exhibit that same obsession with comprehensiveness which we find in medieval 'universal histories' which claim to tell the story of mankind from Adam to the moment of their writing – or even beyond that to the end of the world and the Day of Judgment. The same all-embracing tendencies are present in the structure of the cathedral, which is designed to be a complete and perfect model, a palpable and visible embodiment of the divinely ordered cosmos. The universalism of medieval knowledge is an expression of the medieval conviction that the unity and order of the world can be rationally comprehended. Thus, philosophy could only be the handmaiden of theology; and, far from being seen as degrading, this role was actually felt as a distinction – first of all, because medieval man did not regard voluntary service as degrading, and secondly because service to theology could not but help philosophy to approximate to divine truth. By the same token, universal history was seen as the history of salvation; and any work dealing with knowledge of nature turned sooner or later into a compendium of all that was supposed to be known about the structure of the world (cf. the many treatises bearing such titles as *Imago mundi*, *De creatura mundi*, *De aeternitate mundi*, *De mundi universitate*, *De processione mundi* – but also *De vanitate mundi*, *De contemptu mundi*). The purpose of these encyclopaedias was to give, not the sum of knowledge about the world in an arithmetical sense – 'sum' as the result of simple addition – but to exhibit the unity of the world: *summa* in the meaning of 'highest', 'principal', 'most perfect'. Medieval encyclopaedism is a consequence of the belief that the world is knowable and accessible to reason.

The awareness, or perhaps we should say the feeling that all things share a unity, which lies at the roots of all the component elements of medieval culture, can be traced in everything down to the smallest details. Let us take the concept of time as an example. Time is perceived in terms of spatial categories. Past, present and future could be comprehended as simultaneous: a simultaneity finding visual embodiment in the structure of the cathedral which transmutes the history of mankind into the world picture: the cathedral is the 'microcosm of time' (F. Ohly). Time also proves to be an essential characteristic of law: true law is that which goes back to ancient times, which has been established since time immemorial, so that its antiquity is just as much an organic element in law as justice or rectitude. The theory of the sinfulness of usury also turns upon the concept of time; time is God's creation, it is God's gift to all, and cannot be used as something to bargain with.

It is not simply that all the categories of the medieval world-view are mutually intertwined. What is far more important is that in the Middle Ages, such concepts as time and law which we regard as abstract were held to be just as concrete, as tangible, to have just as much 'materiality', as material objects. Hence general concepts and material objects were regarded by the people of the Middle Ages as manifestations, homogeneous and comparable, of one and the same order. People have rights, but so too do places. Time consists of atoms, as do bodies. Time is spent in the same way as money. Often the same word is used to denote an abstract category and a tangible object. For example, *honor* signifies both 'honour' and 'a fief'; *gratia* is not only 'love' and 'grace' but also 'gift' and 'compensation'. It is well known how a faulty translation of one such word started an international conflict: a statement made by Pope Hadrian IV on the good offices he had shown Frederick Barbarossa was translated from Latin into German in such a way as to make it appear that the pope was presuming to be the feudal seigneur of the emperor (this turns on the dual meaning of the term *beneficium*, which can mean either 'good deed' (*bonum factum*) or '*fief*', 'feudal donation/grant'). The moral and conceptual categories could be illustrated in a sort of blueprint in the shape of geometrical figures joined to each other by lines of force.*

Numbers and geometrical shapes and diagrams (circles, spheres, squares, etc.) had more than merely mathematical significance. In them, the harmony of the world was expressed, and they possessed definite magical and moral significance. What was important to a consciousness that had not yet fully 'desemanticised' numbers was 'sacral arithmetic'. Augustine's concept of the number system as the thoughts of God was taken over; a knowledge of numbers was the key to a knowledge of the universe itself. The Bible was full of sacred and mysterious numbers which were constantly studied and deciphered in an effort to discover the essence of the cosmos.

The best-known example of medieval number mysticism is Dante's *Divina Commedia*, which is built up on the numbers three, nine and thirty-three: these numbers were believed to symbolise the divine rhythm which the universe obeys. Here are some of the most important medieval beliefs concerning numbers – beliefs which were held to be evidently and unquestionably true. Three was the number of the Holy Trinity and the symbol of all that was spiritual. Four was the symbol of the four great prophets and of the four evangelists. Four was also the number of the world elements and therefore the symbol of the material world. Hence, multiplication of three by four indicated the mystical penetration of matter by spirit, the proclamation to the world of the truths of the faith, the establishment of the church universal, symbolised by the twelve apostles. Four plus three equals seven, the human number, the union of two natures, the spiritual and the bodily. In addition, seven is the sign of the seven sacraments, the seven virtues and the seven deadly sins; further, the harmony of the human being and the harmony of his relationship with the universe; seven planets direct human fortunes, the world was created in seven days, and there are seven modes in Gregorian music – the audible expression of universal order.

Words too had magical power. In the Middle Ages, etymologies were as popular as encyclopaedias (indeed, they often coincided). The etymology of a word disclosed the hidden essence of the manifestation it denoted. From the standpoint of scientific linguistics, medieval etymologies are simply absurd, but for the people of the age they served as pointers and guides to penetration into the secrets of things. *Occidens* is the west, the place where the sun goes down; but the medieval etymologists derived the word, not from *occĭdere* (*ob* + *cadere*), meaning 'to fall down', 'to set', 'to wane', but from *occīdere* (*ob* + *caedere*), meaning 'to kill', 'destroy', and in the symbolism of the heavenly directions which finds such graphic representation in cathedral lay-out, the west façade was associated with the Last Judgment. Isidore of Seville derived the word *homo* from *humus*, meaning 'earth', for God created man from the dust of the earth, and to dust man returns. *Reges*, or 'kings', was derived from *regere*, from *re[cte a]gere*, meaning to act correctly, justly; that is, a king had to act in accordance with his essence, in other words 'justly'. *Decorus*, meaning 'proper', 'decorous', 'beautiful', was derived from *dec[us] cor[dis]*, meaning 'spiritual beauty', 'moral virtue', for bodily, purely earthly, beauty lacking a firm moral basis was accounted as evil and the work of the devil.

What is for us no more than a metaphor, which it would be foolish to accept literally, had symbolic import for the people of the Middle Ages; it was the tangible embodiment of invisible essences. As understood in the Middle Ages, the symbol is not simply a convention but is powerfully charged with the most profound significance. For it is not only certain separate acts or objects that are symbolic; the whole of this world is no more than a symbol of the world above. Hence, everything has dual or manifold significance: along with its practical use it has a symbolic application.

The world is a book written by the hand of God, in which everything is a meaningful word. 'Every created thing shadows forth truth and life', said Honorius Augustodunensis. The rose, the dove, precious stones – these are among the most important religious symbols. The lion symbolises the evangelist Mark, the eagle symbolises John, Matthew is symbolised by the human figure, and Luke by a calf. But these same four creatures also symbolise Christ in the four crucial moments of his life: Jesus Christ 'was born as man, sacrificed as a calf, rose as a lion and ascended as an eagle'. The same four beings symbolise the human virtues.

According to Hugh of St Victor (twelfth century) the symbol is a focusing of visible forms, so that what is invisible may be bodied forth. This 'demonstration' is not to be understood formally in terms of categorical syllogistic: rather, it is a direct expression of a reality which is inaccessible to reason.[1]

Conclusion

Medieval symbolism is very far from being an empty intellectual exercise. As P. Bitsilli points out, 'it is not simply that things *can* be used as symbols, it is not we who invest them with symbolic content; they *are* symbols, and the task of the percipient subject is to discover their true meaning'.[2] Accordingly, the symbol is not subjective but objective and of general compulsory significance. The way to understanding of the world lies through comprehension of symbols, of their hidden meaning. Medieval symbolism is a means whereby reality may be intellectually appropriated.

But why should 'understanding' take this particular form? Is it not because the world was not perceived to be in motion or development, but rather immovable and unaltering in its essentials? Not time but eternity was the determining category of consciousness; time measures motion, eternity signifies constancy and permanence. Change was a superficial thing, and what was novel rarely met with approval. Since the problems of change did not bulk very large in the minds of medieval people, the connections between phenomena were not perceived in a causal nexus that could be pragmatically investigated and checked. The world was perceived as a whole, whose parts were bound together in a system of symbolic analogues. Hence, causal explanations played a very minor role, being limited to elucidation of only the most concrete of cases; the world as a whole, as medieval man saw it, was not subject to the principles of causality. Events are linked not horizontally (in terms of 'cause – effect', 'action – reaction') but vertically through a hierarchy: every material object has its transcendental prototype, which does not 'explain' that object (if we take 'explain' in its modern sense) but rather discloses its deeper meaning.[3] The relations between the prototype and the event or object are stable and unchanging; they are functional, not dynamic relationships. This way of looking at the relationship between material things and the higher reality of which they are copies gave medieval man a theory of cognition which he found satisfactory for most of the period. The domination of the symbolic way of thinking was bound up with its universalism. The medieval mind starts from the principle that *universitas* – wholeness, whether it be society, nation, church, corporation, kingdom – is conceptual and therefore takes precedence in the real world over its individual members. It is the wholeness that is real; the individual parts comprised in it are its derivative contingencies. Paraphrasing the thesis of the medieval realists – *universalia ante rem* – we may say that the principle informing medieval society is *universitas ante membra*. Medieval theoretical analysis always started from the whole, never from the individual case. And hence the individual was seen as a symbol of the general.

The medieval symbol is never ethically neutral; the hierarchy of symbols is at the same time a hierarchy of values. Everything on earth, every being, has its determinate and determining value or worth depending on its locus in the universal hierarchy. The centre and the apex of this hierarchy is God, whom all creation serves, from the highest to the lowest, from the angels to the insects and the stones.

In this context it would be quite wrong to speak of the 'backwardness' of medieval thought, of its 'primitive' understanding of nature, or of the unsatisfactory standards of pre-scientific thought – these are all relative assessments which do not help us to grasp what is specific to medieval culture. By modern standards, these ways of construing reality are of course absurd and unacceptable; but our medieval predecessors would probably have found our contemporary methods of scientific elucidation equally alien, and the (for us) unquestioned advantages of the scientific approach would not have seemed so indisputable to a theocentric society. In a theocentric society the world does not need explanation; it is directly apprehended. This way of spiritual appropriation of reality and of its syntactic relationships is deeply mystical. In the medieval setting mysticism and logic were not opposites; logic helped in the mystical discovery of 'the divine secret' – the structure of the universe and the place occupied therein by man.

This medieval form of the symbolic reading of the universe is Christian Neo-Platonism. However, as we have seen, symbolism – albeit in a much coarser and more naive form – was also characteristic of barbarian society in the pre-Christian stages. And even in the Middle Ages, side by side with the subtle symbolism of the theologians we find countless symbolical representations, rituals and formulas which derive from the beliefs and practices of the barbarian age, or which have taken on a new lease of life and show us a stratum of medieval thought underlying the Christian. Many judicial practices – ordeals, single combat, oaths, incantations, sorcery – either had nothing at all to do with Christianity or had merely taken on a Christian veneer. The symbolical way of thinking of the Middle Ages was not engendered by Christianity; rather it is a variety of that archaic 'primitive' way of thinking found all over the planet in societies which are in a pre-class or early class state. The social practice of feudalism provided a rich soil not only for the retention of symbolism but also for a new and vigorous upsurge in its development. The symbolical apprehension of space and time, the ritualisation of all relationships between lords and vassals including service as a knight, the exchange of gifts and even courtly love, the semiotic function of wealth, the strict formalism of law which recognised as legal and effective only those ordinances and acts executed or performed under strict observance of all the due ceremonial – these are examples of the all-embracing medieval symbolism which we have considered in this book. Christianity proved conducive to the reinforcement and the philosophical sublimation of certain symbols with which medieval man was already very familiar, and also introduced some new elements into this complex of heterogeneous images.

As a normative and generally significant system, the semiology of the material world is paralleled by the semiology of the social world. The social symbolism and the ritualised behaviour of medieval man are generated by the specific relationship between individual and group, by the position of the personality in society. The view, popular up to a few decades ago, that not until the Renaissance was there anything that we would call 'personality', that the individual was completely absorbed in the socium, is no longer tenable. Of course there was nothing comparable to the 'personality' which has developed *pari passu* with the atomisation of society in modern Europe; an 'individuality' which likes to regard itself as completely autonomous and imagines itself as enjoying sovereign rights *vis-à-vis* society was unknown in the Middle Ages. But this modern type of personality is equally determined by its historical parameters; it is not the only possible hypostasis of the human personality. Throughout history, the human personality has in one way or another always identified itself as such; whether standing aside in a group or merging into it, man has never been a faceless item in a herd. As Marx put it: 'Man is not only a sociable animal, but also an animal which can become a separate individual only in society.'[4]

Coming back to the Middle Ages, we have to realise that it is precisely in this period that the concept of the human personality takes definitive shape. In antiquity, the Greek πρόσωπον, the Roman *persona*, originally meant a theatrical mask, or the mask worn in religious ritual. *Persona* is here understood as 'guise' or 'mask'; the mask is not the person's face, but between the mask and its wearer there exists a certain complex relationship. The fact that at high points of individual or social life, if not as a regular practice, peoples all over the world conceal the face by a mask (donned, tattooed, painted) is directly connected with the way in which these peoples understand human individuality. To follow this theme in all its ramifications would take us beyond the limits of the task in hand; it is sufficient if we recall that it was in Rome that the concept of *persona* developed into the concept of the sovereign personality, especially in the legal sense. The Roman jurists taught that in law there are only persons (*personae*), things and actions. From the juridical and religious point of view, the Roman citizen was a *persona*, who possessed ancestors, a name and property; hence, the slave, who did not own his body and had none of the other indices of the free man, had no *persona* (*servus non habet personam*).[5] For all the development of the free personality in the ancient polis, none of the ancient philosophers made any attempt at defining it. The transition from the theatrical mask to the moral personality possessed of inner unity took place in Christianity. For it was then that the *persona* acquired a soul, seen as the basis of human individuality and the indestructible, metaphysical core of the person.[6]

The definition of the personality given by Boethius at the

beginning of the sixth century, 'a rational and indivisible substance' (*rationalis naturae individua substantia*, PL t. 64 col. 1343), remained in force throughout the Middle Ages. The word *persona* was held to be derived from *per se una* (united in itself). Man had been made in the image of God, and was God-like. The concept of *persona* is bound up with the nature of God and of the Trinity, and St Thomas's arguments that *persona* is the name given to what is most perfect in nature, that is to say in rational nature ('persona significat id, quod est perfectissimum in tota natura, scilicet subsistens in rationali natura') are with direct reference to the *persona divina*. The word *persona* is most fittingly applied to God.[7] The religious nature of the concept is retained in the name given to the parish priest in English (parson, from Latin *persona*).[8] As always in the Middle Ages, the real anthropological problem is transferred to a 'higher' plane.

It was Christianity that gave rise to the contradictory situation in which the 'personality' now finds itself. On the one hand, man proclaims himself to be like God – like his creator. The medieval period witnesses the transition from the theory according to which men were created to replace the fallen angels, to a conception of man's own independent dignity, of man created as a being in his own right. Far from man being created for some other purpose, it is the universe that is created for man, who represents the crown of creation.[9] Since the world is created for the sake of man, in man may be found the whole world and its unity. The works of the Creator may exist but not live (e.g. stones); they may both exist and live but have no sensation (plants, for example); a third class exists, lives and has sensation, but does not have reason (e.g. the animals). Man shares with the rest of the created world the categories of existing, living, and feeling, but he shares with the angels the power to understand and reason. Man is the crown of creation. On the other hand, man is God's slave. But serving God does not degrade man; on the contrary, it elevates him and saves him. But service requires humility, the suppression of those personal inclinations which are contrary to the rigorous ideals of Christianity; and since the redemption and the perfecting of man can only come about in another world, the free development of the personality on earth is excluded. The freedom of will proclaimed by Christianity is annulled by the commandment to avoid everything that might hinder the salvation of the soul. And although the theologians held that the human being is a unity of body and soul, the Christian was supposed to devote all his attention and care to the first component of his personality, even at the very clear cost of the second. The soul and the body belonged to different dimensions: the soul was of eternity, while the body was subject to the ravages of time.

The specificity, the historical identity of medieval man's 'personality', is, however, not a derivative of Christianity alone. Like Christian symbolism, Christian 'personalism' turned out to correspond in many ways to the stage which had been reached in the evolution of human individuality in medieval Europe. Starting from the stage of 'kindred personality' characteristic of the age of barbarism, the people of the feudal society formed themselves into collectives of a new type, which dominated them not only on the material and political plane but also on the socio-psychological plane. Man in feudal society is corporate man. In greater or lesser degree, he seeks integration in the group to which he belongs, adopting its standards, its ideals and its values, its ways of thought, its patterns of behaviour and the symbolism which imbues it. The categories of the medieval world-view which we have examined are among the factors which came together to produce the form or cast in which human individuality was to be moulded – always of course as a function of its social matrix.

All the elements of medieval culture which we have studied – time, space, law, labour, wealth – are of interest for us precisely from this point of view: they are of interest as the parameters of the medieval human personality, the guidelines of its world-view and of its behaviour patterns, as ways in which human beings came to be aware of themselves. But it hardly needs to be pointed out that an analysis of these categories is not enough to identify this specific human personality; at best, it can help us to pose the problem, So, if we are in no position to reach any definitive conclusions about medieval man, a few general remarks may be in order.

The way in which human personality is institutionalised in different social systems differs from one system to another: the integration of the individual into the social matrix or into any of the groups forming it proceeds by way of mechanisms determined by the socio-cultural nature of the society. The cardinal condition for integration into medieval society was the act whereby an individual was received into the Christian fellowship. Exceptional sacramental significance was given to the act of baptism, and a soul which had not participated in this mystery could not enter heaven, even if it was the soul of an innocent infant. Thus we find Dante placing the souls of unbaptised newborn babes in limbo, along with the souls of the great men of pagan antiquity:

> They sinned not; yet their merit lacked its chiefest
> Fulfilment, lacking baptism which is
> The gateway to the faith which thou believest.[10]

Parents who did not have a newborn child baptised without delay were severely punished, as were priests who failed to perform this part of their duty. The ceremony of baptism had more than purely religious significance; it signified a kind of second birth, a renewal – from the natural state one was transformed by baptism into a member of a society made up of baptised Christians alone. From the early years of Christianity onwards a sharp distinction was made between *homo carnis* or *homo naturalis* ('natural man') and *homo Christianus* – a member of the community of believers. Baptism was seen as a metamorphosis profoundly affecting the human being, whose life thereafter would be entirely guided not by his inborn instincts and inclinations but by his adherence to and participation in a social community which was also a religious one; for commitment to the body of the faithful was at the same time commitment to God. In medieval eyes, society did not merely consist of people, society was that which united the people to God. Neither in the Pauline doctrine nor in the teaching of St Augustine is there any place for natural man. The member of society is *Christianus*.[11] Augustine seeks knowledge of the self. But his answer to the question he addresses to himself, 'What do you thirst to know?', is 'God and the soul and nothing else' (*Soliloquia*, 1, 2). So, only that part of the personality which is supra-individual, the part linked through the Christian community to God, is deserving of attention.

By entering the Christian fellowship and concentrating on the prospects of spiritual salvation which now opened before him, a man renounced his own individuality. Henceforward, he would be obedient and subject to the law as given him, and he would remain faithful to it. We have already seen how important a part, religious and socio-political alike, fidelity played in the medieval consciousness. *Fides, fidelitas* meant both belief in God and fealty to one's feudal lord or ruler, the earthly embodiment of God-given law. Man was not aware of himself as an autonomous individuality; he belonged to a whole, in whose framework he had to perform the part duly allotted to him. The social roles in feudal society were strictly laid down and all-embracing; the individual was absorbed in the role without remainder. The social role allotted to a man was seen as his vocation (*vocatio*); he was summoned by a higher power to pursue this vocation, and to correspond in all things faithfully to this role in life. His personal qualities, his individual talents, are used by him to ensure that he carries out his allotted social duty (his vocation) as efficiently and successfully as possible.

What is wanted from the individual, what constitutes his social virtue, is not originality, not difference from others, but rather the degree to which he can make himself an efficient unit in the social group, in the corporation, and in *ordo* – the God-given order of things. The outstanding man is he who, more than others, incorporates the Christian virtues; he whose behaviour corresponds most closely to the established canons and who approximates most nearly to the type of person accepted in society. Individual traits deviating from the sanctified norm were frowned upon, not only because a conservative society distrusts and despises the eccentric, but mainly because the mental attitudes and the behaviour associated with such traits were regarded as being contradictory to Christian example and dangerous to faith. Hence, in the restriction of individual opinion and the individual will the Middle Ages saw no infringement of the rights of man, no diminution of his dignity. The public utterance of views contradicting the established belief constitutes heresy. The heretic's crime, as is explained in the most important of the canonical law codes, Gratian's *Decretum*, is that he displays intellectual arrogance in that he prefers his own opinion to the authority of those who are specifically qualified to pronounce on matters of faith.[12]

Like the concepts of baptism, faith, fidelity, vocation, the concept of excommunication had religious and socio-political significance. The expulsion of the heretic from the Christian fellowship was equivalent to his exclusion from human society. He was then outside religion and outside the earthly law. It is essential to bear in mind the social aspects of all of these concepts: *religio*, 'link', 'tie', 'bond'; *communio*, 'community', 'eucharist', 'sacrament'; *excommunicatio*, 'exclusion from bond', the abrogation of all social communication.

These are some of the mechanisms which feudal society used to act upon the individual and to subordinate him to the ruling system. But there was more to this than simple suppression of the individual by society. We must ask, to what degree was this individual conscious of himself as an individual?* As a rule, medieval man did not see himself as the centre, as the coordinating agent at the core of actions affecting other persons. The inner life of the medieval individual did not 'jell' as an autonomous unity. In this respect, a study of medieval autobiography can be particularly illuminating. Strictly speaking, autobiography did not exist as a separate genre; the small number of works that might be put under this heading – sermons, letters which tell us something about their authors – give at best only fragmentary information on their characters. It would be difficult to give a rounded picture on the basis of the separate traits recorded, but one thing is certain: these traits are never individual but rather typical. The monk, for example, or other man writing about himself, sees himself in terms of this or that type – sinner, righteous man, ecclesiastic, etc. – and makes no attempt to isolate the traits that go to make him the man he is; it is as though he were unaware of their existence.[13] As a

[301]

result, medieval man as seen by himself emerges as an aggregate of uncoordinated traits.

In his far-ranging and splendidly documented history of autobiography, Georg Misch very aptly speaks of the 'incoherence' (or 'heterogeneity') of the medieval personality and points out that the whole of the medieval period is characterised not by 'organic' but by 'morphological' individualisation, or type-casting: the individual is known only through what is common to a whole category of persons, not through the organisational centre of his own individual inner life. Thus, a man's spiritual odyssey will be described in literary stereotypes, and moral judgments will be not those which the author might have arrived at by himself, but simply borrowings from the morality of the day. Misch compares the different ways used to depict human personality in the Middle Ages and in the Renaissance; the great figures of the Renaissance affirm their own personality 'centripetally', drawing the world into themselves, while their predecessors affirmed themselves 'centrifugally', projecting their own ego into the surrounding world so that it absorbed their personality. Abbot Suger, desirous of glory, dissolved his ego in his great abbey. The characteristic method of self-affirmation for the Christian personality of the Middle Ages was self-abasement, self-denial. In a few cases where a particularly strong individuality defied attempts to pigeonhole or classify him completely as a ready-made type, he simply remained undefined. The inscription carved by friends of Abelard on his gravestone read: 'He alone knows what he was.'[14]

We get the same impression from reading the medieval Lives of the Saints: there is no attempt at an analysis of the inner life, the spiritual progress of a man who is supposed to move steadily and consistently from a state of sinfulness to a state of saintliness. As I said above, the transition seems to take place all of a sudden, without any sort of psychological preparation; the sinner suddenly repents and begins to lead the righteous life of a 'model' saint, or saintliness is miraculously discovered in him. In this latter case, conversion is depicted either as recovery from a severe physical illness or as a battle between the forces of good and of evil in the inner passive arena of the human soul. The hagiographer may indeed remark on and record certain individual traits of the saint,[15] but the task he has set himself – to give an *example* of saintliness – excludes almost by definition the possibility of too much value being placed on unique features and departures from the norm. The literary conventionality shows the author's lack of interest in what is individual.*

The medieval chronicles are concerned with people. But even the historians, for all their lively interest in the human race, pay very little attention to individual human beings. For them, individuals are above all bearers of specific characteristics: pride, bravery, nobility or cowardice, baseness and malice. It is not so much concrete individuals as personified moral values that figure in the medieval narratives. In the Middle Ages the concept of *persona* was no longer linked with the theatrical mask as it was in classical antiquity, and yet the personages of the chronicles appear to be actors, seriously and studiously playing their parts. Their actions, being public, are dictated by the public, not by individual intentions or inclinations; they centre on a norm which is accepted in a given social setting. A knight's behaviour is aimed at his audience, and is dictated by the requirements of the role he is playing; he would prefer to be taken captive but will not appear to hurry when quitting the field of battle lest he be accused of cowardice. Accordingly, the chronicler like the hagiographer, explains the actions of his heroes not in terms of personal peculiarities or individual talents but in terms of the basic motives by which a noble *must* be guided if he is to remain faithful to the code of conduct accepted in courtly society. W. Brandt is not wide of the mark when he writes, 'the personalism of the medieval aristocracy was actually very impersonal'.[16] Primarily, what these people were concerned with was their reputation, good name, their status in their society. In this context, individual human qualities could be taken into account only in so far as they harmonised with the social role of their bearers. What was essential was not the individual traits of the knight but the obligatory attributes he embodied. There was no division between the 'actor' and the role he played. He grew, as it were, with the part which he was continually called upon to undertake in the social game.

Another favourite convention of the chroniclers (especially the ecclesiastical scribes) when describing actions and people's behaviour is to ascribe these actions not to the protagonists themselves, but to their moral virtues or shortcomings. Such and such an action is due to such and such a quality of the doer. These qualities are not connected with each other, which means that when the hero does something, it is not his personality as a whole that is acting but an aggregate of uncoordinated qualities and forces acting independently. Medieval realism personified vices and virtues, like any other abstractions, and conferred independent status on them. Thus for the ecclesiastical chronicler it is a man's several attributes that take turns to act, not one integrated self.

These qualities are easily detachable from the human character. Not for nothing did the Middle Ages love to depict the personified vices and virtues: Goodness and Greed, Pride and Wisdom, Meekness and Justice, like Time, Old Age and so on, are constantly shown in human guise, disporting themselves in coloured miniatures on the pages of poems and romances, or in sculptured form. These allegorical beings appear in the role of man's guides and teachers: they urge him to take this or that action, and get him into the proper emotional mood. Man, in fact, appears as a sort of puppet, to which these personified qualities lend life. At a given moment, a man finds himself in the power of one or other of these moral forces, and it is under its influence that he acts. The initiative comes from these forces, and is not a product of the integral personality as a whole. Various forces struggle for supremacy in man's soul, but they are not activated or called into play by the personality. Hence, these forces or moral qualities are themselves impersonal, and vices and virtues are general concepts. They take on no individual colouring from the individual in whom they are housed; on the contrary, it is their presence in him that determines his mental condition and his conduct. They move into him just as a devil may take possession of a man, and then leave him just as an evil spirit may leave the human integument. The medieval moralists compared man's soul to a fortress, in which the virtues are besieged by the attacking forces of the vices. The image of man as a vessel filled with a varying content which is exterior to his own being at best reflects the total lack in the Middle Ages of any concept of the individual as a morally unique and sovereign agent.

In this context it would be wrong to leave out of consideration the special nature of the literary genres which we have used to reach these conclusions. The literature of the Middle Ages did not set out to reflect living reality as in a mirror; rather, it provided an idealised view of the person and a stereotyped version of his actions, preferring to select only those which suited the author's purposes – the selection of edifying examples from history or from the Lives of the Saints. Hence the literary material at our disposal provides us mainly with a picture of the ideals by which society was guided. The reality was incomparably richer and more varied. But let us once more emphasise that this ideal served an essential social function and reflects for us an authentic tendency in the life of medieval society, orientated as it was on the world beyond.

Medieval man could find himself, become aware of himself and of his own possibilities, only within the framework of the collective; through his adherence to a social group he associated himself with the values accepted in that group. His knowledge, skills, experience, convictions, conduct were then his personal characteristics in so far as they were acceptable to his social group.

A man was rarely called upon to act quite individually. The group to which he belonged was constantly uppermost in his mind, for to act contrary to its norms and designs would be reprehensible. Where voting took place it was by no means simply a way of establishing a proportionate relationship between conflicting individual wills. Either unanimity was required or the motion was carried by the vote of 'the larger and better part' of voters – that is to say, not only their number was taken into consideration but also their 'quality', their status and degree of social privilege. Opposition to the group, to society, counted as the impardonable sin of pride. A man could assert his own individuality only by fitting in with his social group.

Medieval man had a clear concept of the human personality: this personality is answerable to God and it possesses an indestructible metaphysical core – the soul; but it is not an individuality in our sense of the word. The insistence on what is common to all, typical, on the universal, on deconcretisation, militated against the formulation of any clear idea of human individuality.

In the eyes of the medieval writer, the spiritual world is like the physical one, immobile and discrete. Man does not evolve; he merely passes from one age to another, not in a graduated evolutionary process involving qualitative change, but in a succession of internally unrelated states. Children in the Middle Ages were looked upon as small adults, and the question of the growth and education of the human personality simply never arose.[17] Ph. Aries, who has made a study of the treatment of children in medieval and early modern Europe, describes medieval civilisation as 'a civilisation of adults',[18] pointing out that in the Middle Ages children were not recognised as a qualitatively separate category of human beings. In art, up to the twelfth and thirteenth centuries, children are depicted as undersized adults, with adult physique and dressed in the same clothes as their elders.* Education was not geared to age; adults and juveniles studied together. Games were for knights and nobles before they were for children. The child, the youth, were regarded as natural companions of the adult.

Lacking the initiation ceremonies of primitive peoples and the educational principles of classical antiquity, the Middle Ages for a long time simply ignored childhood and the transition from it to adulthood. As we have seen, the child was made a social being by the act of baptism. Throughout the Middle Ages, the family was the formative production cell of society, but the feeling of belonging to a family – unlike the feeling for kindred – was weakly if at all developed. The love hymned in courtly lyrics is explicitly contrasted with the marriage relationship. Christian moralists on the other hand warned against an excess of passion in relations between spouses, and treated sexual love as something very dangerous and better subdued if it could not be totally avoided. It is not until the transition to modern times that the family begins to be viewed not simply as a union of spouses but as a cell entrusted with the socially important function of bringing up children. But by then the family is the bourgeois family.*

The treatment of childhood in the Middle Ages is a good example of the period's specific attitude to the human personality. It shows that medieval man was not yet in a position to be aware of himself as a unified developing being. His life was a series of successive states, whose sequence was not internally motivated. Does this not link up with what we said earlier about the 'ages' of human history? In essence, history does not evolve; the transitions from 'infancy' to 'childhood', from 'childhood' to 'adolescence' and thence to 'youth', 'maturity' and 'old age', are not prepared in the previous stage, but take place suddenly as leaps from one static stage to another. Let us recall also the 'selective time' or 'spasmodic time' of medieval poetry, which shows a failure to grasp the connection between time and events: time is broken up into mutually unrelated fragments.

So, though it is true to say – as I have tried to show above – that medieval man experienced the world as a unity, it must not be forgotten that this unity existed on the metaphysical plane alone; it was not formed by human practice, nor did it arise directly from things themselves; it was rooted in God. Feudal society, torn and broken up by political particularism, found its ideal unity in the Empire and in the '*Civitas Dei*' and in the same way medieval concepts of man and his place in the world, fragmentary and unconnected as they were on the empirical plane, became unified and ordered in the concept of God's preordained harmony.

The personal self in the Middle Ages was not seen as an integrated whole whose faculties, properties and attributes are inwardly and indissolubly bound together, nor is it a unique individuality valued precisely because of its individual peculiarities. The personal self was positively valued in so far as it partook of what was typical and recurrent, and those of its qualities were acceptable which rendered it acceptable to society and to collective action with its fellow members of the social group or corporation. Not the part but the whole, not individuality but *universitas* is in the foreground. *'Indivi-duum est ineffabile'* – 'what is individual is inexpressible'; thus did the medieval philosophers concede the preference of their age for demonstration of what is typical, general and supra-individual.

At a certain stage in the development of medieval society, however, the individual begins to find ways of expressing himself. The turning-point comes in the thirteenth century. [19] In all walks of life we find evidence that the claims of the personal self to be recognised are becoming more and more pressing. In art we see people individually depicted, the beginnings of portraiture; in literature, more and more is written in the vernacular languages, which show themselves to be more capable than Latin of expressing the various shades of human emotion; individual styles in handwriting begin to appear. There is an upsurge in the natural sciences, which put experimentation in the place of authority. The spread of Aristotelianism is linked with a partial revaluation of the content and purpose of philosophy. Where the theologians of the preceding epoch had devoted all their attention to the soul housed in man's body, the philosophers of the thirteenth century turn their attention to the indissoluble unity of body and soul, the unity which constitutes the personal self. St Thomas Aquinas develops and sharpens a definition of the personal self which goes back to Boethius: the personal (*persona*) self not only behaves rationally and is aware of itself as a person, it also takes responsibility for its behaviour, it is guided by divine providence in such a way that it takes decisions and its actions are therefore personal actions. [20] According to St Thomas the *persona* is characterised not only by indivisibility into other essences but also by the fact that it possesses a certain definite dignity – man's rationality, which is the basis of that degree of freedom which man possesses. Complete freedom will be achieved only in the world to come, where man will be made perfect.

Dealing with the problem of the individual's relationship with society, St Thomas proclaims the primacy of the common good over individual good. At the same time, however, he does not consider society as an independent substance, in contradistinction to the individual; for society consists of persons who have come together for the purpose of attaining a specific aim. The personal self possesses an immortal soul and is capable of seeing God face to face; society is not capable of this. Society is a means to an end, the personal self is an end in itself, and thus society serves the person.[21] The shift of interest to a new field of philosophical enquiry is thus clearly attested in the work of St Thomas. It is still clearer in the system elaborated by Duns Scotus, who asserted that every separate individual was unique, and especially in Dante, who postulated the principle of the inner value of the personal self.

While admitting the theological constraint on the medieval doctrine of the personal self and the tendency to extol the typical at the expense of the individual, we must not forget that certain contemporary Oriental philosophical and ethical systems shared these attitudes. In Oriental thought (if we may generalise where so much is particular) individualism is not generally regarded favourably, being often taken as equivalent to selfishness; correct behaviour requires a man to give priority to his duties and obligations rather than to his rights.[22] In the sequel, however, the Western and the Oriental traditions diverged widely, thanks to the enormous increase in and importance of the role of the individual in the West attendant upon the rise of the bourgeoisie.*

More than once in our discussion of the ways in which the personal self was apprehended and treated in the Middle Ages, we have had to proceed by way of negation; trying to establish what medieval man took himself to be, we have found ourselves forced to say what he was not. Comparison with what is meant by 'personal' and 'self' in modern parlance is inescapable. But the comparison must not give the impression either that there was no such thing as 'personal self' in the Middle Ages or that it was undeveloped. Such an inference is justifiable only if we take the individuality of modern man to be, not a function of our own space and time, but an invariant, the only possible model. Would it not be better to treat the human personality as it emerges in medieval Europe as a special case in terms of its own characteristics? Should we not see in it something more than the mere absence of those characteristics which are necessary constituents of modern man's personal self?

The specific limitation of the personal self in the Middle Ages which emerges in comparison with modern man was at the same time the manifestation of the qualities which medieval man possessed and which were later lost. In this book we have had much to say about the close relationship between medieval man and nature, a relationship so close indeed that often it is impossible to draw a clear dividing line between man and his natural environment (we recall once again the 'grotesque body'). We have tried to identify the exact way in which medieval man apprehended time – not as mere duration or as an abstraction but as an indissoluble attribute of being, as material as life itself. All this bears witness to a feeling for the fullness of being, of being not yet fragmented by human experimentation and introspection into its constituent parts and not yet rigorously compartmentalised. Man had not yet become *subject*, the cognisant matrix ensuring veridical perception of all *cognoscenda* related to it. A direct relationship with living processes, organic experiencing of them – this is what is characteristic of people living in a society which has not yet been eroded by a dominance of things over man.

In our analysis of the categories of labour, wealth, property, etc. in the Middle Ages, one thing has become obvious: not one of these categories appears as an end in itself; they are all means to an end, means whereby man supports himself and affirms himself as a fully qualified member of a collective or corporation. Labour must satisfy the current needs of the society, but the concept of the designed growth of means of production is alien to the Middle Ages, because it is not increased production but reproduction that is both norm and ideal. Wealth is used largely as an index of social standing and as a means of enhancing social intercourse. The social functions of labour, property and wealth in the feudal period can be properly understood only when we consider them in the light of relations between individual people. These are not relations which can be reduced to the formula 'goods – money – goods' but relations between socially determinate individuals. The world-view of medieval man corresponded to his limited activity in a relatively narrow space, in intercourse with the relatively small number of other members of his society with whom he was in personal, non-anonymous relations as expressed in direct contact. The money and goods that circulated in this society had not yet become a universal means of social intercourse dominating man.

In short, the medieval individual lived in a society which knew nothing of 'alienation' in its advanced forms. Thanks to this, his social existence and practice were integrated and amalgamated in a way that was lost in the transition to a more developed and more differentiated bourgeois society. Progress is always and inevitably dialectical. Here it is paid for by the loss of certain values which embodied a more direct relationship with life.

The world-view which predominated in the Middle Ages was in many ways illusory. But let us repeat once more: the fact that it was illusory does not mean that it was ineffective; the illusions of a period go to form social practice and move people to act in certain ways. The shortcomings of a culture are most easily identified either from the standpoint of another culture (for example, in the Middle Ages the Catholic and the Orthodox churches abused each other as schismatics, while both attacked the pagans) or *post factum* by a successor culture convinced of its own superiority and rejecting the views of its predecessor as superstition. All of this is historically demonstrable. Scientifically, what matters is that every historical nexus should be assessed with the adequate yardstick. The medieval period has not been well treated in this respect; it tends to be compared either with classical antiquity or with the Renaissance, two 'resonating' epochs, whose criteria can hardly be applied to the Middle Ages. From the world-historical point of view, medieval culture is as significant and worthy of attention as the cultures of classical antiquity and of modern Europe, and it is my conviction that a due assessment of its value can only take shape in the light of the accumulation of objective facts, including its own self-appraisal, the attitudes and ideas of medieval people about themselves and their world.

AUTHOR'S NOTE

The English edition of this book is published a dozen years after its appearance in Russian. As might be expected, I should now like to amend the text, and indeed rewrite parts of it. The 1970s and the early 1980s have seen intensive development of that trend in the study of medieval culture to which my book belongs. A number of important works have appeared in which various aspects of the medieval mentality are investigated. However, since it was not possible for me to change and expand the text of my book, it is here presented in almost the same form in which it appeared in Moscow in 1972. I have, however, made a few small additions to the text. More substantial additions are indicated in the text by asterisks and are listed below as addenda (see p. 315). In addition I have updated some of the references.

My own recent studies have resulted in two books. One is the second, revised and enlarged, Russian edition of *Categories of Medieval Culture* (Moscow, 1984), which appeared when this translation was already in proof, too late to make major changes to the text. The second book is entitled *Problems of Medieval Popular Culture* (Moscow, 1981). It has now been translated into English and will, I hope, soon be published. The new book is closely connected with its predecessor but differs in the standpoint from which medieval culture is studied. Attention in the new book is focused on that layer of the collective consciousness of the Middle Ages which was concealed by the culture of the educated elite, and which is therefore hardly studied by historians. Thus the ideas presented in *Categories of Medieval Culture* are considerably developed in the new book. The two books complement each other. In some ways, this consideration

[313]

may serve as an excuse for my offering English readers the present translation of *Categories* without additional material and without drawing upon recent historiography of which I am well aware.

It is, however, my hope that even so my book may prove acceptable to English readers interested in the history of culture. This hope rests on the assumption that the world picture of medieval people is insufficiently studied. At the same time, I must suppose that not every English historian is ready to agree with my approach, which considers culture as a system: highly complex and inwardly contradictory, but nevertheless a system. There is a tendency in contemporary humanities to try to reconstruct the mental *universum* of people of other epochs and civilisations. The method I apply in my book to the investigation of culture proceeds by an analysis of several of its categories and in the elucidation of their meaning as elements of the social and cultural whole. My attention is directed, first and foremost, to the study of mental attitudes and orientations, customs of thought, the 'psychic instruments' of medieval people: in other words, of that stratum of the intellectual life of the society which was not fully realised and reflected on by its members.

People's social behaviour is greatly influenced by their mentality; and the peculiarities in the conduct of medieval man can be explained only in the light of his world-view. In this respect, cultural and social studies of the life of medieval people are closely interconnected. The socio-cultural point of view embodies an attempt to overcome the onesidedness of traditional historical studies of the economy, the culture and the religion of past societies, and to offer an approach which tries to unite all of them. Of course, it is much easier to formulate such an approach than to fulfil it. Nevertheless, I am convinced that anthropologically orientated history is a developing field of study which has every right to exist.

Finally, I should like to express my gratitude to the translator.

Moscow, July 1984

ADDENDA

p. 195, line 28:
It could hardly be claimed that the trifunctional scheme of the
social whole described its complex structure in all its diversity.
But it was an attempt at a theoretical organisation of this whole,
and therefore reflects an important aspect of the self-
consciousness of medieval society. (See G. Duby, *Les trois ordres
ou l'imaginaire du féodalisme*, Paris, 1978; J. Le Goff, 'Les trois
fonctions indoeuropéennes: L'historien et l'Europe féodale',
Annales. E.S.C., 1979, 34, no. 1, pp. 1187–1215.)

p. 200, line 12:
Only very rarely is the historian given the chance to penetrate
into the world of peasant beliefs and attitudes, and in these
exceptional cases a most peculiar fusion of the elements of
Christian and of folklore culture is revealed to him. (See E. Le
Roy Ladurie, *Montaillou, Paris*, 1975, London, 1978; J.-C.
Schmitt, *Le saint lévrier. Guinefort, guérisseur d'enfants depuis
le XIIIᵉ siècle*, Paris, 1979.)

p. 200, line 34:
But it would be an oversimplification to imagine that the belief
in miracles and in help from saints was simply imposed on the
minds of their parishioners by the clergy. It was the common folk
themselves who felt the urge to place their hopes in the
supernatural. Very often, the cult of saints was a natural growth;
while fear of hell and a craving for salvation drove people to go
on pilgrimages, and to lend a devout ear to tales of devils' tricks
and journeys to hell and purgatory.

[315]

p. 288, line 2:
Our study could be continued by introducing certain new themes.
Analysis could be differentiated – and this is desirable – by
taking into account the peculiarities of certain regions of Europe
and particular periods of the Middle Ages. However, my main
aim has been to examine whether the notion of the 'world picture'
is indeed workable, whether, that is, it affords a possibility of
seeing medieval culture in its entirety as a system; and, further,
whether it is plausible to search for a connection between culture
and socio-economic structures.

p. 290, line 5 from bottom:
The exchange of gifts, characteristic of all pre-capitalist societies,
was inherent, as we have seen, in European medieval civilisation
also. But this exchange did not necessarily presuppose the mutual
transfer of material goods. It could take the form of the exchange
of material goods against panegyric, song, prayer, fasting, mass,
ritual, since sacral or poetic texts and concomitant acts were
apprehended as phenomena of the same order as tangible things,
such as weapons, fine clothes, sums of money, food or land
tenure.

p. 301, line 23:
The notion of 'medieval man' is, of course, an abstraction. The
question arises whether such an abstraction is plausible.
Common sense tells us that no two human beings are exactly
alike; and as for the Middle Ages, it was a long period during
which Europe and the peoples inhabiting it changed radically.
Consequently, our 'medieval man' seems to be an abstraction
which is void of content. But what we are studying is neither
concrete varying types of personality, nor their transformations
during the epoch. We are trying to establish certain basic features
of a culture which, through all its change and development,
retained the same structural parameters. Is it not possible to define
culture as the self-reflection of social man, man in society, as the
revelation of his essence? From this viewpoint, study of the
idiosyncrasies of medieval culture brings us necessarily to the
problem of the personality which conformed with, fitted into
such a culture. May I then venture upon some generalisations.

p. 303, line 7:
Moreover, the author is frightened by the very idea of the
individual, as though it were something inadmissible. When writing
a *vita*, Odo of Cluny used the first person singular, and some
hundred years later, an editor of his text diligently crossed out

the 'ego'. (See C. Carozzi, 'De l'enfance à la maturité: étude d'après les vies de Geraud d'Aurillac et d'Odon de Cluny', *Etudes sur la sensibilité*, Paris, 1979, pp. 103–16.)

p. 306, line 24:
Pupillage was connected with the prolonged removal of the child from his parents, and therefore the socialisation of children and the transmission to them of values and knowledge were not controlled by the family.

p. 307, line 5:
It was only in the fifteenth and sixteenth centuries that the family became an object of iconography: the family portrait 'at home' in the domestic interior makes its appearance, a symptom of the growing importance of private life. The 'privatisation of space' takes place (Ph. Ariès).

p. 309, line 24:
For European culture is the culture of a man 'at the cross-roads', constantly facing the necessity of choosing his way. It is a culture which does not schedule an existence without change; rather, it is a culture which goes beyond its own bounds, a culture of search and open possibilities. And is it not in this respect that medieval European culture differs radically from all other cultures of the epoch?

NOTES

Chapter II Ideas of space and time in the Middle Ages

1 R. Alexander, *Space, Time and Deity*, London, 1947, vol. I, p. 36; W. Lewis, *Time and Western Man*, Boston, 1957, pp. x, xii, 211 ff.; H. H. Parkhurst, *The Cult of Chronology. Essays in Honor of John Dewey*, New York, 1929, p. 294; W. Weischedel, 'Das heutige Denken zwischen Raum und Zeit', *Universitas* 22 Jg, H. 12, 1967, S. 1234 ff.

2 G. J. Whitrow, *The Natural Philosophy of Time*, 2nd edn, Oxford University Press, 1980, p. 55.

3 E. Cassirer, *Philosophie der symbolischen Formen*, II. Teil, Berlin, 1925, S. 103 ff.; A. Hallowell, *Culture and Experience*, Philadelphia, 1955; B. L. Whorf, *Language, Thought, and Reality*, New York, 1956; O. F. Bollnow, *Mensch und Raum*, Stuttgart, 1963.

4 M. Granet, *La pensée chinoise*, Paris, 1934, pp. 86, 90, 97, 103.

5 H. Frankfort, *The Birth of Civilization in the Near East*, London, 1951, p. 20.

6 J. Needham, *Time and Eastern Man*, Glasgow, 1965, pp. 44 f.

7 J.-P. Vernant, *Mythe et pensée chez les grecs. Etudes de psychologie historique*, Paris, 1965, pp. 22 ss., 57, 71 ss., 99 ss. (English edition, *Myth and Thought among the Greeks*, Routledge & Kegan Paul, London, 1983.)

8 A. F. Losev, *Istoriya antichnoj estetiki (rannaya klassika)*, Moscow, 1963, p. 50.

9 *Ibid.*, pp. 38, 55. Cf. A. F. Losev, *Istoriya antichnoj estetiki. Sofisty, Sokrat, Platon*, Moscow, 1969, pp. 598–600, 612–13, etc.

10 B. A. Van Groningen, *In the Grip of the Past. Essays on an Aspect of Greek Thought*, Leiden, 1953.

11 W. den Boer, 'Graeco-Roman Historiography in its Relation to Biblical and Modern Thinking', *History and Theory*, vol. VII, no. 1, 1968, p. 72. Cf. E. Ch. Weiskopf, *Gedanken über den gesellschaftlichen Fortschritt im Altertum*. XIII. Internationaler Kongress der historischen Wissenschaften, Moscow, 1970.

12 M. M. Bakhtin, *Rabelais and His World*, Cambridge, Mass., and London, 1968.

13 N. I. Konrad, *Zapad i Vostok*, Moscow, 1966, p. 79.

14 O. Spengler, *Decline of the West*, vol. I, London, 1929, p. 15.

15 D. S. Likhachev, *Poetika drevnerusskoj literatury*, Leningrad, 1967.

16 J. Le Goff, *La civilisation de l'Occident médiéval*, Paris, 1965, pp. 126, 440.

17 E. Mâle, *L'art religieux du XIIIᵉ siècle en France*, Paris, 1925 (6 éd.), pp. 1–5.

Chapter III Macrocosm and microcosm

1 O. A. Dobiash-Rozhdestvenskaya, *Zapadnye palomnichestva v srednie veka*, Petrograd, 1924, pp. 49 ff. Ch. H. Haskins, *Studies in Mediaeval Culture*, New York, 1929, p. 101; M. N. Boyer, 'A Day's Journey in Mediaeval France', *Speculum*, vol. XXVI, 1951; *Cambridge Economic History of Europe*, vol. III, Cambridge, 1963, p. 128.

2 O. Szemerenyi, 'The Etymology of German Adel', *Word*, vol. 8, 1952; W. Krogmann, 'Handmahal', *Zeitschrift der Savigny Stiftung für Rechtsgeschichte. Germanistische Abteilung*, 71 Bd, 1954. O. Behagel, 'Odal', *Forschungen und Fortschritte*, 11 Jg, N. 29, 1935, S. 369–70.

3 O. v. Dungern, 'Über die Freiheit des Eigentums im Mittelalter', *Zeitschrift der Savigny Stiftung für Rechtsgeschichte. Germanistische Abteilung*, 53 Bd, 1933, S. 291; H. Ebner, *Das Freie Eigen*, Klagenfurt, 1969, S. 129 ff., 227; F. Mezger, 'Zur Frühgeschichte von Freiheit und Frieden', *Fragen und Forschungen im Bereich und Umkreis der germanischen Philologie*, 1956, S. 15–16.

4 V. Grönbech, *Vor Folkeaet i Oldtiden*, Bd II, Copenhagen, 1912, S. 6–9; R. Kummer, *Midgards Untergang*, Leipzig, 1927.

5 J. de Vries, 'Ginnungagap', *Acta Philologica Scandinavica*, V, 1929.

6 Snorri Sturluson, *Edda*, c. 14, utg. av Anne Holtsmark og Jón Helgason, Copenhagen, Oslo and Stockholm, 1965.

7 *Grímnismál*, 12. *The Prose Edda of Snorri Sturluson*, trans. J. I. Young, Berkeley, 1971, p. 51.

8 Snorri Sturluson, *Heimskringla*, I, Bjarni Aðalbjarnarson gaf út, Reykjavík, 1941, bls. 22.

9 *Heimskringla, History of the Kings of Norway*, trans. Lee M. Hollander, New York, 1964.

10 *The Saga of Grettir the Strong*, ch. 72, trans. G. Voght, ed. P. Foote, London and New York, 1965, p. 189.

11 *Njáls saga*, trans. Magnus Magnusson and Hermann Palsson, London, 1960, p. 166.

12 *Njáls saga*, ch. 75, *Islandskie sagi*, ed. with notes and introductory essay by M. I. Steblin-Kamenskij, Moscow, 1956, p. 778.

13 J. Baltrušaitis, *Le Moyen Age fantastique*, Paris, 1955.

14 M. M. Bakhtin, *op. cit.*, chs 5, 6.

15 F. W. Maitland, *Domesday Book and Beyond*, Cambridge, 1907, p. 371.

16 L. Musset, 'Observations historiques sur une mesure agraire: le bonnier', *Mélanges d'histoire du Moyen Age dédiés à la mémoire de Louis Halphen*, Paris, 1951, p. 541.

17 J. Le Goff, *La civilisation de l'Occident médiéval*, p. 405.

18 A. Meyer, *Wesen und Geschichte der Theorie vom Mikro- und Makrokosmos*, Bern, 1900; G. P. Conger, *Theories of Macrocosms and Microcosms in the History of Philosophy*, New York, 1922; R. Allers, 'Microcosmos', *Traditio*, 2, 1944.

19 W. Kranz, 'Kosmos', *Archiv für Begriffsgeschichte*, Bonn, 1958.

20 Sanctae Hildegardis, *Liber Divinorum Operum Simplicis Hominis*, J. P. Migne, *Patrologia Latina* (hereafter cited as PL), t. 197, Paris, 1855, col. 862.

21 M.-M. Davy, *Essai sur la symbolique romane (XIIe siècle)*, Paris, 1955, p. 103.

22 Alani ab Insulis, *Liber de Planctu Naturae*, PL, t. 210, Paris, 1855, col. 443 b.

23 M.-Th. D'Alverny, 'Le cosmos symbolique du XIIe siècle', *Archives d'histoire doctrinale et littéraire du Moyen Age*, 28 année, 1954.

24 C.-M. Edsman, 'Arbor inversa. Heiland, Welt und Mensch

als Himmelspflanzen', *Festschrift Walter Baetke*, Weimar, 1966.

25 PL t. 210, col. 579a.

26 L. Spitzer, 'Classical and Christian Ideas of World Harmony', *Traditio*, vol. II, New York, 1944, pp. 434 ff.

27 E. Gilson, 'Le Moyen Age et le naturalisme antique', *Archives d'histoire doctrinale et littéraire du Moyen Age*, 7 année, 1933, pp. 22 ss.

28 L. Kirchenbauer, *Raumvorstellungen in der frühmittel-hochdeutschen Epik*, Heidelberg, 1931, S. 17.

29 O. Lauffer, *Das Landschaftsbild Deutschlands im Zeitalter der Karolinger*, Göttingen, 1896.

30 Quoted from R. A. Fridman, 'Lyubovnaya lirika trubadurov i ee istolkovanie', *Uchenye zapiski Ryazanskogo gospedinstituta*, vol. 34, Trudy kathedry literatury, Moscow, 1965, p. 288.

31 A. Biese, *Die Entwicklung des Naturgefühls im Mittelalter und in der Neuzeit*, Leipzig, 1888. Cf. E. Pons, *Le thème et le sentiment de la nature dans la poésie anglo-saxonne*, Strasbourg and Paris, 1925.

32 G. Stockmayer, *Über Naturgefühl in Deutschland im 10. und 11. Jahrhundert*, Leipzig and Berlin, 1910.

33 W. Ganzenmüller, *Das Naturgefühl im Mittelalter*, Leipzig and Berlin, 1914.

34 K. Wührer, *Romantik im Mittelalter. Beitrag zur Geschichte des Naturgefühls, im besonderen des 10. und 11. Jahrhunderts*, Baden, Vienna, Leipzig and Brünn, 1930.

35 L. Schneider, 'Die Naturdichtung des deutschen Minnesangs', *Neue deutsche Forschungen, Abteilung Deutsche Philologie*, Bd 6, Berlin, 1938.

36 E. R. Curtius, 'Rhetorische Naturschilderung im Mittelalter', *Romanische Forschungen*, 56, 1942, S. 221 ff.; M. Gsteiger, *Die Landschaftsschilderungen in den Romanen Chrestiens de Troyes*, Bern, 1958.

37 I. Hahn, 'Raum und Landschaft in Gottfrieds Tristan. Ein Beitrag zur Werkdeutung', *Medium Aevum. Philologische Studien*, Bd 3, Munich, 1963, S. 7 ff.

38 R. Gruenter, 'Zum Problem der Landschaftsdarstellung im höfischen Versroman', *Euphorion*, 56 Bd, 3 H., 1962.

39 E. Kobel, *Untersuchung zum gelebten Raum in der mittelhochdeutschen Dichtung*, Zürich, 1950.

40 Ch.-V. Langlois, *La connaissance de la nature et du monde au Moyen Age*, Paris, 1911, p. xii.

41 P. M. Bitsilli, *Salimbene*, Odessa, 1916, pp. 300–1.

42 W. Homuth, 'Vom Einfluss des Lehnswesens und Rittertums auf den französischen Sprachschatz', *Romanische Forschungen*, XXXIX Bd, 2 Heft, Erlangen, 1925.

43 Sancti Dionysii Areopagitae, *De Caelesti Ierarchia*, I, 7–9, PL, t. 122, Paris, 1865, col. 1050–8.

44 J. Sauer, *Symbolik des Kirchengebaüdes und seiner Ausstattung in der Auffassung des Mittelalters*, Freiburg, 1924; G. Bandmann, *Mittelalterliche Architektur als Bedeutungsträger*, Berlin, 1951; E. Baldwin Smith, *Architectural Symbolism of Imperial Rome and the Middle Ages*, New York, 1956.

45 As 'handmaid of theology', the allegorical geography of the Middle Ages combined biblical story and earthly history on one and the same plane. 'Maps of the world' show paradise with Adam and Eve, the great figures of the Bible, Troy, the campaigns of Alexander, the Roman provinces, the Holy Places, the Christian states and the Last Judgment. See A.-D. v. den Brincken, ' "ut discriberetur universus orbis". Zur Universal-kartographie des Mittelalters', *Methoden in Wissenschaft und Kunst des Mittelalters*, Berlin, 1970.

46 W. Harms, *Homo viator in bivio*, Munich, 1970.

47 Y. M. Lotman, 'O ponyatii geographicheskogo prostranstva v russkikh srednevekovykh tekstakh', *Trudy po znakovym sistemam*, II, Tartu, 1965, pp. 210–16.

48 P. Alphandery, *La Chrétienté et l'idée de Croisade*, I, Paris, 1954, p. 7.

49 R. W. Southern, *The Making of the Middle Ages*, New Haven, 1953, pp. 241–5.

50 S. D. Katznel'son, *Istoriko-grammaticheskie issledovaniya*, Moscow and Leningrad, 1949, pp. 80–1, 91–4.

51 *Bandamanna saga und Qlkofra þáttr*, hrsg. von Baetke, *Altnordische Textbibliothek*, N. F., 4 Bd, Halle (Saale), 1960, S. 52, 54.

52 Beati Rabani Mauri . . . , *Allegoriae in Universam Sacram Scripturam*, PL, t. 112, Paris, 1852, col. 849–50.

53 Dante Alighieri, *Epistle to Can Grande della Scala*, 7. Cf. *Convivio*, II, 1.

54 For a detailed decoding of the symbolism found in medieval ecclesiastical architecture, see Auber, *Histoire et théorie du symbolisme religieux avant et depuis le Christianisme*, t. 3–4, Paris and Poitiers, 1871.

55 Franco Sacchetti, *Opere*, vol. I, Florence, 1857, p. 87.

56 I. Döllinger, *Beiträge zur Sektengeschichte des Mittelalters*, Bd 2, Munich, 1890, S. 151.

57 G. Poulet, *Les métamorphoses du cercle*, Paris, 1961, p. iii.

58 A. Grabar, 'Plotin et les origines de l'esthétique médiévale', *Cahiers archéologiques*, I, 1945, p. 22.

59 E. Trubetskoj, *Dva mira v drevnerusskoj ikonopisi*, Moscow, 1916, pp. 17, 23.

60 See P. A. Florenskij, 'Obratnaya perspektiva', *Trudy po znakovym sistemam*, III, Tartu, 1967, p. 397. Cf. L. F. Zhegin, *Yazyk zhivopisnogo proizvedeniya*, Moscow, 1970.

61 On perspective as variously perceived in the ancient world, in the Middle Ages and in the Renaissance period, see M. Schild Bunim, *Space in Medieval Painting and the Forerunners of Perspective*, New York, 1940. On 'spiritual perspective' in medieval art, see W. Messerer, 'Einige Darstellungsprinzipien der Kunst im Mittelalter', *Deutsche Vierteljahrschrift für Literaturwissenschaft und Geistesgeschichte*, 36 Jg, H. 2, 1962.

62 E. Panofsky, 'Die Perspektive als symbolische Form', *Aufsätze zu Grundfragen der Kunstwissenschaft*, Berlin, 1961, S. 110.

63 E. de Bruyne, *Etudes d'esthétique médiévale*, t. 3, Bruges, 1946, ch. 1.

64 E. Panofsky, *op. cit.*, S. 111–15; *idem*, *Gothic Architecture and Scholasticism*, New York, 1957, pp. 44 ff., 58.

65 A. Koyré, 'Le vide et l'espace infini au XIVᵉ siècle', *Archives d'histoire doctrinale et littéraire du Moyen Age*, 24 année, 1949, p. 50; E. Cassirer, *The Individual and the Cosmos in Renaissance Philosophy*, New York, 1963.

66 E. Whittaker, *Space and Spirit*, London, 1946, pp. 73 ff.

67 Honorii Augustodunensis, *De Philosophia Mundi*, I, 23, PL, t. 172, Paris, 1854, col. 56.

68 *Raumordnung im Aufbau des mittelalterlichen Staates*, Bremen, 1961; B. Guenée, 'Espace et Etat dans la France du Bas Moyen Age', *Annales. Économies, Sociétés, Civilisations*, 23, no. 4, 1968.

69 A. Dupront, 'Espace et humanisme', *Bibliothèque d'humanisme et Renaissance*, t. VIII, Paris, 1946; J. Delumeau, 'Le développement de l'esprit d'organisation et de la pensée méthodique dans la mentalité occidentale à l'époque de la Renaissance', *XIIIᵉ congrès international des sciences historiques*, Moscow, 1970.

Chapter IV What is time?

1 K. Weinhold, *Über die deutsche Jahrtheilung*, Kiel, 1862; idem, *Die deutschen Monatnamen*, Halle, 1869; J. Grimm, *Geschichte der deutschen Sprache*, I Bd, Leipzig, 1868; M. P. Nilsson, *Primitive Time-reckoning*, Lund, 1920.

2 G. Bilfinger, *Untersuchungen über die Zeitrechnung der alten Germanen*, I, *Das altnordische Jahr*, Stuttgart, 1899.

3 K. Weinhold, *Altnordisches Leben*, bearb. von G. Siefert, Stuttgart, 1938, S. 258.

4 *The Prose Edda of Snorri Sturluson*, trans. J. I. Young, Berkeley, Los Angeles and London, 1971.

5 *Ibid.*

6 Snorri Sturluson, *Heimskringla*, I, *Prologus*, bls. 4–5.

7 *Sverris saga*, kap. 38, udg. ved G. Indrebø, Kristiania, 1920.

8 Snorri Sturluson, *Heimskringla*, I, *Ynglinga saga*, kap. 15.

9 Å. V. Ström, 'The King God and His Connection with Sacrifice in Old Norse Religion', *La Regalita sacra*, Leiden, 1959, S. 714–15.

10 *Ynglinga saga*, kap. 25.

11 Snorri Sturluson, *Edda*, kap. 26.

12 M. Eliade, *Le mythe de l'éternel retour*, Paris, 1949.

13 Th. Finkenstaedt, 'Das Zeitgefühl im altenglischen Beowulf-Epos', *Antaios*, Bd III, Stuttgart, 1962, S. 226 ff.

14 M. Halbwachs, 'La mémoire collective et le temps', *Cahiers internationaux de sociologie*, vol. II, 1947, p. 8.

15 K. A. Eckhard, *Irdische Unsterblichkeit. Germanischer Glaube an die Wiederverkörperung in der Sippe*, Weimar, 1937.

16 M. I. Steblin-Kamenskij, 'Tidsforestillingene i Islendingasagaene, *Edda*, Bd LXVIII, H. 6, 1968, s. 358–9.

17 R. Glasser, 'Verborgene und vordringliche Zeit in der Sprache' *Romanische Forschungen*, 56 Bd, 3 H., 1942, pp. 386–7; E. Leisi, 'Die Darstellung der Zeit in der Sprache', *Das Zeitproblem im 20. Jahrhundert*, hrsg. von R. W. Meyer, Bern and Munich, 1964, pp. 17 ff. In Old Russian, the word *mĕsto* meant both 'place' (locus) and 'time' (hence, *pokamest*). I. I. Sreznevskij, *Materialy dlya slovarya drevnerusskogo yazyka*, Moscow, 1958 (2nd edn), vol. II, p. 247.

18 W. Mannhardt, *Germanische Mythen. Forschungen*, Berlin, 1858, S. 606.

19 Snorri Sturluson, *Edda*, kap. 8. Cf. M. Ciklamini, 'The

Chronological Conception in Norse Mythology',
Neophilologus, 47 Jaargang, Afl. 2, 1963, pp. 142–3.
20 Snorri Sturluson, *Edda*, kap. 15.
21 'Grágás, I, 10, hrsg. von A. Heusler', *Germanenrechte*, Bd 9,
Weimar, 1937.
22 *King Alfred's Orosius*, ed. H. Sweet, London, 1883, pp.
17–19.
23 W. H. Vogt, 'Aldartryggđir ok aevintryggđir. Zur
Entwicklung von germ. ald- und aiw- zu "immerdar" und
"ewig" ', *Beiträge zur Geschichte der deutschen Sprache und
Literatur*, 58 Bd, 1934.
24 Ari Thorgilsson, *The Book of the Icelanders* (*Íslendingabók*),
ed. H. Hermannsson, Ithaca, New York, 1930 (*Islandica*, vol.
XX).
25 G. Bilfinger, *Untersuchungen über die Zeitrechnung* . . ., S.
38 f.
26 M. C. van den Toorn, 'Zeit und Tempus in der Saga', *Arkiv
för nordisk filologi*, LXXVI Bd, 1961, s. 136, 137.
27 Lynn Thorndike, *A History of Magic and Experimental
Science*, vol. II, New York, 1923, p. 68.
28 G. Bilfinger, *Die mittelalterlichen Horen und die modernen
Stunden. Ein Beitrag zur Kulturgeschichte*, Stuttgart, 1892;
W. Rothwell, 'The Hours of the Day in Medieval French',
French Studies, XIII, no. 3, 1959.
29 Quoted from: J. Le Goff, *La civilisation de l'Occident
médiéval*, p. 229.
30 M. Bloch, *La société féodale*, Paris, 1968, pp. 117–18.
31 Honorii Augustodunensis, *De Imagine Mundi*, libri tres, II,
4–10, PL, t. 172, col. 172 ss.
32 J. C. Webster, *The Labors of the Months in Antique and
Mediaeval Art*, Princeton, 1938; H. Stern, 'Poésies et
représentations carolingiennes et byzantines des mois', *Revue
archéologique*, 6 sér., t. XLV, 1955.
33 O. Cullmann, *Christ et le temps*, Neuchâtel and Paris, 1947.
34 St Augustine, *De civitate Dei*, book XII chs 13, 17.
35 St Augustine, *Confessiones*, book XI, ch. 14.
36 *Ibid.*, book XI, ch. 22.
37 *Ibid.*, book XI, ch. 27.
38 *Ibid.*, book XI, chs 20, 28.
39 St Augustine, *De civitate Dei*, book XII, ch. 12; *idem*,
Confessiones, book XI, ch. 13.
40 Honorius Augustodunensis, *Clauis Physicae*, f. 4v–5. Quoted

from: M.-Th. D'Alverny, *Le Cosmos symbolique . . .*, p. 39.
Cf. Ioannis Scoti, *De Divisione Naturae libri quinque*, I, 1,
PL, t. 122, col., 442.

41 J. F. Callahan, *Four Views of Time in Ancient Philosophy*,
Cambridge, 1948, pp. 152–3, 192–202.

42 *De civ.*, XXII, 24.

43 Quoted from H.-I. Marrou, *L'ambivalence du temps de
l'histoire chez Saint Augustin*, Montreal and Paris, 1950, p.
22.

44 A.-D. v. den Brincken, *Studien zur lateinischen Weltchronistik
bis in das Zeitalter Ottos von Freising*, Düsseldorf, 1957, S.
38.

45 *De civ.*, XVII, 1.

46 P. Rousset, 'La conception de l'histoire à l'époque féodale',
*Mélanges d'histoire du Moyen Age dédiés à la mémoire de
Louis Halphen*, Paris, 1951, pp. 630–3.

47 G. Schoebe, 'Was gilt im frühen Mittelalter als geschichtliche
Wirklichkeit? Ein Versuch zur Kirchengeschichte des Baeda
venerabilis', *Festschrift Hermann Aubin zum 80. Geburtstag*,
Bd II, Wiesbaden, 1965, S. 640–3.

48 J. M. Wallace-Hadrill, 'Gregory of Tours and Bede: their
views on the personal qualities of kings', *Frühmittelalterliche
Studien*, Bd 12, 1960, S. 36–7.

49 A. Dempf, *Sacrum Imperium. Geschichts- und
Staatsphilosophie des Mittelalters und der politischen
Renaissance*, Munich and Berlin, 1929, S. 251.

50 Thomae Aquinatis, *Summa Theologica*, Pars I, quaest. V, art.
V.

51 Honorii Augustodunensis, *De Imagine Mundi*, II, 1–3.

52 *Ibid.*, II, 3.

53 Quoted from: M.-D. Chenu, *La théologie au douzième siècle*,
Paris, 1957, pp. 67, 87.

54 E. Jeauneau, 'Nains et géants', *Entretiens sur la Renaissance
du 12ᵉ siècle*, Paris and The Hague, 1968.

55 Thomae Aquinatis, *Summa Theologica*, pars I, quaest. X, art.
I.

56 J. Ratzinger, 'Der Mensch und die Zeit im Denken des
Heiligen Bonaventura', *L'homme et son destin d'après les
penseurs du Moyen Age*, Louvain and Paris, 1960, pp. 476,
483.

57 Z. Zawirski, *L'évolution de la notion du temps*, Cracow, 1936,
pp. 35–42.

58 M.-D. Chenu, 'Situation humaine, corporalité et temporalité', *L'homme et son destin d'après les penseurs du Moyen Age*, pp. 39–40, 49.

59 M.-D. Chenu, *La théologie au douzième siècle*, p. 93.

60 F. S. Lear, 'The Mediaeval Attitude Toward History', *The Rice Institute Pamphlet*, vol. XX, no. 2, 1933, pp. 160–71.

61 *De civ.*, XI, 6.

62 Honorii Augustodunensis, *Elucidarium*, PL, t. 172, col. 1119.

63 Sancti Isidori Hispalensis episcopi, *Etymologiarum libri*, XX, PL, t. 82, Paris, 1878, col. 223.

64 *De civ.*, XVIII, 53; XXII, 30.

65 G. Duby, *L'an mil*, Paris, 1980; J. Delumeau, *La peur en Occident (XIVe–XVIIIe siècles. Une cité assiégée*, Paris, 1978, p. 199.

66 Dante Alighieri, *Paradiso*, XXX, 131–2.

67 J. E. Cross, 'Aspects of Microcosm and Macrocosm in Old English Literature', *Studies in Old English Literature in Honor of A. G. Brodeur*, Univ. of Oregon, 1963, pp. 2–3.

68 E. R. Curtius, *Europäische Literatur und lateinisches Mittelalter*, Bern, 1948, S. 103. (English edn, *European Literature and the Latin Middle Ages*, Routledge, London, 1953.)

69 Quoted from J. Spörl, *Grundformen hochmittelalterlicher Geschichtsanschauung. Studien zum Weltbild der Geschichtsschreiber des 12. Jahrhunderts*, Munich, 1935, S. 59.

70 Dante Alighieri, *Convivio*, IV, XXIII–XXIV.

71 W. Freund, *Modernus und andere Zeitbegriffe des Mittelalters*, Cologne and Graz, 1957, S. 108.

72 Walter Map, *De nugis curial*. Quoted from E. R. Curtius, *op. cit.*, S. 259.

73 J. Spörl, *Grundformen . . .*, S. 30.

74 E. Jeauneau, *op. cit.*, p. 26. We have to remember that such statements cannot always be taken at their face value. Adelard of Bath admits that, in view of the widespread prejudice against anything smacking of novelty, he felt it wiser to ascribe his thoughts to others – i.e. to ancient writers or to Arab scholars. See J. Le Goff, *Les intellectuels au Moyen Age*, Paris, 1960, p. 60.

75 H. Beumann, 'Der Schriftsteller und seine Kritiker im frühen Mittelalter', *Studium Generale*, 12 Jg, H. 8, 1959, S. 502, 509.

76 H. Grundmann, 'Die Grundzüge der mittelalterlichen Geschichtsanschauungen', *Geschichtsdenken und Geschichtsbild im Mittelalter*, hrsg. von W. Lammers. (*Wege der Forschung*, XXI), Darmstadt, 1961, S. 424.

77 Quoted from H. Grundmann, 'Geschichtsschreibung im Mittelalter', *Deutsche Philologie im Aufriss*, hrsg. von W. Stammler, 35. Lieferung, Berlin, Bielefeld, Munich, 1961, S. 2283.

78 E. Gilson, *L'esprit de la philosophie médiévale*, Paris, 1948, ch. XIX.

79 Quoted from S. M. Stam, 'Uchenie Ioakhima Kalbrijskogo', *Voprosy istorii religii i ateizma*, VII, Moscow, 1959, p. 348.

80 Quoted from: E. Gilson, *op. cit.*, p. 377.

81 Thomae Aquinatis, *Summa Theologica*, II, 1, quaest. 106, art. 4; II, 2, quaest. I, art. 7.

82 A. Borst, *Der Turmbau von Babel. Geschichte der Meinungen über Ursprung und Vielfalt der Sprachen und Völker*, Bd II, 1–2, Stuttgart, 1958–9.

83 H. Beumann, 'Topos und Gedankengefüge bei Einhard', *Archiv für Kulturgeschichte*, 33 Bd, 3 H., 1951, S. 349–50.

84 A. Funkenstein, *Heilsplan und natürliche Entwicklung. Formen der Gegenwartsbestimmung im Geschichtsdenken des hohen Mittelalters*, Munich, 1965, S. 76.

85 'La morale de l'histoire', *Le Moyen Age*, t. LXIX, 1963, p. 366.

86 E. Meuthen, 'Der Geschichtssymbolismus Gerhohs von Reichersberg', *Geschichtsdenken und Geschichtsbild im Mittelalter*, S. 241–6.

87 Ottonis episcopi Frisingensis, *Chronica*, Prol. I, hrsg. von W. Lammers, Berlin, 1960, S. 8.

88 Chrétien de Troyes, 'Chevalerie et clergie', *Anthologie poétique française. Moyen Age*, 1. Choix, introduction, traduction et notes par A. Mary, Paris, 1967, p. 102.

89 Ottonis episcopi Frisingensis, *Chronica*, S. 11–17. See H. M. Klinkenberg, 'Der Sinn der Chronik Ottos von Freising', *Aus Mittelalter und Neuzeit*, Bonn, 1957.

90 B. Widmer, *Heilsordnung und Zeitgeschehen in der Mystik Hildegards von Bingen*, Basel and Stuttgart, 1955, S. 132 ff.

91 W. J. Brandt, *The Shape of Medieval History. Studies in Modes of Perception*, New Haven and London, 1966, p. 171.

92 M. Kemmerich, *Die frühmittelalterliche Porträtmalerei in Deutschland bis zur Mitte des XIII. Jahrhunderts*, Munich, 1907.

93 G. Poulet, *Etudes sur le temps humain*, I, Paris, 1965, pp. I–VI.

94 P. M. Bitsilli, *Salimbene*, p. 132.

95 H.-H. Steinhof, *Die Darstellung gleichzeitiger Geschehnisse im mittelhochdeutschen Epos*, Munich, 1964.
96 U. Ruberg, 'Raum und Zeit im Prosa-Lancelot', *Medium Aevum. Philologische Studien*, Bd 9, Munich, 1965, S. 16, 164, 182–3.
97 Guillaume de Lorris, 'Le jardin de déduit', *Anthologie poétique française. Moyen Age*, 1, p. 394.
98 Ph. Ménard, 'Le temps et la durée dans les romans de Chrétien de Troyes', *Le Moyen Age*, t. 73, no. 3–4, 1967.
99 E. Koehler, 'Observations historiques et sociologiques sur la poésie des troubadours', *Cahiers de civilisation médiévale*, VIIᵉ année, no. 1, 1964, p. 43.
100 G. Quispel, 'Time and History in Patristic Christianity', *Man and Time*. Papers from the Eranos Yearbooks, Bollingen Series XXX, 3, New York, 1957, p. 101.
101 Ph. Ménard, *op. cit.*, p. 393 ss.
102 *The Elder Edda*, trans. Paul B. Taylor and W. H. Auden, New York, 1969, p. 124.
103 D. S. Likhachev, *op. cit.*, p. 254.
104 S. Hinterkausen, 'Die Auffassung von Zeit und Geschichte in Konrads Rolandslied', Inaugural-Diss., Bonn, 1967.
105 R. Glasser, 'Studien zur Geschichte des französischen Zeitbegriffs', *Münchner Romanistische Arbeiten*, 5, Munich, 1936, S. 5; K. von Ettmayer, *Analytische Syntax der französischen Sprache*, II Bd, Halle (Saale), 1936, S. 886; G. Lechner, 'Zur "Zeit" und zur stilistischen und topologischen Funktion der "Tempora" in der früheren altfranzösischen Heldenepik', Inaugural-Diss., Munich, 1961, S. 251.
106 M. Huby, 'La structure numérique et sa valeur symbolique dans la poésie religieuse allemande du Moyen Age', *Etudes germaniques*, 22, no. 2, 1967, p. 244.
107 E. Kobel, *op. cit.*, S. 8 ff., 14–15.
108 H. Werner, 'Raum und Zeit in den Urformen der Künste', *Vierter Kongress für Ästhetik und allgemeine Kunstwissenschaft. Berichte*, Stuttgart, 1931, S. 69–83.
109 O. Mandelstam, 'Conversation on Dante', in *The Complete Critical Prose and Letters*, trans. Harris and Link, Ann Arbor, Mich., 1979, p. 422.
110 V. Shklovskij, *Tetiva. O neskhodstve skhodnogo*, Moscow, 1970, p. 175.
111 Dante Alighieri, *Inferno*, XV, 85–7.
112 Dante Alighieri, *Purgatorio*, XI, 106–8.

113 Dante Alighieri, *Paradiso*, XXIX, 12–32; XXXIII, 94–5.
114 P. A. Michelis, *An Aesthetic Approach to Byzantine Art*, London, 1964, p. 118.
115 See *Istoriya Vizantii*, t. 1, Moscow, 1967, p. 433.
116 S. Stelling-Michaud, 'Quelques aspects du problème du temps au moyen âge', *Schweizer Beiträge zur Allgemeinen Geschichte*, Bd 17, Bern, 1959, S. 25–6.
117 J. Le Goff, 'Temps de l'Eglise et temps du marchand', *Annales. Économies, Sociétés, Civilisations*, 15, no. 3, 1960.
118 A. Doren, *Fortuna im Mittelalter und in der Renaissance*, Leipzig, 1924; K. Hampe, 'Zur Auffassung der Fortuna im Mittelalter', *Archiv für Kulturgeschichte*, 17, 1927; D. M. Robinson, 'The Wheel of Fortune', *Classical Philology*, vol. XLI, no. 4, 1946; H. R. Patch, *The Goddess Fortuna in Mediaeval Literature*, New York, 1967 (2nd edn).
119 P. Mandonnet, *Siger de Brabant et l'averroïsme latin au XIIIᵉ siècle*, Louvain, 1911, pp. 170–1; P. Duhem, *Le système du monde*, t. II, Paris, 1914, p. 447 ss; t. V, 1917, p. 61; t. VII, 1956, p. 441 ss; H. Ley, *Studie zur Geschichte des Materialismus im Mittelalter*, Berlin, 1957, S. 267, 298.
120 Dante Alighieri, *Inferno*, VII, 77–81, 96.
121 W. von den Steinen, *Menschen im Mittelalter*, Bern and Munich, 1967, S. 231 ff.
122 W. Gent, *Die Philosophie des Raumes und der Zeit*, Berlin, 1926; idem, *Das Problem der Zeit*, Frankfurt a. M., 1934.
123 Heinrich Böll, *Irisches Tagebuch*, Berlin, 1957.
124 J. Le Goff, *La civilisation de l'Occident médiéval*, p. 223.
125 G. Gurvitch, *The Spectrum of Social Time*, Dordrecht, 1964.
126 P. Browe, *Beiträge zur Sexualethik des Mittelalters*, Breslau, 1932; J. T. Noonan, *Contraception, a History of Its Treatment by the Catholic Theologians and Canonists*, Cambridge, Mass., 1966; J.-L. Flandrin, 'Contraception, mariage et relations amoureuses dans l'Occident chrétien', *Annales. Économies, sociétés, civilisations*, 24, no. 6, 1969.
127 N. Cohn, *The Pursuit of the Millennium*, London, 1970; T. Manteuffel, *Naissance d'une hérésie*, Paris and The Hague, 1970.
128 M. de Gandillac, *Valeur du temps dans la pédagogie spirituelle de Jean Tauler*, Montreal and Paris, 1956, p. 42.
129 O. Spengler, *Decline of the West*, vol. I, London, 1929.
130 J. Le Goff, 'Le temps du travail dans la crise du XVIᵉ siècle: du temps médiéval au temps moderne', *Le Moyen Age*, t. LXIX, 1963.

131 C. M. Cipolla, *Clocks and Culture, 1300–1700*, London, 1967, pp. 80–7.

132 L. B. Alberti, 'Della famiglia', *Opere volgari*, vol. I, Bari, 1960, pp. 168–70. We find the new attitude to time powerfully expressed at the close of the Renaissance in the poems of John Donne and in Shakespeare. 'The time is out of joint,' cries Hamlet. 'Oh cursed spite, That ever I was born to set it right.'

133 G. Paris, *La Littérature française au Moyen Age.* 2ᵉ éd., Paris, 1890, p. 30; L. Febvre, *Le problème de l'incroyance au XVIᵉ siècle. La religion de Rabelais*, Paris, 1942, pp. 426–34; M. Bloch, *op. cit.*, p. 118.

Chapter V 'The country is built on law . . .'

1 R. David, *Les grands systèmes de droit contemporains*, Paris, 1971.

2 F. Joüon des Longrais, *L'Est et l'Ouest. Institutions du Japon et de l'Occident comparées*, Tokyo and Paris, 1958, p. 256.

3 R. David, *op. cit.*

4 M. I. Steblin-Kamenskij, 'Proiskhozhdenie poezii skal'dov', *Skandinavskij Sbornik*, III, Tallinn, 1958, p. 188.

5 See Einar Ol'geirsson, *Iz proshlogo islandskogo naroda. Rodovoj stroj i gosudarstvo v Islandii*, Moscow, 1957.

6 G. Ch. von Unruh, 'Wargus. Friedlosigkeit und magischkultische Vorstellungen bei den Germanen', *Zeitschrift der Savigny Stiftung für Rechtsgeschichte. Germanistische Abteilung*, 74 Bd, 1957.

7 E. Leisi, 'Aufschlussreiche altenglische Wortinhalte', *Sprache–Schlüssel zur Welt*, Düsseldorf, 1959.

8 W. Ullmann, *The Individual and Society in the Middle Ages*, Baltimore, Maryland, 1966, p. 38.

9 A. Dempf, *Sacrum Imperium*, S. 8 ff., 147 ff.

10 E. H. Kantorowicz, *Laudes Regiae. A Study in Liturgical Acclamations and Mediaeval Ruler Worship*, Berkeley and Los Angeles, 1946; P. E. Schramm, *Herrschaftszeichen und Staatssymbolik*, Stuttgart, Bd I–III, 1954–6.

11 G. Post, 'Sovereignty and its Limitations in the Middle Ages (1150–1350)', *XIII International Congress of Historical Sciences*, Moscow, 1970.

12 G. Tellenbach, *Church, State and Christian Society at the Time of the Investiture Contest*, Oxford, 1940, p. 22.

13 W. Ullmann, 'Law and the Medieval Historian', *XIe Congrès International des Sciences Historiques, Stockholm, 21–28 août 1960. Rapports. III. Moyen Age*, Göteborg, Stockholm and Uppsala, 1960, p. 36.

14 Quoted from B. Jarrett, *Social Theories of the Middle Ages, 1200–1500*, New York, 1966, p. 17.

15 F. Kern, 'Recht und Verfassung im Mittelalter', *Historische Zeitschrift*, 120 Bd, 1919, S. 3 ff.

16 'Das Rüstringer Recht, hrsg. von W. J. Buma und W. Ebel', *Altfriesische Rechtsquellen*, Bd I, Göttingen, Berlin and Frankfurt, 1963, S. 24–32.

17 F. Liebermann, *Die Gesetze der Angelsachsen*, Bd I, Halle a. S., 1898, S. 26 ff., 46.

18 *Die Gesetze der Langobarden*, hrsg. von F. Beyerle, Weimar, 1947, S. 2.

19 Quoted from F. Kern, *Gottesgnadentum und Widerstandsrecht im früheren Mittelalter*, Leipzig, 1914, S. 167. Anhang XVII, S. 372–6.

20 *Etymolog.*, IX, 3, § 4, PL, t. 82, col. 342.

21 S. B. Chrimes, *English Constitutional History*, London, 1967, p. 69.

22 F. Kern, *Gottesgnadentum . . .*, S. 177–8, 389–92.

23 See F. J. Dölger, *Antike und Christentum. Kultur- und Religionsgeschichtliche Studien*, Bd I, 1, Münster, 1929, S. 79 f.

24 P. Meinhold, *Geschichte der kirchlichen Historiographie*, Bd I, Munich, 1967, S. 155–6.

25 J. Spörl, 'Das Alte und das Neue im Mittelalter. Studien zum Problem des mittelalterlichen Fortschrittsbewußtseins', *Historisches Jahrbuch*, 50 Bd, 3 H., 1930.

26 E. Goldmann, 'Cartam levare', *Mitteilungen des Instituts für Österreichischen Geschichtsforschung*, 35 Bd, 1 H., 1914.

27 M. Kos, 'Carta sine litteris', *Mitteilungen des Instituts für Österreichischen Geschichtsforschung*, 62 Bd, 1954, S. 98–100.

28 J. Grimm, *Deutsche Rechtsalterthümer*, Bd I, Berlin, 1956, S. 550.

29 H. Fuhrmann, *Einfluss und Verbreitung der pseudoisidorischen Fälschungen*, I–III, Stuttgart, 1972–4.

30 M. Bloch, *op. cit.*, p. 142.

31 T. F. Tout, 'Mediaeval Forgers and Forgeries', *Bulletin of the John Rylands Library, Manchester*, vol. 5, 1919.

32 O. L. Vainshtein, *Zapadnoevropejskaya srednevekovaya istoriographiya*, pp. 87 f.

33 K. Bosl, 'Zu einer Soziologie der mittelalterlichen Falschung', *Frühformen der Gesellschaft im mittelalterlichen Europa*, Munich and Vienna, 1964, S. 414 ff.

34 P. Rousset, 'La croyance en la justice immanente à l'époque féodale', *Le Moyen Age*, t. LIV, no. 3–4, 1948, p. 227 ss.

35 P. Rousset, 'Le sens du merveilleux à l'époque féodale', *Le Moyen Age*, t. LXII, no. 1–2, 1956, pp. 32–3.

36 M. A. Zaborov, *Vvedenie v istoriographiyu krestovykh pokhodov*, Moscow, 1966, pp. 70 f., 89.

37 L. Genicot, 'Valeur de la personne ou sens du concret. A la base de la société du haut moyen âge', *Miscellanea Mediaevalia in memoriam Jan Frederic Niermeyer*, Groningen, 1967.

38 A. P. Kazhdan, *Vizantijskaya kul'tura (X–XII vv.)*, Moscow, 1968, pp. 49 f.

39 A. P. Kazhdan, 'O sotsial'noj prirode vizantijskogo samoderzhaviya', *Narody Azii i Afriki*, 1966, no. 6, pp. 52–64.

40 Anne Comnena, *The Alexiad of Anne Comnena*, Penguin Books, Harmondsworth, 1969.

41 K. Bosl, *Frühformen der Gesellschaft im mittelalterlichen Europa*, pp. 39, 58, 185.

42 P. Vinogradoff, *Villeinage in England*, Oxford, 1892, ch. II; E. A. Kosminsky, *Studies in the Agrarian History of England in the Thirteenth Century*, Oxford, 1956; M. A. Barg, *Issledovaniya po istorii anglijskogo feodalizma v XI–XIII vv*, Moscow, 1962, pp. 254 f.

43 Quoted in R. W. Southern, *The Making of the Middle Ages*, London, 1953, p. 104.

44 Adalberonis, *Carmen ad Rotbertum regem Francorum*, PL, t. 141, Paris, 1853, col. 781–2.

45 G. Gusdorf, *Signification humaine de la liberté*, Paris, 1962, pp. 81 ss.

46 F. Graus, 'Littérature et mentalité médiévales: le roi et le peuple', *Historica*, XVI, Prague, 1969, pp. 58 ss.

47 E. Fromm, *Escape from Freedom*, New York and Toronto, 1941, pp. 41–3.

48 F. Graus, *Volk, Herrscher und Heiliger im Reich der Merowinger*, Prague, 1965, S. 300 f.

49 J. Huizinga, *Le Déclin du Moyen Age*, Paris, 1948, p. 51.

50 P. A. Fridman, ' "Kodeks" i "zakony" kurtuaznogo sluzheniya dame v lyubovnoj lirike trubadurov', *Uchenye*

zapiski Ryazanskogo gospedinstituta, t. 34, vyp. II, Moscow, 1966, pp. 64 f.

51 E. de Bruyne, *Etudes d'esthétique médiévale*, t. 2, Bruges, 1946, pp. 177–80.

52 E. Koehler, 'Observations historiques et sociologiques sur la poésie des troubadours', p. 34.

53 M. B. Meilach, *Jazyk trubadurov*, Moscow, 1975.

54 A. Kelly, *Eleanor of Aquitaine and the Four Kings*, New York, 1967, pp. 207–10.

55 V. Shishmarev, *Lirika i liriki pozdnego srednevekov'ya. Ocherki po istorii poezii Frantsii i Provansa*, Paris, 1911, pp. 296–7; E. Wechsler, *Das Kulturproblem des Minnesangs*, Bd 1, Halle a. S., 1909, p. 105 ff.; E. Koehler, *op. cit.*, p. 45.

56 M.-D. Chenu, 'L'homme et la nature. Perspectives sur la Renaissance du XIIᵉ siècle', *Archives d'histoire doctrinale et littéraire du Moyen Age*, 27 année, 1953, p. 62.

57 *Das Stadtbuch von Augsburg*, hrsg. von Chr. Meyer, Augsburg, 1872, S. 240–4.

58 *Documents relatifs à l'histoire de l'industrie et du commerce en France*, publiés par G. Fagniez, I, Paris, 1898, no. 130.

59 Snorri Sturluson, *Heimskringla*, II, *Ólafs saga Tryggvasonar*, kap. 88.

60 F. Tönnies, *Gemeinschaft und Gesellschaft*, Berlin, 1926, S. 22, 35–8.

Chapter VI Medieval attitudes to wealth and labour

1 S. Bolin, *Ur penningens historia*, Stockholm, 1962.

2 *Edda*, hrsg. von G. Neckel und H. Kuhn, Heidelberg, 1962, S. 131.

3 *Gulathings-Lov*, 223, 270. *Norges gamle Love indtil 1387.* Bd 1, Christiania, 1846.

4 F. T. Harmer, *Select English Historical Documents of the 9th and 10th Centuries*, Manchester, 1914, n. 2.

5 K. H. Ganahl, 'Hufe und Wergeld', *Zeitschrift der Savigny Stiftung für Rechtsgeschichte. Germanistische Abteilung*, 53 Bd, 1933.

6 *Hávamál. Elder Edda*, trans P. B. Taylor and W. H. Auden, New York, 1969, p. 57.

7 A. Val de Lièvre, *Launegild und Wadia*, Innsbruck, 1877; K. v. Amira, *Nordgermanisches Obligationenrecht*, I Bd, Leipzig, 1882, S. 506 ff.; M. Pappenheim, 'Über die Rechtsnatur der altgermanischen Schenkung', *Zeitschrift der*

Savigny Stiftung für Rechtsgeschichte. Germanistische Abteilung, 53 Bd, 1933.

8 E. Benveniste, 'Don et échange dans le vocabulaire indoeuropéen', *Problèmes de linguistique générale*, Paris, 1966, pp. 317 ss.

9 R. Thurnwald, *Economies in Primitive Communities*, Oxford, 1932; M. J. Herskovits, *Economic Anthropology*, New York, 1952; J. H. Michel, *La gratuité dans le droit romain*, Brussels, 1962; J. Bardach, 'La donation reciproque en Lituanie aux XVᵉ et XVIᵉ siècles', *Studi in onore di Edoardo Volterra*, vol. I, 1969; A. Ja. Gurevič, *Le origini del feudalismo*, Rome and Beri, 1982.

10 V. Grönbech, *The Culture of the Teutons*, vol. II, pp. 6 f., 16 f., 54.

11 *Hávamál. Elder Edda*, *op. cit.*, p. 37.

12 *Ibid.*, p. 43.

13 *Ibid.*, p. 44.

14 *Edda*, hrsg. von G. Neckel und H. Kuhn, S. 39.

15 V. Machek, 'Sl. gospod', lat. hostes et lit. viešpats', *Slavica*, VIII, Debrecen, 1968.

16 M. Mauss, 'Essai sur le don. Forme et raison de l'échange dans les sociétés archaiques', *Sociologie et anthropologie*, Paris, 1950.

17 J. Blumenstengel, *Wesen und Funktion des Banketts im Beowulf*, Marburg, 1964. Ritual feasts were also held in the Middle Ages. See K. Hauck, 'Rituelle Speisegemeinschaft im 10 und 11 Jahrhundert', *Studium generale*, 3 Jg, H. 11, 1950.

18 H. C. Peyer, 'Das Reisekönigtum des Mittelalters', *Vierteljahrschrift für Sozial- und Wirtschaftsgeschichte*, 51 Bd, 1 H., 1964; C. Brühl, *Fodrum, Gistum, Servitium Regis*, I–II, Cologne and Graz, 1968.

19 A kenning for 'bracelets'.

20 A kenning for 'hand'.

21 *Egils saga*, ch. 55, trans. Gwyn Jones, New York, 1960. pp. 132–3.

22 *Heimskringla, History of the Kings of Norway*, trans. Lee M. Hollander, New York, 1964, p. 71.

23 *Gulathings-Lov*, 270.

24 A. Y. Gurevich, *Svobodnoe krest'yanstvo feodal'noj Norvegii*, Moscow, 1967, pp. 139–49, 249–50.

25 *Gulathings-Lov*, 126, 141.

26 *Gulathings-Lov*, 6, 7.

27 Aethelbert, 3. *The Laws of the Earliest English Kings*, ed. F. L. Attenborough, New York, 1963, p. 4.

28 Hlothhere and Eadric, 12–14; Ine, 6, § 5; *ibid.*, pp. 20, 38.
29 VI Aethelstan, 8 § 1. *Ibid.*, p. 162.
30 *Grágás*, 115.
31 *Grímnismál. Elder Edda, op. cit.*, p. 61.
32 *Hávamál. Ibid.*, p. 38.
33 St Piekarczyk, *Barbarzyńcy i chrześcijaństwo. Konfrontacie społecznych postaw i wzorców u Germanów*, Warsaw, 1968, s. 98 ss.
34 *Hávamál. Elder Edda, op. cit.*, p. 45.
35 *Ibid.*, p. 42.
36 *Edda*, hrsg. von G. Neckel und H. Kuhn, S. 281.
37 *Ibid.*, S. 283.
38 *Gulathings-Lov*, 145.
39 *Frostathings-Lov*, XV, 8.
40 *Landnámabók Islands. Einar Arnorsson bjó til prentunar*, Reykjavík, 1948, bls. 13, 14, 24, 207, 211, 221.
41 The meaning is unclear; perhaps 'rich', 'fat', or it may be a proper name.
42 *Hávamál. Elder Edda, op. cit.*, p. 47.
43 *Ibid.*, pp. 47, 48.
44 *Ibid.*, p. 47.
45 St. Piekarczyk, 'Zur Frage der internen und externen Funktionen des frühmittelalterlichen Staates und der Ideologie verschiedener Gesellschaftsschichten im Lichte der skandinavischen Quellen', *L'Europe aux IXe–XIe siècles*, Warsaw, 1968, s. 441, n. 33; *idem, Barbarzyńcy i chrześcijaństwo*, s. 141–2, 240–1.
46 Thomae Aquinatis, *Summa Theologica*, II, 2, quaest. 186, art. 3.
47 H. v. Eicken, *Geschichte und System der mittelalterlichen Weltanschauung*, Stuttgart, 1887, S. 500.
48 Thomae Aquinatis, *Summa Theologica*, II, 2, quaest. 66, art. 2.
49 *Ibid.*, quaest. 118, art. 1, 2.
50 R. Le Jan-Hennebicque, ' "Pauperes" et "paupertas" dans l'Occident carolingien aux IX et X siècles', *Revue du Nord*, t. L, no. 197, 1968, p. 186.
51 M. Mollat, *Les pauvres au Moyen Age*, Paris, 1978.
52 S. Painter, *French Chivalry. Chivalric Ideas and Practices in Mediaeval France*, Ithaca, New York, 1957.
53 M. Bloch, *La société féodale*, pp. 432–3.
54 J. Frappier, 'Vues sur les conceptions courtoises dans les littératures d'oc et d'oil au XIIe siècle', *Cahiers de civilisation*

médiévale, II, no. 2, 1959, p. 141.

55 E. Köhler, *Trobadorlyrik und höfischer Roman. Aufsätze zur französischen und provenzalischen Literatur des Mittelalters*, Berlin, 1962, S. 48, 73.

56 R. A. Fridman, *Lyubovnaya lirika* . . ., str. 178.

57 G. Duby, *Hommes et structures du Moyen Age*, Paris and The Hague, 1973, pp. 213–25.

58 R. A. Fridman, *Lyubovnaya Iirika* . . ., str. 180, 323, 327.

59 R. A. Fridman, *'Kodeks' i 'zakony' kurtuaznogo sluzheniya dame* . . ., str. 74 f., 83.

60 L. J. Paetow, *Morale Scolarium of John of Garland*, Berkeley, 1927, pp. 195–6; Petri Cantoris, *Verbum Abbreviatum*, PL, t. 205, Paris, 1855, col. 78–82.

61 Quoted from M. Bloch, *Seigneurie française et manoir anglais*, Paris, 1960, p. 555.

62 K. Marx, *Early Writings*, Penguin Books, Harmondsworth, 1975, p. 318.

63 *Ibid.*, p. 317.

64 H. v. Eicken, *op. cit.*, S. 490. Bernard of Clairvaux, 'De modo bene vivendi', Sermo 53.

65 H. v. Eicken, *op. cit.*

66 *Die Klosterregel des Heiligen Benedikt*, Beuron, 1947, Kap. 57.

67 K. Thomas, 'Work and Leisure in Pre-Industrial Society', *Past and Present*, 1964, no. 29, p. 56.

68 *The Cambridge Economic History of Europe*, vol. III, Cambridge, 1963, p. 574.

69 *Aelfric's Colloquy*, ed. G. N. Garmonsway, London, 1939, 219–37.

70 J. Gilchrist, *The Church and Economic Activity in the Middle Ages*, London, 1969, p. 78.

71 J. A. Yunck, 'Economic Conservatism, Papal Finance, and the Medieval Satires on Rome', *Change in Medieval Society*, ed. S. Thrupp, London, 1965.

72 E. Mâle, *L'art religieux du XIIIᵉ siècle en France*, pp. 28, 64 ss., 131.

73 J. Le Goff, 'Métier et profession d'après les manuels de confesseurs au moyen âge', *Beiträge zum Berufsbewusstsein des mittelalterlichen Menschen*, Berlin, 1964, S. 49–60.

74 G. Post, K. Giocarinis and R. Kay, 'The Medieval Heritage of a Humanistic Ideal: "scientia, donum dei est, unde vendi non potest" ', *Traditio*, vol. XI, no. 4, 1955, pp. 232 ff.

75 See E. R. Curtius, *op. cit.*, S. 465.

76 O. Jodogne, 'La personnalité de l'écrivain d'oil du XIIᵉ au

XIVᵉ siècle', *L'humanisme médiéval dans les littératures romanes du XIIᵉ au XIVᵉ siècle*, Paris, 1964; F. Tschirch, 'Das Selbstverständnis des mittelalterlichen deutschen Dichters', *Beiträge zum Berufsbewusstsein des mittelalterlichen Menschen*, Berlin, 1964.

77 K. Marx, *Early Writings*, p. 337.

78 W. Sombart, *Der Bourgeois*, Munich and Leipzig, 1913, S. 19.

79 *Reformation Kaiser Siegmunds*, hrsg. von H. Keller, Stuttgart, 1964, S. 270.

80 K. Thomas, *op. cit.*, p. 55.

81 John Milton, *Paradise Lost*.

82 William Langland, *The Vision of Piers Plowman*, VII, 6–7.

83 Adalberonis, *Carmen . . .*, PL, t. 141, col. 781–2.

84 *Histoire générale du travail*, II, p. 9.

85 H. Grundmann, 'Adelsbekehrungen im Hochmittelalter', *Adel und Kirche. Festschrift für Gerd Tellenbach*, Freiburg, Basel and Vienna, 1968.

86 *Riches et pauvres dans l'église ancienne*, Paris, 1962.

87 Thomae Aquinatis, *Summa Theologica*, II, 2, quaest. 50, art. 3.

88 *Ibid.*, II, 2, quaest. 77, art. 4.

89 J. Le Goff, *La civilisation de l'Occident médiéval*, p. 326.

90 Thomae Aquinatis, *Summa Theologica*, II, 2, quaest. 47, art. 10; quaest. 152, art. 4.

91 J. A. Schumpeter, *History of Economic Analysis*, London, 1955, p. 85 ff.

92 J. W. Baldwin, *The Medieval Theories of the Just Price*, Philadelphia, 1959, p. 60.

93 Thomae Aquinatis, *Summa Theologica*, II, 2, quaest. 58, art. 11.

94 J. Ibanès, *La doctrine de l'église et les réalités économiques au XIIIᵉ siècle*, Paris, 1967, pp. 33, 39, 57, 100, 102.

95 Quoted in W. J. Ashley, *Introduction to English Economic History*, 1888–93.

96 *Ibid.*

97 See J. T. Noonan, *The Scholastic Analysis of Usury*, Cambridge, Mass., 1957, pp. 38–9.

98 J. W. Baldwin, *op. cit.*, p. 27–9.

99 Thomae Aquinatis, *Summa Theologica*, II, 2, quaest. 78.

100 Robert de Curzon, William of Auxerre (early thirteenth century). Quoted from J. T. Noonan, *op. cit.*, pp. 39, 41, 43. The Roman lawyers already give this etymology.

101 *Ibid.*, pp. 43–4 f.

102 Dante Alighieri, *Inferno* XI, 49–50, 95–96, 109–10.

103 J. T. Noonan, *op. cit.*, p. 79.

104 R. De Roover, *San Bernardino of Siena and Sant' Antonino of Florence: the Two Great Economic Thinkers of the Middle Ages*, Boston, 1967.

105 R. De Roover, 'The Decline of the Medici Bank', *Journal of Economic History*, vol. VII, N 1, 1947, p. 73 ff.; *idem, The Rise and Decline of the Medici Bank 1397–1494*, Cambridge, Mass., 1963, pp. 13 ff., 112, 121.

106 H. Lapeyre, *Une Famille de Marchands les Ruiz*, Paris, 1955.

107 A. Sapori, *Le marchand italien au Moyen Age*, Paris, 1952, p. XVIII.

108 H. Pirenne, *Histoire économique et sociale du Moyen Age*, Paris, 1963, pp. 99–100, 115.

109 E. Troeltsch, *Die Soziallehren der christlichen Kirchen und Gruppen*, Tübingen, 1919, S. 244 ff., 295 ff., 329.

Chapter VII Conclusion: In search of human personality

1 M.-D. Chenu, *La théologie au douzième siècle*, p. 162.

2 P. Bitsilli, *Elementy srednevekovoj kul'tury*, pp. 4–5.

3 W. J. Brandt, *op. cit.*, pp. 33 ff.

4 K. Marx, *Grundrisse der Kritik der politischen Ökonomie (Rohentwurf), 1857–1858*, Moscow, 1939, S. 6.

5 *Paulys Realencyclopädie der Classischen Altertumswissenschaft*, 37 Halbb., Stuttgart, 1937, col. 1040–1.

6 M. Mauss, 'Une catégorie de l'esprit humain: la notion de personne, celle de moi', *Sociologie et anthropologie*, p. 335–62.

7 Thomae Aquinatis, *Summa Theologica*, I, quaest. 29, art. 3.

8 See *Persönlichkeitsforschung und Persönlichkeitstheorie*, hrsg. von Ph. Lersch und H. Thomae, Göttingen, 1960, S. 8–9; H. Rheinfelder, *Das Wort persona. Geschichte seiner Bedeutungen mit besonderer Berücksichtigung des französischen und italienischen Mittelalters*, Halle (Saale), 1928.

9 M.-D. Chenu, *La théologie au douzième siècle*, p. 52 ss.

10 Dante Alighieri, *Inferno*, IV, 34–6, trans. Dorothy L. Sayers.

11 W. Ullmann, 'Some Observations on the Medieval Evaluation of the Homo Naturalis and the Christianus', *L'homme et son destin d'après les penseurs du moyen âge*, p. 145 ss.

12 W. Ullmann, *The Individual and Society in the Middle Ages*, p. 37.

13 P. Lehmann, 'Autobiographies of the Middle Ages', *Transactions of the Royal Historical Society*, 5th series, vol. 3, London, 1953, p. 47.

14 G. Misch, *Geschichte der Autobiographie*, III Bd, 1 H., Frankfurt am Main, 1959, S. 529.

15 L. Zoepf, *Das Heiligen-Leben im 10. Jahrhundert*, Leipzig and Berlin, 1908; R. Teuffel, *Individuelle Persönlichkeits-schilderung in den deutschen Geschichtswerken des 10. und 11. Jahrhunderts*, Berlin, 1914.

16 W. J. Brandt, *op. cit.*, p. 109.

17 H. Winkel, *Aspekte mittelalterlicher Erziehung*, Munich, 1968, S. 67, 74 ff.

18 Ph. Ariès, *L'enfant et la vie familiale sous l'ancien régime*, Paris, 1960.

19 See: L. Genicot, *Le XIIIᵉ siècle européen*, Paris, 1968, p. 212 ss.

20 Thomae Aquinatis, *Contra gentil.*, III, 113. See also E. Gilson, *L'esprit de la philosophie médiévale*, pp. 174–5.

21 A. Krempel, 'Hiérarchie des fins d'une société d'après Saint Thomas', *L'homme et son destin* . . ., pp. 611–18.

22 *The Status of the Individual in East and West*, ed. Ch. A. Moore, Honolulu, 1968, p. 563.

INDEX

Abelard, Peter, 85, 302
Adalberon, Bishop, 195, 269
Adam of Bremen, 73
Adhémar of Chabannes, 68
Aelfric, Bishop, 262
'age', in barbarian society, 95–7
age, average, in Middle Ages, 123–4
Aidan, Saint, 85
Alan of Lille, 59, 61
Alberti, Leone Battista, 50
Alcuin, 243
Alfred, King of England, 166
alms, 242–3
anachronism, 129–30
ancestors, cult of, 99–101
Anselm of Canterbury, 143, 195
Anselm of Havelberg, 124
Antoninus, Archbishop, 281
Apocalypse, 122–3
Ari Þorgilsson, 103
Ariès, P., 306
Aristotle, 89, 120, 213, 398
art: anonymity in, 37–8; barbarian,
  78–9; illustrating law codes, 256–7;
  landscape in, 62, 66–7; microcosm/
  macrocosm depicted in, 59–60;
  theology of, 38 f.; time and space in,
  35–7, 86–90
Arthurian romances, 75, 76–7, 134, 253
asceticism, 244–6
Ásgarðr, 47, 49–50
atomisation, 107
Augustine, Saint: on dualism, 58; on
  freedom, 196; on possessions, 241;

on time, 113–17, 121–2, 127, 131,
  136; on the self, 299–300
autobiography, 301–2
Averroism, 142

Bakhtin, M. M., 33, 53
banking, 281–4
baptism, 162, 299
barbarian society: age, concept of,
  95–7; art, 35–7, 78–80, 86–90;
  calendars, 94–5; feasts and gifts,
  221–39; labour and property, 235–9;
  law, 156–62; relationship with
  nature, 45–53; spatial symbolism,
  78–80; time, concept of, 94–104,
  147–50; wealth, 215–39; see also
  Scandinavia
Basil, Saint, 73
Bede, 71, 73, 109, 118, 122
Benedictines, 241
Benzo of Alba, Bishop, 126
Bernard of Chartres, 119
Bernard of Clairvaux, Saint, 61–2, 143,
  240, 260, 261
Bertran de Born, 63
bestiaries, 68
Biese, A., 62, 63
Bitsilli, P. M., 68–9, 293
Bloch, Marc, 177, 248
Boethius, 296, 308
Böll, Heinrich, 143
Bonaventura, Saint, 120, 127, 279
Boniface VIII, Pope, 171
Bosch, H., 53
Brandt, W., 303